## Critical Acclaim from Across Disciplines for
### *The Practical Art of Suicide Assessment*

**From the Experts:**

"At last! A readable book that melds established principles of suicide assessment with an innovative method of data collection. This book provides the best systematic approach to suicide assessment and the tools to sharply reduce the risk of malpractice liability."

>Phillip J. Resnick, MD
>Professor and Director of Forensic Psychiatry
>Case Western Reserve University, School of Medicine

"If readers follow the principles of the main text of this book they will save lives. If they follow the principles outlined in the appendix, "How to Document a Suicide Assessment," they will stay out of court. Quite literally, nobody has ever written sounder or more practical principles for documenting suicide assessments. Nobody. Ever. Period."

>Skip Simpson, JD
>Practice Limited to Psychiatric and Psychological Malpractice

". . . . The CASE Approach moves the clinician almost imperceptibly into the secret internal workings of the mind and soul of the patient tormented by suicidal ideation. I believe that the CASE Approach is a remarkable conceptual and clinical contribution to the field of suicidology. It should be routinely taught to any front-line clinician. It has the power to meaningfully save lives."

>David A. Jobes, PhD
>Past President, American Association of Suicidology

"Written with compassion and understanding, *The Practical Art of Suicide Assessment* combines the brilliance of clinical innovation with great writing. The result is both poignant and imminently useful. I couldn't put it down."

>Charlotte Anderson
>Director, Crisis Center Division
>American Association of Suicidology

**From the Reviewers:**

"In this highly readable, engaging volume, Dr. Shea makes the process of discovering suicidality come alive. Even if you are not directly involved in suicide risk assessment, this is a very worthwhile read. If you are directly involved, this is a must read."

>School Psychology Resources Online, August 2000

". . . a concise, carefully conceptualized, well-written book . . . highly recommended for all psychiatric residents and all other mental health students. Their teachers, as well, will profit greatly by reading it."

>*Journal of Clinical Psychiatry,* September 2000

# The Practical Art of Suicide Assessment

## A Guide for Mental Health Professionals and Substance Abuse Counselors

Shawn Christopher Shea

John Wiley & Sons, Inc.

Copyright © 2002, 1999 by John Wiley & Sons, Inc., Hoboken, New Jersey.
All rights reserved.

Published simultaneously in Canada.

This publication is designed to provide accurate and authoritative information in
regard to the subject matter covered. It is sold with the understanding that the
publisher is not engaged in rendering professional services. If professional advice or
other expert assistance is required, the services of a competent professional person
should be sought.

Designations used by companies to distinguish their products are often claimed as
trademarks. In all instances where John Wiley & Sons, Inc. is aware of a claim, the
product names appear in initial capital or all capital letters. Readers, however, should
contact the appropriate companies for more complete information regarding
trademarks and registration.

Wiley also publishes its books in a variety of electronic formats. Some content that
appears in print may not be available in electronic books. For more information about
Wiley products visit our Web site at www.wiley.com.

*Library of Congress Cataloging-in-Publication Data:*

Shea, Shawn C.
    The practical art of suicide assessment : a guide for mental
  health professionals and substance abuse counselors / Shawn
  Christopher Shea.
      p.    cm.
    Includes bibliographical references and index.
    ISBN 0-471-18363-6 (cloth : alk. paper)
    ISBN 0-471-23761-2 (pbk. : alk. paper)
    1. Suicide—Risk factors.   2. Suicide—Prevention.   I. Title.
  RC569.S46    1999
  616.85′8445—dc21                                    98-55218

Printed in the United States of America.

10  9  8  7  6  5  4  3  2

To the memory of Peter Henderson, my residency director at WPIC, who taught me much about the delicate art of interweaving skill and compassion.

# Foreword

A s A reader, I often find myself skipping over much of a book's Foreword, so let me get straight to the point. With the publication of this book, there is now no better guide for learning about and clinically assessing the phenomenology of suicidal states. Penned with compelling elegance and charm, *The Practical Art of Suicide Assessment* is brimming with clinical wisdom, enlightening case illustrations, and a vibrant sense of compassion. Writers of Forewords have a tendency to proclaim that the book in hand is a "must-read" for every clinician. This time it is actually true.

Shea has an almost unparalleled way of making sense out of the complex interplay of the biopsychosocial and philosophical forces that lead a human to take his or her own life. What at first glance seemed senseless, murky, and intangible becomes palpably real to the beginning clinician. Shea then offers a practical, commonsense, and accessible approach to systematically assessing the nuances and essentials of suicidal thoughts, plans, and behaviors. He walks the student through this process step by step, offering numerous examples of useful questions and fascinating excerpts of clinical dialogue.

For the seasoned clinician, this book is no less valuable. The most daunting and complicated clinical scenarios are dealt with plainly and with a no-nonsense approach, from emergency-room assessments of psychotic patients to borderline "suicide talk" at 2:00 A.M. Controversial topics such as the usefulness or uselessness of safety contracts and the role of the clinician's own thoughts and biases toward the topic of suicide are discussed head-on and with a refreshing candor. Shea never talks down to his readers; rather, he shares himself and his techniques with matter-of-fact openness.

He reminds us of the inherent challenges and rewards that are central to the life-and-death arena of clinical work with suicidal patients.

As the seasoned clinician reads, old facts are suddenly seen with a new light. Seemingly disparate clinical encounters garnered over years of clinical experience become connected by underlying principles that can be immediately applied to the next clinic day. There is an earnest quality to the writing. Shea's sharing of his clinical vignettes highlights the importance of timing, patience, technique, and the acceptance of our own mistakes and failures.

No less would be expected from this author. This same sense of an always-welcome "beginner's mind" was one of the irresistible qualities of his first book, *Psychiatric Interviewing: The Art of Understanding*, now in its second edition. That classic text was my original introduction to Shea. As a teacher of graduate students in clinical psychology and counseling, I was delighted when I discovered it. The book is rich with case presentations, vivid clinical dialogues, theoretical eclecticism, empirical underpinnings, literary style, personal wit, clinical acumen, and undeniable readability. I can't think of any other book that my graduate students enjoy as much, or talk about with more enthusiasm. In my view, *Psychiatric Interviewing: The Art of Understanding* is unequivocally the best beginning text for mental health professionals, no matter what their discipline. I am delighted to say that the present effort is a worthy successor to this previous work.

As a career suicidologist, I marvel at Shea's almost uncanny ability to grasp, embrace, and extend what we know about effective clinical work with suicidal patients. While plainly a master clinician, Shea is nevertheless a relative newcomer to the subspecialization of clinical suicidology. The freshness and vitality of his approach take us to a new level of clinical understanding.

His most striking contribution to the practical assessment of risk is his innovative interview strategy for eliciting suicidal ideation itself, a strategy he calls the Chronological Assessment of Suicide Events (the CASE Approach). The CASE Approach is a remarkably pragmatic and systematic interview strategy that enables clinicians to flexibly and comprehensively assess the nooks and crannies, the ins and outs, of different suicidal states. The CASE Approach moves the clinician almost imperceptibly into the secret internal workings of the mind and soul of a patient tormented by suicidal ideation. From this shared phenomenological exploration, the client's immediate risk becomes much clearer. I believe that the CASE Approach is a remarkable conceptual and clinical contribution to the field of suicidology. It should be routinely taught to any frontline clinician. It has the power to meaningfully save lives.

Shea's work complements other recent work by leading clinical suicidologists who are increasingly emphasizing the importance of understanding the power and seduction of suicide for those who are experiencing unbearable pain and despair. Shea wisely walks us through a nonjudgmental, systematic, thoughtful approach to appreciating the attraction of suicide as an apparently viable solution to ending this pain. In so doing, he helps us understand how we can help a patient to seek alternative solutions. This search—not always, but often—leads to hope, renewal, and the choice of life over death.

In the last analysis, this is a very human book about the very human struggles of people who find themselves standing at the precipice of eternity. Shea helps us to understand their exquisite pain, and that understanding gives us the capacity to reach out to those who are at this precipice. I have no doubt that the reader will find herein the skills and the confidence to enter the world of these acutely suicidal patients, to sensitively yet tenaciously ask the right questions at the right times, and to enter their world of suicidality with as little pre-judgment, fear, or bias as one can manage. The gentle wisdom of this book allows us to discover within ourselves the capacity and courage to help such patients make seemingly unlivable lives once again livable, creating new life and new hope—an important, if not noble pursuit.

DAVID A. JOBES, PhD
President, American Association of Suicidology
Associate Professor of Psychology
The Catholic University of America
Washington, DC

# Preface to the Paperback Edition

The purpose of life is to serve and to show compassion and the will to help others. Only then have we ourselves become true human beings.

Albert Schweitzer, MD

I t is with great pleasure that I sit down to write the Preface to the paperback edition of *The Practical Art of Suicide Assessment.* It has been a delight to see the enthusiastic reception of both the original book and of the Chronological Assessment of Suicide Events (the CASE Approach), the interviewing strategy for eliciting suicidal ideation that was introduced in the first book. By producing a paperback, at a significantly lowered price, it is our hope that many more clinicians may learn about the CASE Approach and use it in their everyday practices.

This book is not a second edition of The Practical Art of Suicide Assessment, since the main body of the text has not been changed at all. On the other hand, this is not your typical re-release of a hardback into paperback format, for three brand new appendices have been added that were not present in the original book. These three appendices consist of over 60 pages of new information. The topics include: (1) How to Document a Suicide Assessment, (2) Safety Contracting Revisited: Pros, Cons, and Documentation, and (3) A Quick Guide to Suicide Prevention Web Sites.

As with the original edition, the goal of the paperback edition of *The Practical Art of Suicide Assessment* is to provide the busy clinician, with a no-nonsense set of principles for spotting and assessing suicidal ideation, planning, and intent. It is my hope that such principles may help us to save lives—a goal that lies at the very heart of our mission— a mission that lies at the very heart of our souls.

SHAWN CHRISTOPHER SHEA, MD

# Preface

Currently, the major bottleneck in suicide prevention is not remediation, for there are fairly well-known and effective treatment procedures for many types of suicidal states; rather it is in diagnosis and identification.

Edwin Shneidman, Father of modern suicidology

THIS IS a book designed specifically for front-line clinicians. Few clinical challenges are as daunting nor as critical as the art of suicide assessment. This book is 0intended to be a fast-paced and practical guide to this art. Much has been written about suicide, but the field lacks a single concise introduction for busy everyday clinicians in the fields of mental health, substance abuse, and school counseling. This book attempts to fill this gap.

In particular surprisingly little has been written about the actual elicitation of suicidal ideation, yet there can be little doubt that clients can provide strikingly different databases to different clinicians depending on how the clinicians phrase their questions and establish a sense of safety. This book focuses directly on this art of eliciting suicidal ideation. It introduces an innovative interview strategy, the Chronological Assessment of Suicide Events (the CASE Approach), that was initially developed in the "clinical trenches" of a busy urban emergency room at Western Psychiatric Institute and Clinic in Pittsburgh Pennsylvania, and subsequently refined doing community mental health work in the rural settings of southern New Hampshire.

In addition an attempt is made to help the reader gain a clearer understanding of the complex inner worlds of both the client contemplating suicide and the clinician trying to prevent it. These two worlds invariably interact and change one another. Whether the client and the clinician choose to acknowledge it, both are changed by the act of sharing such intimate material. Towards this end the fascinating world of suicidal etiology and phenomenology is explored in detail. A heavy emphasis is placed on illustrating potentially confusing clinical presentations ranging from suicide assessments in ongoing therapy to emergency room settings.

Part One, *The Experience of Suicide: Etiology, Phenomenology, and Risk Factors*, is composed of three chapters. In Chapter 1 an effort is made to highlight the impact of suicide and to demonstrate some of our current limitations at its prediction while pointing out that there is hope that our predictive abilities can be improved. In the second chapter we will embark upon a detailed examination of the etiology of suicide and the phenomenology of people who are contemplating it. An understanding of the diversity of the etiologic roots of suicide can help the clinician to recognize its many faces. By exploring the phenomenology of the inner world of the acutely suicidal client, I believe a clinician can increase his or her "intuitive ear" perhaps hearing a danger that others, less trained, would miss. In the third chapter we will look at two illustrative clinical presentations which bring suicidal risk factors into sharper focus.

In Part Two, *Uncovering Suicidal Ideation: Principles, Techniques, and Strategies,* we will address the interview itself, getting down to the nitty gritty of everyday assessment. In Chapter 4 we will explore the resistances and biases of both the client and the clinician that can disrupt the uncovering of suicidal intent. In Chapter 5 six validity techniques will be illustrated that the reader can use immediately, and which will serve as the foundation stones for the CASE Approach. In Chapter 6 the CASE Approach itself is carefully delineated. Chapters 5 and 6 rely heavily upon the direct demonstration of the techniques described in the book via carefully designed sample interviews and numerous examples of specific questions. In addition, in Chapter 6 we will look at an actual transcript of an assessment using the CASE Approach from front to back, illustrating and discussing the nuances of the techniques as they unfold.

Part Three, *Practical Assessment of Risk: Flexible Strategies and Sound Formulations,* consists solely of Chapter 7. In this chapter we will explore the complicated variables that can make arriving at a sound clinical judgment of risk so daunting. This chapter explores critical issues such as contradictory data, client deceit, the role of corroborative sources of information, and the always vexing issues of forensic liability. All of these complicating "real-life" difficulties in suicide assessment are looked at via seven clinical case presentations from a variety of settings.

Please note that the names of all clients have been changed, and at times distinguishing characteristics or facts have been altered to further protect their identity.

In closing I should emphasize that this book is not an attempt to review the vast body of literature on suicide. It is my hope that it will stir readers to explore this fascinating reading for themselves. The focus in this book is on a no nonsense approach to suicide assessment for the busy clinician of today. Edward Shneidman, in the opening epigram, pointedly referred to a bottleneck in suicide prevention. It is my sincere hope that the principles delineated in the following pages will serve as one step toward the dismantling of this bottleneck and ultimately help us to save lives.

SHAWN CHRISTOPHER SHEA, MD

*Dartmouth School of Medicine*
*Hanover, New Hampshire*

# Acknowledgments to the Paperback Edition

FIRST, I WOULD like to thank my editor, Tracey Belmont for all of her support; without it, there would not have been a paperback edition in the first place. I could not ask for a better editor. I would also like to thank Judi Knott my marketing manager for her support and belief in the paperback edition.

Thanks go to both Nancy Marcus Land and Maryan Malone at Publications Development Company, who once again have clearly improved the text of the new appendices with the same exquisite skill they demonstrated in the original hardback.

I would also like to especially thank Phillip J. Resnick, MD, for his useful feedback on Appendix B, as well as for all of his support throughout the years, and to Skip Simpson, JD, for his meticulous, and greatly appreciated, input on Appendices A and B, as well as his warm friendship.

As always, a special thanks to my wife Susan for all of her love and support and for her irrepressible belief in The Practical Art of Suicide Assessment and its mission.

Thanks again to all.

S.C.S.

# Acknowledgments

I WOULD like to begin by thanking the Department of Psychiatry at the Dartmouth Medical School, and its Chairman, Peter Silberfarb, M.D., for supporting my interviewing training ideas over the past ten years. In particular, I would like to thank the Director of Residency Training, Ron Green, M.D., for all his support in the implementation of our interviewing mentorship program. Through his help, I feel that I have truly found an academic home at Dartmouth.

I would also like to thank all the Dartmouth faculty who have served as interviewing mentors during the writing of this book—the so-called "Phantom Gate Club." In addition to Ron Green, this group includes Bruce Baker, Ph.D., Christine Barney, M.D., Stephen Cole, Ph.D., and Suzanne Brooks, M.D. They have been enthusiastic supporters of the CASE Approach and have helped many residents to understand its nuances. They have also been great colleagues and friends whom I genuinely admire. They are the best set of teachers with whom I have ever had the pleasure to be associated.

I would also like to thank my colleagues, from many years back, at Western Psychiatric Institute and Clinic in Pittsburgh, Pennsylvania. It was in the clinical trenches of the DEC (the Diagnostic and Evaluation Center) that the CASE Approach first began to evolve. All of the following colleagues provided both unflagging support and sound feedback on the early development of the CASE model. I owe them a lot, not only for their ideas, but for all the fun we had together: Juan Mezzich, M.D., Ph.D., Karen Evanczuk, R.N., Ph.D., Scott Bohon, M.D., Anita Zeiders, M.S., and Patty McHugh, M.S.W.

A special thanks goes to my good friend Barnes Peterson, M.Ed., for the delightful Easter afternoon we spent in the Keene State cafeteria, during which he offered many excellent suggestions on the manuscript. Thanks go also to another friend, Tom Ellis, Ph.D., for his enthusiastic support of the CASE Approach over the years.

It has been a great personal pleasure to get to know David Jobes, Ph.D. I offer many thanks for his enthusiastic support of my work and for taking the time, from his very busy schedule, to write his wonderful Foreword to the book.

Final thanks go to Kelly Franklin and Dorothy Lin, the editorial team at John Wiley & Sons, as well as to Nancy Marcus Land and Maryan Malone at Publications Development Company, whose outstanding editorial work has clearly improved the manuscript.

As always, a very special thanks to my wife Susan, for both her love and her editorial acumen. Her belief in the mission of this book and the CASE Approach, in particular, has been an unending source of support.

Thanks again, to all.

S.C.S.

# Contents

# THE EXPERIENCE OF SUICIDE: ETIOLOGY, PHENOMENOLOGY, AND RISK FACTORS

# CHAPTER 1

# Suicide:
# The Ultimate Paradox

In this life it is not difficult to die.
It is more difficult to live.

> Vladimir Mayakovsky, Russian revolutionary[1]
> (Died by suicide, 1931)

## A SUNDAY AFTERNOON PRELUDE

THIS EXPLORATION of suicide began on a Sunday in a most unlikely place: a drafty old bookshop on the outskirts of a small town in southern New Hampshire. As I entered the shop, the welcoming heat of the woodstove provided a sharp counterpoint to the crisp autumn air. I am a lover of books, and on that particular Sunday I spent the better part of the morning browsing the shelves and chatting with Henry, the always amiable shop owner.

I wandered about the aisles, hoping to stumble upon some secret treasure that others had unwittingly passed by. When I reached the section on psychology, I spotted what looked like a promising find. I pulled the book down and flicked it open to the title page. I stopped. For a moment, not a muscle in my body moved. My eyes held the name in sharp focus. I blinked and looked again at the name.

It was not the name of the author that caught my attention. It was the name of the previous owner, scrawled across the upper tip of the title page. Jackie, as I shall call her, had been a colleague in our small community of mental health professionals. Jackie had killed herself some months before.

I placed the book back on the pine shelf. Perhaps a morbid sense of curiosity propelled me to pull out the volume sitting beside it. Different tip of a different page in a different book; same name. Next book, same name. Next book, same name. I realized then that either Jackie, in desperation, had sold off her book collection as her alcoholism swallowed her dreams, or else the books had been bought cheap from her estate. I quietly left the bookshop and drove home.

## CLINICIANS AND THEIR EMOTIONAL RESPONSES TO SUICIDE

I begin with this incident because I believe that the chill that it created in me, and still creates in me as I write about it now, serves a useful purpose. It highlights the power of suicide to engender intense emotional reaction in all of us. For mental health professionals, an understanding of this reaction is one of the cornerstones of effective assessment and management of a suicidal patient. Many emotional currents dart beneath this chill: fear, grief, anger, puzzlement, and even condemnation. When unrecognized, these feelings can drag an unwary clinician into a sea of countertransferential responses and unproductive interventions. The potentially dangerous undertow, beneath this sea, can pull us away from the very people who most need our help: acutely suicidal patients.

When a clinician begins to understand his or her own attitudes, biases, and responses to suicide, he or she can become more psychologically and emotionally available to a suicidal client. Clients seem to be able to sense when a clinician is comfortable with the topic of suicide. At that point, and with such a clinician, clients may feel safe enough to share the immediacy of their pull toward death.

One of the goals of this book is to help readers become more comfortable with their own emotional responses to the topic of suicide. Hopefully, the reading of the book will also spur clinicians to discuss the topic of suicide in more depth with fellow therapists, supervisors, and trainees, for it is often only through such intimate conversations that we can more clearly see the undertows beneath our own personal seas. And here we meet one of the first paradoxes of suicide. As a topic for discussion, it is often avoided by clinicians; yet, discussion of it offers us one of the greatest gateways into personal, spiritual, and professional growth.

The opening vignette about Jackie is a reminder of the ubiquitous nature of suicide. No group of humans has a monopoly on suicidal behavior. It is seen in the rich and the poor, the famous and the unknown, male and female, older adult and child. Mental health professionals are far from immune to its draw; many of us have been touched by suicides among our friends, family members, and colleagues. Contemplation of suicide may even be part of our own past or future history.

It is important to realize that suicide "works" at some level; it provides a solution to intense personal pain. As life ends, the pain ends. Acceptance of the effectiveness of suicide is an important first step in a clinician's understanding of why suicide is relatively common. We humans are a solution-oriented species.

This does not mean that the clinician must agree with or accept the solution. We are all entitled to our own moral beliefs. But, without conveying judgment, the clinician can recognize why suicide presents as a natural solution for many people. When clients sense that they are not being "put down" for their choice of a solution, but rather, the clinician is seeking a more effective and life-enhancing solution, they may be more willing to explore other alternatives. The clinician's ability to convey a nonjudgmental understanding of the client's right to view suicide as a rational solution may introduce the rapport that is needed to help the client choose another solution. This irony is just one of the many contradictory elements of suicide.

## THE PARADOX OF SUICIDE

The implementation of suicide is often one of the most private of all human actions, yet its impact on the people left behind could not be more profound. Self-destruction frequently crosses the minds of vast numbers of humans, but it remains among the most taboo of topics. Mental health professionals encourage the public to feel comfortable discussing suicidal thoughts, yet many of these same professionals are hesitant to ask family members or colleagues whether they are having such thoughts. Death is sometimes chosen as the only alternative by people who feel deeply alone or shamed, yet are profoundly loved and respected. The manner of suicide adds to the paradox. If a businessman takes his life in an effort to avoid scandal and the pain of admitting his wrongdoing to his family, he may be labeled as a coward; yet a soldier who jumps on a land mine to save fellow troops will undoubtedly be called a hero.

The paradoxical nature of suicide has not been lost on philosophers. Arthur Schopenhauer cogently captured the essence of the most ironic paradox of the suicidal act:

> Suicide may also be regarded as an experiment—a question which man puts to Nature, trying to force her to answer. The question is this: What change will death produce in a man's existence and in his insight into the nature of things? It is a clumsy experiment to make, for it involves the destruction of the very consciousness which puts the question and awaits the answer.[2]

Its paradoxical nature is one of the reasons that exploration and discussion of suicide, within the clinical interview, raise such powerful emotions in both patients and clinicians. Some of its greatest paradoxes still await us. They will surface as we begin to more carefully explore the nature of suicide by looking, first, at its epidemiology and then at some of the practical problems inherent in its prediction.

## THE EPIDEMIOLOGY OF SUICIDE, AND PROBLEMS WITH ITS PREDICTION

Suicide is one of our most pressing public health concerns. In the United States, suicide is the ninth leading cause of death in adults, with 30,903 suicides in 1996.[3] It has been estimated that a suicide occurs every twenty minutes.[4] In the age group of 15 to 25 years, suicide is the third leading cause of death in America (accidents and homicides are first and second, respectively).[5] Between 1952 and 1992, the rate of suicide among adolescents and young adults tripled.[6] And even though young children are much less likely to commit suicide, they still do. In the United States in 1995, 330 children, ages 10 to 14, killed themselves and seven children, ages 5 to 9, committed suicide.[7]

The development of improved ways of spotting and providing relief to acutely suicidal patients could dramatically decrease one of the leading causes of death in both the United States and the world at large. As a society, we must openly address suicide as a public health problem and, as was done with smoking, aggressively address methods of decreasing its prevalence.

Is such a goal possible? Several studies have shown that roughly 50 percent of people who commit suicide have been seen by a primary care physician within the month prior to their death.[8, 9] This staggering statistic provides hope. If effective screening mechanisms can be developed and are subsequently embraced and effectively utilized by primary care physicians, a marked drop in suicide could result. This is not a pipe dream. It can happen.

But the task is formidable. Current research shows that clinicians have little ability to predict imminent suicide. For a moment, let us look at this problem of prediction more carefully. What are some of the factors that might help us to predict that a person is *not* acutely suicidal? In essence, what are the risk factors and what does the absence of these risk factors mean? (We shall examine these risk factors in much greater detail in Chapter 3, but a glance at them now will prove to be quite useful.)

Reproduced below are two pieces of writing, a letter and a poem. They contrast the types of reassuring circumstances versus risk factors that suggest whether suicide is or is not imminent. The author of the letter, which was addressed to her mother, had been suffering from depression for years. She had recently moved to England from the United States, a move that seemed to ease her ongoing battle, although she acknowledged that the transition was tough. In the letter, she displayed a sense of hope, an intense interest in the parenting of her children, and a deeply held conviction that she needed to be there for them. As you read the letter, note the strong framework for meaning (parental responsibilities, in this case) and the sense of hopefulness that suggest suicide is not near.

February 4, 1963

Dear Mother,

Thanks so much for your letters. I got a sweet letter from Dotty and a lovely hood and mittens for Nick from Warren and Margaret. I just haven't written anybody because I have been feeling a bit grim—the upheaval over, I am seeing the finality of it all, and being catapulted from the cowlike happiness of maternity into loneliness and grim problems is not fun. I got a sweet letter from the Nortons and an absolutely wonderful, understanding one from Betty Aldrich. Marty Plumer is coming over at the end of March, which should be cheering.

I have absolutely no desire ever to return to America. Not now, anyway. I have my beautiful country house, the car, and London is the one city of the world I'd like to live in with its fine doctors, nice neighbors, parks, theatres and the BBC. There is nothing like the BBC in America—over there they do not publish my stuff as they do here, my poems and novel. I have done a commissioned article for *Punch* on my schooldays and have a chance for three weeks in May to be on the BBC Critics program at about $150 a week, a fantastic break I hope I can make good on. Each critic sees the same play, art show, book, radio broadcast each week and discusses it. I am hoping it will finish furnishing this place, and I can go to [Devon] right after. Ask Marty for a copy of the details of the two places and the rent, and maybe you could circulate them among your professor friends, too.

I appreciate your desire to see Frieda, but if you can imagine the emotional upset she has been through in losing her father and moving, you will see what an incredible idea it is to take her away by jet to America. I am her one security and to uproot her would be thoughtless and cruel, however sweetly you treated her at the other end. I could never afford to live in America—I get the best of doctors' care here perfectly free, and with children this is a great blessing. Also, Ted sees the children once a week and this makes him more responsible about our allowance . . . I shall simply have to fight it out on my own over here. Maybe someday I can manage holidays in Europe with the children. . . . The children need me most right now, and so I shall try to go on for the next few years writing mornings, being with them afternoons and seeing friends or studying and reading evenings.

My German "au pair" is food-fussy and boy-gaga, but I am doing my best to discipline her. She does give me some peace mornings and a few free evenings, but I'll have to think up something new for the country as these girls don't want to be so far away from London.

I am going to start seeing a woman doctor, free on the National Health, to whom I've been referred by my very good local doctor, which should help me weather this difficult time. Give my love to all.

Sivvy[10]

Although this letter is a bit lengthy, I have chosen to include the entire piece, for it provides important clues to the types of risk factors that may be of value in suicide assessment. In this case, the absence of these risk factors is striking. It clearly points toward the patient's strengths and increases one's prediction of her safety in the near future.

Still, we must acknowledge that some of the risk factors that are described could suggest lethality. The author is in pain; she openly acknowledges it with her allusion to "feeling a bit grim." She also appears to be suffering from a significant psychiatric disorder, as reflected by her referral to a psychiatrist. Apparently, another risk factor—a recent loss, which sounds like a divorce—is also present.

On the other hand, the letter is filled with reassuring signs of renewed strength. With genuine enthusiasm, the author talks about the many aspects of Britain and London that she loves. She is very excited about her career possibilities, and feels appreciated by both her British peers and the British public. On an interpersonal level, she sounds supported and is grateful for the support: "I got a sweet letter from the Nortons and an absolutely wonderful, understanding one from Betty Aldrich." All of these are good signs suggesting a lowered risk for suicide.

The appearance of hopelessness would serve as a potentially ominous sign. But as we weigh the risk factors reflected in this letter, the absence of this frame of mind is conspicuous. The author sounds hopeful about her medical care and clearly plans to be around for quite a while: ". . . and so I shall try to go on for the next few years writing mornings, being with them [her children] afternoons and seeing friends or studying and reading evenings." Earlier, in this same paragraph, she provides some of the most compelling evidence of her immediate safety when she shares her framework for meaning: her love of her children and their need for that love. This powerful reason for living is poignantly reflected in her reference to her child Freida, "I am her one security and to uproot her would be thoughtless and cruel, however sweetly you treated her at the other end."

In summary, the author's enthusiasm about her career opportunities, her awareness of the availability of both supportive friends and competent mental health professionals, her expressions of hope, and a recognition of her children's dependence on her, all argue against imminent suicide. Conversely, the next piece of writing, although much briefer, should provoke a good deal more concern:

> Dying
> Is an art, like everything else.
> I do it exceptionally well.
> I do it so it feels like hell.
> I do it so it feels real.
> I guess you could say I've a call.[11]

Although not long enough to contain many risk factors, this excerpt speaks directly to the important role of the clinician's intuitive faculties when making a suicide assessment. This poem simply has a bad feel to it. It would be the rare interviewer who would not decide to perform a thorough suicide assessment if presented with such a poem by a client.

Our intuition about this poem's bad feel would have been on the mark. The poet committed suicide roughly one year after penning this verse—a fact that paradoxically hints at the limitations of clinical intuition, for this was not the poem of someone immediately suicidal. A year passed between its writing and the fatal act. The poem was a bit of a red herring, despite its extremely ominous tone.

Conversely, the absence of many of the most foreboding risk factors from the letter would probably provide some reassurance to most clinicians. But there is one problem with this comfort. The letter was written by the same hand that penned the poem. Seven days after writing the letter, the author, Sylvia Plath, the gifted poet, was found dead—her head inside the oven of her gas range.

None of us would do a suicide assessment based on the contents of a single poem or letter. Nevertheless, the letter, for me, is particularly puzzling. Every time I read it, I must remind myself that its author killed herself just seven days later. A weighing of the risk factors revealed in the letter just doesn't seem to point in that direction.

These two examples amply illustrate the difficulties and intrigues of suicide assessment. Intuition is an important tool, but clearly it is not enough. Risk factor analysis, despite its being extensively studied, has yielded a disappointingly low predictive power, as mirrored by our analysis of Plath's letter. Are we then helpless to predict suicide? I think not. But to understand the strategies that may potentially increase our predictive powers, we must return to a study of the three tasks that are actually involved when a clinician attempts to make a suicide assessment in the rigors of everyday clinical practice.

### THE THREE TASKS OF SUICIDE ASSESSMENT

The art of suicide assessment is composed of three tasks: (1) gathering information related to the risk factors for suicide, (2) gathering information related to the patient's suicidal ideation and planning, and (3) the clinical decision making that is subsequently applied to these two databases. Errors can occur in any of these three tasks. Much attention has been given to the first and third tasks. Curiously, much less attention has been given to the practical art of eliciting suicidal ideation and planning itself. For years, the vogue has been the development of instruments for statistical analysis of risk factors.

But people don't kill themselves because statistics suggest that they should. The call to suicide comes not from statistical protocol, but from psychological pain. Each person is unique. Statistical power is at its best when applied to large populations, and at its weakest when applied to individuals. But it is the individual who clinicians must assess in the quietude of their offices or the distracting hubbub of busy emergency rooms.

It is from the patient's individual world, the intimate world of his or her own phenomenology, that suicide is conceived as the correct answer. An obvious point warrants repeating: Most people kill themselves because they *decide* to kill themselves. A given individual can present with very few risk factors, but if that patient has decided to kill himself or herself, that patient will—and the absence of risk factors be damned. Another patient may have an enormous number of risk factors, but if that patient does not want to kill himself or herself, no suicide will occur. No formal risk factor analysis will help us here, any more than it did in the reading of Sylvia Plath's letter to her mother.

Granted, some clients inadvertently kill themselves when a suicidal gesture backfires into a lethal attempt. Other clients, with processes such as borderline pathology, may move with surprising impulsivity into suicide. But these exceptions do not define the rule. Generally, a decision to kill oneself is made after a complex and stressful weighing of the pros and cons by reflective people who would not choose death as the answer if life provided better solutions. The actual behaviors that end life—swallowing pills, pulling triggers, stringing ropes—are preceded by an intricate array of thoughts devoted to the implementation of these plans. These thoughts shape, and ultimately determine, whether these actions will be undertaken.

The sequential unfolding of thought and action, inherent in the process of attempting suicide, offers clinicians a glimmer of hope concerning our attempts at suicide prediction, because it suggests that there are warnings of imminent suicidal action. But these warnings lie deep inside the mind and soul of the client. On one level, an uncovering of the client's internal dialogue, concerning the pros and cons of committing suicide, can provide important clues toward prediction. But on a more practical level, knowledge of the degree of concrete planning and the actions taken on that planning probably serves as a better barometer of how close at hand the act may be. If the clinician is allowed to enter this secretive world of concrete suicidal planning, such an invitation may represent the best window we have into the severity of the client's pain and the proximity of death as an answer to that pain.

## THE WINDOW INTO SUICIDE: CHRONOLOGICAL ASSESSMENT OF SUICIDE EVENTS

A window into the client's world of concrete suicidal planning was missing in the analysis of risk in the two pieces of writing by Sylvia Plath. It wouldn't be surprising to learn that on the very day of writing the letter, Sylvia Plath had been considering various ways of ending her life. But we were not privy to her actual suicidal ideation, which no doubt plays a major role in our lack of predictive validity. If we had been granted access to this world, what would we have seen?

No one can say for sure, but I suspect that during the weeks predating the writing of that letter and the week following it, Plath courageously struggled with the most momentous decision of her life. She was a highly sensitive, responsible, and loving parent; she would not have made the decision to die unless she saw no other solution. What then were the likely thought processes of Sylvia Plath during those last days?

On a practical level, suicide is not easy to do. Plath describes it as an "art" in her poem. As with any art, suicide generally requires thoughtful and sometimes meticulous planning and discipline. The degree of planning and the dedication to detail often provide insight into the likelihood that the task will be accomplished. If we had been privy to the intimate thoughts of Sylvia Plath, especially her concrete planning regarding suicide, I believe we would have found a wealth of harbingers of her death, betraying the benign facade of her letter.

If she was like many others in the same frame of mind, she would have been reviewing her options for death. Various methods of killing herself would have been contemplated, with the pluses and minuses of each method carefully considered. She would have had a myriad of practical considerations to mull over: the degree of pain she wanted, the finality of the plan, where to do it, the prevention of premature discovery, the person whom she wanted to find her body, the protection against her children's finding her body, the time of day (or night) to do it, the decision about writing a suicide note or letters to close friends and to her mother, the possible use of alcohol to buttress her resolve to follow through, and a rehearsal of the method in an effort to perfect it.

Not all patients who are imminently suicidal think such thoughts. But most patients consider some of them—and, at times, all of them— especially in the weeks immediately preceding their suicide attempt. And they think about them a lot.

The greater the degree to which the full extent of this planning can be elicited, the more likely the clinician will gain insight into the seriousness of the client's intent. In my experience, gaining access to a client's concrete suicidal planning provides the most reliable data for a sound suicide assessment. Indeed, it can be argued that the degree with which the patient shares these thoughts, and shares them truthfully, may prove to be the limiting factor in how accurate a clinician can be in predicting suicide.

Looking for ever more effective ways of uncovering this type of acute suicidal ideation is an exciting and challenging mission. In this book, an interview strategy called the Chronological Assessment of Suicide Events (CASE Approach)[12, 13] will be described in detail. At present, this interview strategy has not been studied empirically. Indeed, one of the goals of this book is to invite researchers to vigorously test and evaluate the effectiveness of the CASE Approach. It is designed to provide a practical framework for clinicians' study of what they actually do in a client interview. It is not offered as the "right way" to elicit suicidal ideation, it is "a way" to elicit suicidal ideation. Its study will, I hope, prompt readers to develop their "own way."

In examining the principles of the CASE Approach, clinicians are invited to adapt what is appealing, reject what may not be appealing, and strive constantly for flexibility in its application. The ultimate goal is to creatively match our interviewing style to the needs of each unique client. Through the window provided by the CASE Approach, in conjunction with the clinician's understanding of the client's risk factors, the clinician is best able to begin his or her clinical formulation, the complexities of which form the focus of the concluding chapter of this book.

The next chapter gives a more detailed look at the phenomenology and etiology of suicide. To end here on a positive note, let us look at the results of a clinical encounter in which the types of techniques we have been discussing may have effected a very different outcome.

## A TUESDAY AFTERNOON REPRISE

I was a psychiatric resident at Western Psychiatric Institute and Clinic in Pittsburgh many years ago. One Tuesday afternoon, I was in my office catching up on some long overdue discharge summaries. It was always difficult to get an hour for paperwork in the middle of the day. Invariably, phone calls disrupted the work, or colleagues dropped by to "shoot the breeze."

That afternoon proved to be no different. There was a knock. When I opened the door, I was face-to-face with an unexpected visitor, who smiled warmly. I immediately recognized Judith, a middle-age woman whom I had treated as an inpatient the prior year. Judith lived in Canada, hundreds of miles away. What was she doing in the bustling streets of Pittsburgh?

I remembered how I first met Judith. On the night of her hospital admission, as with this new encounter, Judith had traveled hundreds of miles. But on that night she was tracking down a boyfriend who had unexpectedly jilted her and taken off to Pittsburgh to live with a different woman. According to Judith, he had refused to see her; he slammed his apartment door in her face and threatened to call the cops. Judith drove to a local park, found a secluded area, and popped a bottle of pills, which she promptly chased down with a bottle of wine. The overdose should have been fatal, but a local police officer became suspicious of her parked car.

Once admitted to the inpatient unit, Judith presented with a curious mixture of depression laced with a heated rage. She was furious that her suicide attempt had failed, and even more furious that we were detaining her against her will. Five days later, when I committed her again, she screamed a few innovative expletives. Over the subsequent weeks, her progress in therapy and with medications was slow, although she repeatedly claimed that she was feeling better. As time passed, Judith and I developed a genuine therapeutic bond. Occasionally, a spunky, funny Judith poked out from beneath her depressive shawl. But such pleasant interludes were infrequent. The staff liked Judith. So did I. But as her release date approached, I felt uncomfortable.

After careful formulation and consultation, I decided that I needed to commit her again. It was a very difficult decision; I was worried that I was being overly protective and was infringing on her civil rights, a point she repeatedly made quite clear to me. To complicate matters, some of the staff felt that it was okay for her to go. There was an unpleasant tension on the unit. We all felt stressed. Judith was indeed shocked and outraged at my decision. It was not a good day at work.

Fortunately, the rest of the hospital stay went better. About two weeks later it became clear that the antidepressant power of her medication was kicking in. In her psychotherapy a new will to live emerged. Judith was discharged several weeks later.

And, on that Tuesday afternoon twelve months later, I stood looking at a feisty, small-framed woman with equally feisty eyes. She had bought a new blue business suit. Her hair was neatly trimmed, and just the lightest breath of makeup customized her cheeks. Our conversation went something like this.

"Hi, Dr. Shea. Do you remember me?"

"Of course I do, Judith. How are you? What brings you down here?"

She paused for a moment. "I drove all the way down here to say something to you."

"Well, what's up?" I asked.

"I just wanted to let you know that the day you committed me, you know, the last time? Well, I was going to kill myself. If you'd have let me go, I'd have never made it out of Pittsburgh. I had the whole thing planned, down to the hotel room." She smiled gently, "You really did save my life, and I wanted to thank you again."

I didn't know exactly what to say.

She continued, "You'll be glad to know that I've found a new job and a new guy—who is not half bad either, I might add. I'm truly enjoying myself. And believe it or not, I'm really glad to be alive."

"That's great to hear. I'll tell everybody up on the unit you stopped by. They'll be very pleased."

At this point, there was a bit of an awkward pause.

"Well, that's it," she quipped. Her mission apparently had been accomplished. "Thanks again."

She started down the hallway. After a few steps, she paused and turned. "Hey, Dr. Shea."

"Yes, Judith?"

"Keep up the good work." And she darted down the hallway.

When I sat down again at my desk, I glanced over at the stack of discharge charts. I smiled and told myself they could wait one more day. I had forty minutes left, just long enough to head down to Oakland Avenue to browse the aisles of my favorite bookstore.

## NOTES

1. Alvarez, A.: *The Savage God—A Study in Suicide.* New York, Random House, 1971.

2. Alvarez, A., 1971, p. 138.

3. National Institute of Mental Health: Suicide Fact Sheet (based on 1996 statistics), NIMH Website, April 1999.

4. Roy, A.: Psychiatric emergencies, suicide. In *The Comprehensive Textbook of Psychiatry, 6th Edition,* edited by H.I. Kaplan and B.J. Sadock. Baltimore, Williams and Wilkins, 1995, pp. 1739–1752.

5. NIMH Website, June 1996 update.

6. Hirschfeld, R.M.A.: Algorithms for the evaluation and treatment of suicidal patients. *Primary Psychiatry* 3: 26–29, 1996.

7. Centers for Disease Control and Prevention: Suicide Deaths and Rates per 100,00 (based on 1995 statistics), CDC Website, April 1999.

8. Fawcett, J., Clark, D.C., and Busch, K.A.: Assessing and treating the patient at risk for suicide. *Psychiatric Annals* 23: 244–255, 1993.

9. Rich, C.L., Young, D., and Fowler, R.C.: San Diego suicide study. *Archives of General Psychiatry* 43: 577–582, 1986.

10. Plath, S.: "Final letter" from *Letters Home,* by Sylvia Plath: Correspondence 1950–1963 by Aurelia Schober Plath. Copyright © 1975 by Aurelia Schober Plath. Reprinted by permission of HarperCollins Publishers, Inc., 1975, pp. 498–500.

11. Plath, S.: "Lady Lazarus" in *The Norton Anthology of Modern Poetry,* edited by R. Ellman and R. O'Clair. New York, W.W. Norton & Company, 1973, pp. 1295–1297.

12. Shea, S.C.: *Psychiatric Interviewing: The Art of Understanding, 2nd Edition.* Philadelphia, W.B. Saunders Company, 1998.

13. Shea, S.C.: The chronological assessment of suicide events: A practical interviewing strategy for eliciting suicidal ideation. *The Journal of Clinical Psychiatry (supplement)* 59: 58–72, 1998.

# CHAPTER 2

# Descent into the Maelstrom: Etiology and Phenomenology of Suicide

> It may appear strange, but now, when we were in the very jaws
> of the gulf, I felt more composed than when we were only
> approaching it. Having made up my mind to hope no more, I
> got rid of a great deal of that terror which unmanned me at
> first. I suppose it was despair that strung my nerves.
>
> From "A Descent into the Maelstrom" by Edgar Allan Poe[1]

## THE NATURE OF THE STORM

EDGAR ALLAN Poe based his story on a most intriguing natural phenomenon, the whirlpools known as "maelstroms" that churn off the western coast of Norway. In Poe's story, the protagonist encounters a monstrous variety of maelstrom that sucks his sea vessel into its black depths and furies. A maelstrom is a fitting metaphor to represent the inner suffering and psychological chaos of the descent into suicidal pain. The everyday world is sucked into the blackness of suicidal cognition. All is seen as pointless and hopeless. The world constricts into a tightly funneled vision of endless despair. It is not a nice place to be. And people will do what they need to do to get out.

The opening quote even seems to fit a curious phenomenon sometimes alluded to in the suicide literature. Once they have made the decision to end their lives, some people become suddenly calm. The anxiety accompanying the intimidating decision to end or continue life is over. Relief from pain is in sight.

Another calmness merits our attention when we consider the phenomenology of suicide and suicide prediction, but it bodes well for the *continuation* of life. It is the calmness inside an experienced clinician's mind as he or she approaches the fury of a patient's unique suicidal maelstrom. Not all therapists and assessment clinicians do well with people contemplating suicide; those who do best exhibit an unmistakable trait. They approach the stress generated by a patient's repeated contemplation of suicide with a surprisingly matter-of-fact calmness that is at the very crux of their success in both uncovering and transforming suicidal ideation. It is the calmness of knowledge. It is the calmness of experience. It is the calmness of "been there, done that."

These therapists are familiar with suicidal maelstroms. They realize that they should take nothing for granted, and they conscientiously attend to their maps during the ravages of the storm. They recognize that they cannot save everybody within the maelstrom, but they can save a large number. They are familiar with suicide and not afraid to explore its steep walls. Their calmness casts a refreshing and reassuring lifeline to their patients. They offer a safe haven in which patients share the extent of their suicidal plans but often find a therapeutic trust that allows them to transform and ultimately abandon those very same plans.

As hinted in Chapter 1, this calmness partially comes from knowledge of what triggers suicidal ideation and of the ways in which it is experienced. An understanding of the intricate interactions among the environmental stresses, cognitive distortions, and biochemical influences that are so common in suicidal process helps the experienced clinician to avoid the pitfalls and surprises into which less experienced professionals are apt to stumble. For readers without years of clinical experience, this chapter functions as a "jump start." It is not a replacement for clinical experience, but it is meant to help accelerate the process of learning from such experience. Toward this end, let us begin our study with a "suicide fact" that is not often a topic of discussion.

Arguably, the most startling irony of suicide is that so few people do it. This statement is not made facetiously. It is meant to highlight an often underemphasized, yet ultimately reassuring fact: Roughly less than one percent of people who have had suicidal ideation go on to kill themselves. This is an extraordinarily important number. It is a measure of hope.

To frontline clinicians, this number suggests that most humans are eventually able to transform suicidal ideation. Indeed, for the vast majority of people who experience it, suicidal ideation is usually of a transient nature. If a clinician can spot a client who is acutely suicidal and provide an alternative solution that delays the act, there is a reasonable chance that the person will have a change of mind. But first we have to be able to uncover the hidden suicidal ideations. Once they are uncovered, we have to be able to decide which suicidal ideation is the harbinger of immediate danger and which is not.

Much of this book is dedicated to demonstrating tools for doing both of these tasks. But before we look at the available tools, we need to be acquainted with some more nebulous areas of knowledge that will serve us well.

To understand when and how to effectively utilize interviewing strategies, such as the CASE Approach, we must first descend as the characters in Poe's short story did, into a maelstrom of sorts. This maelstrom is not the maelstrom of an uncontrolled Nature whipping at the sea, it is the maelstrom of an uncrontrolled Nature cutting into the soul. The slide down the turbulent walls of a single person's descent into suicide is a frightening one. It is one that all clinicians who want to become expert at suicide assessment must undertake. Once within the maelstrom, the clinician will come face-to-face with two clarifying frameworks, that will be pivotal in enhancing the clinician's ability to effectively use the interviewing techniques described in the remainder of this book.

## TWO FRAMEWORKS FOR UNDERSTANDING THE NATURE OF SUICIDE

The first framework, the *etiology* of suicidal ideation, is deceptively simple. Suicidal ideation can spring from three main types of factors: (1) situational, (2) psychological, and (3) biological. Each etiologic factor can produce a markedly distinctive presentation of suicidal ideation and behavior. Some presentations facilitate prediction; others cloud the picture. The more a clinician understands these differing etiologies, the less likely that he or she will be caught off guard by the sometimes apparently whimsical nature of a suicidal act. A theoretical understanding of etiology early in a clinician's career can be the foundation for life-saving intuition later.

The second framework of suicidal ideation consists of an ever-growing understanding of the *phenomenology* of suicide. Each person's inner maelstrom harbors unique emotions, cognitions, and nightmares. There is no such thing as a "typical" suicidal patient. This does not mean we should not hunt for similarities in cognition and emotion among suicidal people. But it does mean that we should not become slaves to the stereotypes that such information can create when applied uniformly and simplistically.

The importance of phenomenology is not limited to the inner world of the patient. It is also greatly impacted by the inner world of the interviewer, who automatically becomes part of the interpersonal field from which suicidal ideation arises. A given clinician may or may not feel comfortable with a specific interviewing technique, depending on his or her own history with suicidal ideation in self, family, friends, or patients. Such factors can greatly interfere with the clinician's openness to new ideas of suicide assessment or even to the value of attempting to predict suicide risk in the first place.

The inner worlds of both the patient and the interviewer are also affected by the room in which they meet. The process of eliciting suicidal ideation is indelibly stamped by the constraints of the clinical setting. Each interviewing dyad is uniquely defined by the interplay of variables created by the characteristics of the client, the clinician, and the clinical setting. This unique situational interplay determines which interviewing techniques will be most effective with a given client/clinician dyad interacting in a specific setting—emergency room, school counselor's office, substance abuse clinic.

For example, performing an initial suicide assessment in an emergency room, when the patient is suffering from a major depressive episode, is not the same as assessing the suicide potential in a patient who has undergone years of therapy for a borderline personality disorder. In this book, especially in Chapter 7, the variations in technique that are demanded by the differences in the clinical setting or the clinical relationship will be explored carefully.

No one can pretend to know exactly what causes suicidal thought; even the patients experiencing the suicidal ideation do not know the cause with certainty. But, by piecing together diverse strands of knowledge and carefully heeding the words of suicidal patients and the writings of those who have tried to help them, we can begin to sort out a matrix of factors that cause a person to become acutely suicidal. The key word here is *matrix*. Suicide, more often than not, has multiple causes.

For the purposes of our discussion, the etiologic factors of suicide will be placed into three categories. It is critical to remember that, for most clients, *mixtures* of these categories are at work when suicidal thought is developing. Unraveling the proportion of each etiologic category that is contributing to a given suicidal presentation can help clarify the clinical strategies that will best facilitate both assessment and treatment. Suicidal ideation seems to be triggered by:

1. External stressors (e.g., death of or rejection by a significant other, job loss, public humiliation, serious illness).
2. Internal conflict (e.g., psychological impasses, unconscious conflicts, cognitive distortions and binds).
3. Neurobiological dysfunction (e.g., exogenous toxins such as alcohol and/or cocaine, or endogenous pathophysiology as evidenced during spontaneously arising biologic depressions).

To explore these three etiologic categories and the differing phenomenological responses they create in individuals, we will look at the world of suicidal ideation through the eyes of those who have experienced it.

## PART I: THE ROLE OF EXTERNAL STRESSORS IN THE ETIOLOGY OF SUICIDE

### A HISTORICAL CASE STUDY

Suicidal ideation knows no allegiance to time nor place. Our first exploration begins in England, in 1862, a time very different from our own. The place is London, alive with all of the intrigues and paradoxes of its Queen Mother, Victoria. Our focus is upon a talented and tenacious artist named Elizabeth Siddal. Known as Lizzy to her husband and friends, she has found herself involved with a curious mix of significant others.

In 1848, her then husband-to-be, Dante Gabriel Rossetti, and two of his friends, John Everett Millais and William Holman Hunt, had created a renegade art movement born from the cocky exuberance of late adolescence. They boldly proclaimed themselves the "Pre-Raphaelite Brotherhood," announcing to the world that most of the art created since the time of Raphael, as anyone with much of a brain could pretty well see, had been botched by their elders. In the normal course of events, these twenty-year-old youths should have become mere footnotes of adolescent grandiosity. But there was a catch. All three of them were brilliant.

Rossetti had a knack for capturing the sensuality of women. His startling palette of velvety greens and languid reds seemed to catch the fancy of all of Victorian England. John Everett Millais would go on to become one of the most famous portrait artists in Europe and eventually assumed the presidency of the Royal Academy of the Arts. The fame of William Holman Hunt was perhaps the most astounding. The reclusive Hunt later painted one of the most famous pictures of all time: a picture of Christ called *The Light of the World.* In its day, the painting drew massive crowds to London. Nor did its fame stop at the shores of merry olde England. It captivated the world. It has been estimated that, in Australia alone, four million people, or four-fifths of the population, saw the painting two or three times.[2]

Into this gifted mix, enter one Elizabeth Siddal. In addition to her frail and wispy physical beauty, Elizabeth had a keen artist's eye and an even keener poet's mind. Under the tutelage of Rossetti, she created wonderful watercolors and even more striking poems. Today, she is recognized as a minor but significant Victorian poet.

Unfortunately, Rossetti, the gifted artist, was an equally gifted narcissist. Today, in a book on social conduct, he would be listed under "Men Who Cannot Commit." He repeatedly professed his love to Elizabeth but doggedly refused to marry her. Over the years, the toll on Elizabeth was painfully visible to all within the Pre-Raphaelite circle. Eventually, whether in response to pressure from his peers, shame, or insight, Rossetti proposed marriage.

Her marriage did not prove to be the panacea for which Elizabeth had hoped. As she continued to deal with her husband's self-centeredness, she was confronted with a new enemy—a debilitating case of tuberculosis. The answer to her agonies lay within a quiet hope, barely whispered for fear of scaring it away. Elizabeth desperately wanted a child. Her wish was soon granted; to her great joy, she became pregnant. All of her hopes for happiness were inflamed by the dreams of giving birth and the wonders sure to be waiting for her and her husband. Even her tuberculosis seemed to wane beneath the promise of this miracle.

In the Spring of 1861, Rossetti wrote home to his mother, "Lizzy has just been delivered of a dead child."[3] The resulting agony of Elizabeth Siddal provides a penetrating glimpse into the relationship between external stress and the decision to kill oneself. It is difficult to imagine a more potent external stressor. Her loss triggered her descent into a suicidal maelstrom from which she was not able to arise. We have access to her descent because it was captured in the poetry of her journal and the writings of the artistic circle who loved her.

It did not take long to see the devastation wrought upon Elizabeth by the loss of her child; indeed, there appears to have been a brief interlude of psychotic escape. Shortly after her loss, some close friends visited at her Chatham Place home in London. A more recent newcomer to the Pre-Raphaelite circle, Edward Burne-Jones, who would prove to be as brilliant as the three originators, had become, with his wife "Georgie," close friends of the Rossettis. Elizabeth fondly referred to Edward as "Ned." Ned and Georgie were not fully prepared for the intensity of Elizabeth's pain. They found their dear friend "sitting in a low chair with the childless cradle on the floor beside her, and . . . she cried with a kind of soft wildness as we came in, 'Hush, Ned, you'll waken it!'"[4]

In the months that followed, a second loss rocked the fragile world of Elizabeth and her husband. They had decided to adopt a child, but the adoption fell through at the very last moment, a loss that proved to be too much for the beleaguered Elizabeth. Following this disappointment, Elizabeth's poetry took on an ominous tone:

> I am gazing upwards to the sun,
> Lord, Lord, remembering my lost one.
>    O Lord, remember me!
> How is it in the unknown land?
> Do the dead wander hand in hand?
> Do we clasp dead hands, and quiver
> With an endless joy for ever?[5]

The image of Elizabeth touching her beloved child's hand is chilling. In a fragment of one of her later poems, the tone soon becomes even more foreboding. This subsequent poem was written as her spirits tumbled and tossed in the currents of the cold winter winds of 1861:

> Laden autumn, here I stand
> With my sheaves in either hand.
> Speak the word that sets me free,
> Naught but rest seems good to me.[6]

"Laden autumn" is an eerie play on words in the first line; Laudanum would prove to be the agent of her death shortly afterward. On a late Monday night, February 10, 1862, Rossetti returned home to find Lizzy comatose on her bed. A phial of laudanum was found sitting on a bed-side table. It was empty.

From Elizabeth Siddal's death, much can be learned to prevent future deaths. Elizabeth stands as a powerful reminder that people do indeed kill themselves in direct response to stressors. At one level, that fact seems so obvious that it almost doesn't bear mentioning. But there is a pitfall to keep in mind. Elizabeth Siddal killed herself in response to the stillbirth of her child, an admittedly horrific experience but one that others have undergone without killing themselves. The stressor per se does not result in suicide. The individual's *interpretation* of the stressor will guide the patient's hand either toward the bottle of laudanum or away from it.

---

PRACTICAL TIPS FOR EVALUATING THE PSYCHOLOGICAL IMPACT OF STRESSORS

Of particular importance is the fact that any given patient may cognitively distort a relatively small stressor into a lethal stressor. I believe all of us might be wary of suicidal intent in the presence of a distraught mother who has just lost her child at birth. But how do we view an adolescent boy who has just lost the lead in his high school's musical, or a 16-year-old girl whose parents will not let her drive other kids in the family car despite her newly obtained driver's license? Adults might easily be lulled into a false sense of security in such situations because of the seemingly insubstantial gravity of the stressor. But the clinician must assiduously remember that the individual patient's unique interpretation of an event determines whether a stressor may prove to be a lethal trigger.

For purposes of illustration, let us look more closely at the hypothetical adolescent boy who did not land the lead role in the high school musical. Most adolescents would eventually relegate this disappointment to its appropriate role as one of life's many setbacks. But assume that the boy came from an abusive home, where he was constantly belittled by his alcoholic father. Further, imagine that he lay awake at nights dreaming of escaping his personal nightmare by landing a scholarship to college for acting. To him, the loss of the role could easily be viewed as eliminating the hope of escape and the even more pressing hope for self-vindication. The loss of the acting role has become transformed from a disappointment into a psychologically catastrophic event perhaps as devastating as a stillbirth to a woman. But its significance is only apparent if one enters the client's world and views the event through the client's unique perspective toward the stressors of daily life.

Family and friends may be able to provide invaluable insight on the severity of a stressor in the patient's mind. However, the most effective way to evaluate perceived stress is to ask the patient about it directly. The following questions, which can be rephrased to apply to any specific stressor, can be of use:

1. What do you feel will be the impact of this loss on you?
2. Do you see any way that this loss can be replaced for you?
3. On a scale from one to ten, with "one" being no pain and "ten" being unbearable pain, where would you place your pain?
4. Do you see any way that this pain will lessen or end for you?

As the patient answers these questions, a vivid window may begin to open, revealing the cognitive interpretation that the patient is giving to the stressor. It is here that a clinician may stumble upon a potentially lethal stressor that would not have seemed dangerous at first glance.

## EVALUATING THE ALLURE OF THE HEREAFTER

The degree with which a client views suicide as a viable solution for escaping the pain inherent with a life stressor is sometimes directly affected by the client's perception of what will happen following the act of suicide. Is there a hereafter, and what does it hold? Elizabeth Siddal highlighted how enticing the pull to death can be, if a person truly believes in an afterlife and is confident that God is tolerant of suicide if it is done for appropriate reasons. The chance to be reunited with a loved one is a powerful lure. For Elizabeth, death offered the opportunity to hold once again the hand of her child and to smell the sweetness of his head. The prospect of feeling the warmth of his cheek against hers would prove to be too compelling for her to resist. Such a deeply held belief of reunion with loved ones in heaven is a convincing argument for suicide, but some clinicians do not intuitively grasp it because it is foreign to their spiritual point of view. It is important not only to grasp it, but to truly respect the power of its draw. Questions such as the following can help:

1. Do you believe in an afterlife?
2. Do you believe you will see your [loved one] again in heaven?
3. Do you picture yourself seeing [the loved one] again?
4. Share with me what you think it will be like.
5. How much time do you spend thinking about seeing your [loved one] again?
6. Do you think God approves of suicide?
7. Do you think that God will forgive you if you kill yourself?

Matter-of-fact explorations can lead to some surprises—bad and good. A belief in heaven, because it offers the hope of a reunion with loved ones, might support a decision to end one's life. Conversely, a belief in the hereafter may forbid suicide as an option among people who fear that suicide is punishable with damnation and would thus eternally prevent a reunion with loved ones.

## EVALUATING THE RAVAGES OF AGE

The case of Elizabeth Siddal illustrates the role of the loss of a loved one in triggering suicidal ideation. But other losses can also function as powerful external stressors that decrease the desire to continue the ongoing battle of life. These losses can occur at any age, but they are most striking as one grows older. For some people, the aging process is surprisingly benign; the last years of life are filled with vigor and relatively good health. For many others, the passing of time is marked by a series of losses, behind whose wake the lust for life disappears.

The suicide of the eloquent and charming psychoanalyst, Bruno Bettelheim, provides insight to this process. Bettelheim, a true lover of life, was perhaps best known for his thought-provoking book, the 1976 National Book Award winner, *The Uses of Enchantment*, which delved into the role of fairy tales as a means of wrestling with the fears and bogeymen of childhood. Near the end of his life, Bettelheim lost his wife. This loss was followed by several strokes, which made it difficult for him to write. His mobility and strength declined. He feared the loss of his role as a mentor and, ultimately, the meaning of his life itself.

In a series of interviews with Celeste Fremon from *The Los Angeles Times Magazine*, Bettelheim, then approaching his eighty-seventh year, was surprisingly open about his thoughts of suicide. He repeatedly referred to the "ravages of age." When asked whether he was afraid of dying, he answered with simple Bettelheimian elegance, "No. I fear suffering. The older one gets, the greater the likelihood that one will be kept alive without purpose."[7] He continued:

> Things I enjoyed are no longer available to me, you know. I like to walk. I like to hike. Now when I read, I get tired. Dickens wrote: "It was the best of all times. It was the worst of all times." It all depends on how you look at it. At my age you can no longer look at it and say, "It is the best of all times." At least I find it impossible. However, if I could be sure that I would not be in pain or be a vegetable, then, like most everyone, I believe I would prefer to live. But, of course, there is no such guarantee. This is why the decision is so problematic.

Five months after uttering these words, Bruno Bettelheim made his decision. He was found dead on the bedroom floor of his new apartment in a Maryland nursing home. A plastic bag about his head served to ensure the effectiveness of the barbiturates streaming through his bloodstream.

Bettelheim's series of losses serves as a vivid reminder of the warning signs of dangerousness, especially in the elderly. When performing a suicide assessment, I have found it useful to look for the following types of losses:

1. Loss of health.
2. Loss of mobility, cognitive functioning, ability for self-care.
3. Loss of role within family or society.
4. Loss of skills, job, or job opportunity.
5. Loss of means of self-support.

6. Loss of home or cherished possessions.
7. Loss of loved ones, including pets.

This list of losses represents a good starting platform with a client of any age, if there is suspicion that the client may be developing suicidal ideation in response to external stressors. It is important, especially with elderly clients, to be able to openly discuss this material and its specific ramifications for the individual client. This must be done with a no-nonsense attitude and with the clinician's willing acceptance that the client may be correct in saying that things are only going to get worse.

The psychological pain that occurs when one loses the ability for self-care, as evidenced by incontinence or inability to feed oneself, cannot be overestimated. It is important to openly explore these changes with the client, to note his or her individual response to such personal losses, and to attempt to see the impact of the continuing stress through the eyes of the client. This can be done with a gentle query such as, "John, I know you've lost a lot of functioning from the multiple sclerosis, from your speech to even being able to control your bowels. I know this has got to be very painful for you. I'm wondering how it makes you feel about yourself—who you are and what the future holds." This approach unveils taboo topics. The interviewer's compassionate entry into this taboo area can create a powerful moment for a client. The interviewer may be the first person with whom the pain of such changes in self-image can be shared.

As we close this topic it is refreshing to note that our culture is finally moving toward a long overdue recognition that some of these situations may represent, for disease-ravaged persons, legitimate and rational times for considering ending life with their dignity intact.

### PUBLIC HUMILIATION AS A TRIGGER FOR SUICIDE

The suicides of Elizabeth Siddal and Bruno Bettelheim were triggered by one of the most common external stressors: death or loss. A loss of another kind—the loss of respect or public approval—presents as a real concern. To the degree that the client feels that such approval can never be regained, the risk of suicide probably increases. Even an apparently innocuous loss of approval can prove to be fatal if cognitively transformed into a catastrophic "loss of face." This was apparently the cause for the tragic loss of the distinguished Navy career man, Admiral Robbie Inman, to suicide. In 1997, *Newsweek* purported to have uncovered the fact that Admiral Inman was wearing a medal that indicated active combat duty, which the admiral did not merit. Rather than risk public humiliation and the loss of his colleagues' respect, Inman shot himself in the head.

In some cultures and subcultures, such an action may not carry the same condemnation it frequently earns in American society. Acceptance of suicide or even peer pressure to commit it, can significantly increase the risk of suicide in these circumstances. Suicide can be viewed as an effective means of achieving the following three ends: avoiding public humiliation, accepting responsibility for one's inappropriate actions, or dramatically demonstrating one's conviction behind specific political causes or moral beliefs. Sometimes it can seem to mirror all three of these processes as was the case with the act of *seppuku* by one of the most famous writers of modern Japan, Yukio Mishima.

*Seppuku*, suicide by self-disembowelment, demonstrates the ritual standardization of suicide as a means of "saving face." Until the death of Mishima, there had been no act of *seppuku* in Japan since immediately after World War II adding to the shock on November 25, 1970, when Mishima and an accomplice took their own lives. Mishima, known as a radical reactionary, was brimming with fiery notions of the need for the Japanese to return to the proud and militaristic past of an idealized age of glorified Emperors.

Mishima and his accomplices concocted and executed a rather bizarre kidnapping of Kanetoshi Mashita, a Japanese general. As a prerequisite for his safe return, they demanded that a large group of youthful Japanese soldiers be assembled to hear a speech by Mishima, that was naively designed to bring the soldiers to an uprising. After the speech, Mishima planned to commit *seppuku*. Behind the external illogic of this almost surreal plan, one can discern the three suicidal motivators described above, providing a sort of internal logic—avoidance of humiliation, acceptance of responsibility for wrong-doing, and demonstration of one's political or moral convictions.

The months of careful planning suggest that the suicide itself may well have represented not only a means of avoiding the humiliation of the public trial that was sure to follow, but also a display of the willingness to self-sacrifice for the "cause at hand." It may have even included an almost polite acknowledgment that any disruption caused to the general and the country was due solely to Mishima's actions. In this regard, Mishima was quite concerned that the general might subsequently attempt suicide, and he went to great lengths to make sure that his followers kept the general safe following his own death. As Mishima addressed the crowd of Japanese soldiers, to his disappointment his ideas were met with condescension and jeers. This humiliation may have further fueled his need for a "way out." Mishima promptly stepped inside and proceeded to quietly commit suicide, aided by his carefully chosen "second" who mercifully quickened the end via decapitation.

Before leaving Mishima, it is worth focusing upon the rather strange twist that his death provides to the concept of suicide as a response to shame or humiliation. In some instances, the act of suicide is so glorified—to oneself, to one's peers, or to both—that it becomes an act of shame or humiliation to not do it. Suicide becomes not the way but the goal. I don't believe I have ever seen this glamorization better illustrated than in Mishima's essay "Sun and Steel":

> Such is the beauty of the suicide squad, which is recognized as beauty not only in the spiritual sense but, by men in general, in an ultra-erotic sense also . . . No moment is so dazzling as when everyday imaginings concerning death and danger and world destruction are transformed into duty . . . To keep death in mind from day to day, to focus each moment upon inevitable death, to make sure one's worst forebodings coincided with one's dreams of glory.[8]

Clinicians need not be overly concerned with cross-cultural fears of seppuku when counseling Japanese students. But there is a good reason I have chosen to emphasize it. An understanding of seppuku provides an important and often understated reminder that suicide risk can be related to external stressors, especially public humiliation or fear that public humiliation is inevitable. The proclivity of an individual to try to escape the pain of an external stressor by committing suicide is not determined solely by the degree of the individual's pain. It can be greatly spurred by the individual's perception that the subculture within which he or she lives condones or even romanticizes suicide as an appropriate "out." Nowhere is such romanticization as prevalent as in the adolescent population.

## EVALUATING THE ROLE OF HUMILIATION AS AN ETIOLOGY FOR SUICIDE AMONG STUDENTS AND OTHER ADOLESCENTS

While working as school counselors, from middle school through college, or while performing psychotherapy with adolescents, it is important for professionals to keep a key principle in mind: Probably during no other period of human development are individuals more apt to be savaged by public humiliation and peer denigration than in the ego-vulnerable years of adolescence. Shame and humiliation may be generated in relation to the perception that one has failed one's parents' expectations, or has been repeatedly humiliated by violence and abuse within the home, or is regarded as an outsider by one's peers. I believe that whereas loss is probably the most common driving force toward suicide among the elderly, public humiliation is probably the more frequent driving force with adolescents. Consequently, making an evaluation of the pressures that encourage using suicide to escape the stress inherent in the client's immediate subculture is of particular importance in this age population. Two distinct situations can signal danger: (1) a relatively recent suicide of a friend or fellow student often in an effort to escape peer denigration or bullying, and (2) a subculture that romanticizes suicide.

As the rate of suicide has increased in the adolescent age group, it has become more common for students contemplating suicide to have firsthand experience of another student's suicide. One suicide can serve as a model for subsequent "cluster" suicides. It can also automatically increase the amount of time that students spend talking about suicide. In a sense, this increased exposure to the topic of suicide serves as a desensitizing agent. Consequently, students become more accepting of the idea that suicide may be an okay solution to the stresses of life, including humiliation.

Even when there is no model for student suicide, be on the lookout for increased risk of suicide in students who may be physically unattractive, uncoordinated, or too short, too tall, or overweight compared to their peers. All of these traits can result in vicious verbal abuse or violence. Another vulnerable group are students who are wrestling with acceptance of their homosexuality, which may also result in aggressive taunting and violence. These students may regard the suicide of a fellow student as a model for obtaining relief, a possible solution for escaping their own pain. This is particularly dangerous if the student identifies in some way with the student who killed himself or herself—for example, both students may have been subjected to verbal and physical abuse because of their short stature.

Regarding another student's suicide, the following questions may be of use ("Jim" is the theoretical student who committed suicide):

1. Did you know Jim very well?
2. Did Jim ever talk to you about suicide?
3. What did Jim say about the pros and cons of killing himself?
4. When was the last time you saw Jim?
5. Were you or other kids at all suspicious that Jim might be thinking of killing himself?
6. Do you have any concerns that somehow you could have prevented Jim from killing himself?
7. Do you think that Jim was right to kill himself?
8. What do you think happened to Jim *after* he killed himself? Do you think he now has an afterlife?
9. Did you and Jim have anything in common?
10. Has Jim's death made you think at all about killing yourself?

A second problem that may drive a student to escape humiliation through an act of suicide is peer glamorization of both death and suicide. Some rock cultures clearly have romanticized suicide, sometimes coupling it with a primitive eroticization—a combination that can prove deadly—not so unlike Mishima's suicidal fantasies. An example of this glamorization of death is reflected in the black garb and vampiric images of the current "goth" scene. Many goths have a love of life and are innocently enjoying the forbidden nature of their alternative lifestyle and the attention it brings. But, for some goths who are dealing with depression and isolation, suicide can appear as a romanticized method of ending life with a dramatic flair. A further complication can be an unconscious fascination with the idea that life after death may be a vampiric existence. The image of a supernaturally endowed vampire may be powerfully attractive to any adolescent who has been repeatedly made to feel weak and vulnerable.

Some rock cultures and specific rock groups have made a business of romanticizing suicide. Repeated references to suicide show up in their lyrics. With an adolescent who seems allied to a subculture that is pushing suicide, the following questions can be useful in raising the topic:

1. You know, suicide comes up a lot in some contemporary music. Are there any groups you like that tend to talk a lot about it?
2. What are some of the lyrics that fascinate you about suicide?
3. Do you know if any of the members of that band have tried to kill themselves or cut themselves?
4. What is your opinion about that?

It is sometimes useful to ask the student to write down the lyrics for you, or even bring in the CD, so that you can listen and then open up a discussion on the feelings generated by the music. This can be done by indicating interest: "Mary, I'd like to learn more about songs like that; maybe you could teach me a little about what is popular now. Would you be able to bring in the lyrics to that song, so I can get a better feel for it?" If the student then discusses the lyrics enthusiastically, the clinician may discover newly proffered feelings about suicide that would otherwise have remained hidden. A careful exploration of the degree to which suicide is sanctioned in the student's peer group can provide invaluable information on the likelihood that the student will attempt to escape his or her current external stressors via suicide.

Having reviewed some of the etiologic and phenomenologic factors related to external stress, let us turn to the role of inner conflict in encouraging suicidal thought.

## PART II: ROLE OF INNER CONFLICT IN THE ETIOLOGY AND PHENOMENOLOGY OF SUICIDE

Although the role of inner conflict overlaps with the role played by the external triggers of suicide, there are some distinctive features to this etiologic region. Inner conflict is defined here as those etiologic factors that are rooted in the turbulent vicissitudes of the patient's inner world and are played out in the cumulative stressors of everyday living, as opposed to being primarily and directly related to a specific devastating life stressor. Most people do not kill themselves in response to a single, catastrophic stressor. It is the stress of living with oneself that more often leads to despair.

We will explore the world of inner conflict by first examining a suicide note, for such notes can sometimes provide a surprisingly clear image of the writer's turmoil directly before committing suicide. We will then discuss two questions that frequently preoccupy a person as he or she wrestles with the decision of whether to proceed with suicide. An understanding of these two questions will provide a unique opportunity to see how the phenomenology of suicide actually unfolds. This section will end with a look at three sets of cognitive distortions that are frequently present in the development of suicidal ideation: (1) cognitive processes commonly seen in both depression and suicide; (2) cognitive processes particularly active in people with severe character disorders who become suicidal; and (3) cognitive processes particularly characteristic of people who have more mature characterological structure but develop suicidal ideation.

## A SUICIDE NOTE

Our exploration of the second etiologic factor, internal conflict, begins on April 8, 1994. The setting is quite a bit different from the streets of Elizabeth Siddal's Victorian London. We find ourselves in the heroin alcoves of contemporary Seattle, and the chaotic world of grunge rock.

On this date, in his home near Lake Washington, one of the most promising and popular rock stars, Kurt Cobain, dead for three days from a single 20-gauge shotgun blast, was found by an electrician. Like the premature deaths of earlier rock stars from the psychedelic era—Janis Joplin, Jim Morrison, and Jimi Hendrix—news of Cobain's death shocked the world of popular culture. Unlike the 1960s, the news did not travel only by television and print. It was rocketed around the world in minutes via the World Wide Web.

Researching the Web for background material for this book, I happened upon the suicide note of Kurt Cobain. Indeed, it seemed to be everywhere in cyberspace. I found the letter to be very disturbing. It was scrawled in a disarmingly sloppy fashion, sans paragraph indentations. Entire lines were crossed out, and the last words, "I LOVE YOU. I LOVE YOU" were printed in large, childlike letters.

Cobain's suicide note provides a tragic, yet powerful, window into the role of inner conflict as an etiology of suicide. "Boddah" is a nickname for his wife, Courtney Love, another gifted rock star. Parts of the letter clearly are written to Courtney, as the salutation suggests. Other parts seem to mirror the confusion wrought by his suicidal anguish. They appear to be addressed to the members of his band or perhaps to his fans:

To Boddah,

Speaking from the tongue of an experienced simpleton who obviously would rather be an emasculated, infantile complain-ee. This note should be pretty easy to understand. All the warnings from the punk rock 101 courses over the years, since my first introduction to the, shall we say, the ethics involved with independence and the embracement of your community has proven to be very true. I haven't felt the excitement of listening to as well as creating music along with reading and writing for too many years now. I feel guilty beyond words about these things. For example when we're backstage and the lights go out and the manic roar of the crowd begins, it doesn't affect me the way in which it did for Freddy Mercury, who seemed to love, and relish in the love and adoration from the crowd, which is something I totally admire and envy. The fact is, I can't fool you, any of you. It simply isn't fair to you or me. The worst crime I can think of would be to rip people off by faking it and pretending as if I'm having 100% fun. Sometimes I feel as if I should have a punch-in time clock before I walk out on stage. I've tried everything within my power to appreciate it (and I do, God believe me I do, but it's not enough). I appreciate the fact that I and we have affected and entertained a lot of people. I must be one of those narcissists who only appreciate things when they're gone. I'm too sensitive. I need to be slightly numb in order to regain the enthusiasm I once had as a child. On our last 3 tours, I've had a much better appreciation for all the people I've known personally and as fans of our music, but I still can't get over the frustration, the guilt and empathy I have for everyone. There's good in all of us and I think I simply love people too much, so much that it makes me feel too fucking sad. The sad little sensitive, unappreciative, Pisces, Jesus man. Why don't you just enjoy it? I don't know! I have a goddess of a wife who sweats ambition and empathy and a daughter who reminds me too much of what I used to be, full of love and joy, kissing every person she meets because everyone is good and will do her no harm. And that terrifies me to the point where I can barely function. I can't stand the thought of Frances becoming the miserable, self-destructive, death rocker that I've become. I have it good, very good, and I'm grateful, but since the age of seven, I've become hateful towards all humans in general. Only because it seems so easy for people to get along and have empathy. Only because I love and feel sorry for people too much I guess. Thank you all from the pit of my burning, nauseous stomach for your letters and concern during the past years. I'm too much of an erratic, moody, baby! I don't have the passion anymore, and so remember, it's better to burn out than to fade away. Peace, Love, Empathy. Kurt Cobain.

Frances and Courtney, I'll be at your altar

Please keep going Courtney,

for Frances.

for her life will be so much happier

without me. I LOVE YOU. I LOVE YOU[9]

Within the paradoxes, self-denigrations, and exhortations of the note, one sees the tattered outlines of the writer's ravaged soul. With this note, we look directly into the gaping jaws of a suicidal maelstrom.

Like Elizabeth Siddal, Kurt Cobain clearly had had enough of pain, sorrow, and suffering. But unlike Elizabeth, his suicidal drive did not arise from an external catastrophic stressor. For Kurt Cobain, the catastrophic stress was unfolding within himself, and the walls of his unique maelstrom were splashed with guilt, self-reprobation, and the lethal loathing of what he perceived to be his own hypocrisy.

Success and fame, not career failure, created the milieu within which this suicide occurred. Cobain delineated his own understanding of this paradox by contrasting the success of the band, the love of his wife, and the joy of his child with the self-reprimand, ". . . Jesus man. Why don't you just enjoy it?" To which he had no real answer. If Kurt Cobain had possessed an answer, he might still be alive today.

Many lessons from this letter can potentially help clinicians to spot acute suicidal risk. The "bottom line" for a person trying to determine whether he or she should end life often comes down to two questions, one practical and the other ethical:

1. Will it work? ("Will my pain end and my problems be solved?")
2. Is it right to do? ("Does committing suicide hurt other people or break my underlying code of ethics?")

These questions may be less powerful for patients who kill themselves impulsively or have problems with affect modulation. Similarly, for people with an antisocial character structure, the second question may be disturbingly moot. But, for the majority of people who are considering killing themselves, these questions help frame the rules of the debate in which the decision will be reached.

Indeed, for someone contemplating suicide, these two questions pose the final hurdles. The more the clinician is invited into the patient's internal debate concerning these two questions, the more likely the clinician will gain insight into the severity of the imminent risk. Ultimately, many people will postpone killing themselves until these questions are answered satisfactorily.

THE FIRST QUESTION OF SUICIDE: WILL IT WORK?

This question is often easier to answer than the second question. For people who do not believe that suicide will result in ultimate retribution in an afterlife, suicide works—it ends their intense personal pain. For people who firmly believe that suicide will result in eternal damnation and a dramatic worsening of their pain, it doesn't. Suicide is not a logical option.

However, be careful because for some people, the pain driving them toward suicide is of such magnitude and intensity that even the risk of eternal pain in the afterlife will not reverse their choice of suicide. Unrelenting pain changes people's minds. Do not assume safety because a client has strongly dismissed suicide on religious grounds. As a precaution, keep checking in.

Odd as it may seem at first, a person contemplating suicide will often ponder whether or not suicide will solve specific practical problems that would seem to be moot if the person were dead. But such is the paradoxical nature of suicide. Practical considerations may include: Will debts become suddenly irrelevant (suicide functioning as the ultimate declaration of bankruptcy)? Will bills be paid off because life insurance will be available (suicide functioning as a source of funding)? Will important life decisions, such as whether or not to marry a specific person, simply evaporate (suicide functioning as a "doctor's excuse note")? Will a challenge in which the patient feels certain of failure, such as a graduate school entrance examination, be avoided (suicide functioning as a permanent "leave of absence")?

Concerns like these reemphasize the fact that suicide is generally a person's attempt to *find solutions,* not a way of "copping out." A person contemplating suicide often sees it as the only logical answer to ending his or her pain. This fact offers a hopeful realization: If people can generate alternative solutions, they will choose them. People wrestling with suicidal ideation are hungry for answers. The urgent need to get away from the pain, as is so poignantly apparent in the final note of Kurt Cobain, makes people act on their ideation.

Because the first question of suicide concerns the pressing need of ending pain, time should be spent in an effort to understand the nature of this pain more fully. The intensity of the pain driving suicidal anguish is so immense that it is hard to conceptualize unless one has experienced it. Some of the readers of this book may have experienced the pain personally; for those who have not, a detailed exploration of its roots is worthwhile.

From a phenomenological viewpoint, Aaron Beck, in his innovative work on cognitive therapy, was the first to document "hopelessness" as one of the most powerful correlates with long-term suicide risk.[10] Hopelessness destroys "the future"—a useful intellectual construct based on a promise, or even a possibility, of change. If one can foresee no potential differences, the future is essentially indistinguishable from the present. It is no longer a relevant concept. Without hope, there is no future. Without the concept of a future, there is no hope.

Once the future is gone, it becomes frustratingly problematic for a human being to generate life-sustaining feelings such as energy, enthusiasm, drive, and motivation. If there is truly no possibility of change, why bother to sustain life? This is a logical argument, not a defeatist one. The pain of a "world sans hope" is very difficult to tolerate for any prolonged length of time no matter how solidly built one is psychologically.

People kill themselves because they see no hope for a solution to their pain. But where does this hopelessness arise? Chiles and Strosahl, in their excellent book, *The Suicidal Patient: Principles of Assessment, Treatment, and Case Management,*[11] help to clarify this question by pointing out that the hopelessness of suicide may arise in any person, with or without a mental disorder, if that person is experiencing intense emotional pain that is perceived as being inescapable, interminable, and intolerable. From our reading of the suicide note of Kurt Cobain, it is easy to project that this is exactly the internal world he found himself experiencing.

A major buffer against the powerful enticement of suicide is the ability of some people to perceive and sustain a counterbelief that there is a spiritual reason for their pain. Consequently, the pain must be tolerated. This life-preserving belief is often rooted in a patient's belief in a soul and in a godhead who guides the growth of this soul and who is deeply concerned for its salvation. Such a belief was the lifeline for Job in the biblical narratives.

Clinicians' understanding of a client's framework for meaning is a task of vital importance while performing a suicide assessment. The patient's framework may be rooted in religious or spiritual beliefs or hard-core practical concerns, such as providing for one's family or suffering for one's country during time of war. Victor Frankl's seminal work, *The Search for Meaning*,[12] elegantly points out the method by which a framework for meaning can help sustain life even in the hostile world of a concentration camp, a world with which Frankl, a survivor of a Nazi death camp, was all too familiar.

Another powerful buffering mechanism helps to keep people alive, even when they experience hopelessness: They will often try to answer the second question of suicide—"Does my committing suicide hurt other people or break my code of ethics?"—before proceeding with the business of concretely planning its method of implementation. Finding this answer takes time. The time it requires for the patient to resolve this complex question can be the time it takes to intervene effectively and save his or her life. Moreover, the patient's answer to this question may remove suicide as a viable option.

## THE SECOND QUESTION OF SUICIDE: IS IT RIGHT TO DO?

I believe that the vast majority of human beings have an internal code of ethics. It might not be well defined, or it may simply manifest itself as an urge to do "what is right." Given this internal code, the process of deciding whether to kill oneself is arguably the most momentous ethical dilemma that a person can face. The decision weighed heavily on the mind of Kurt Cobain; if his suicide note is a valid projection, he had a demanding code of ethics. In fact, his code of ethics eventually demanded that he take his life.

The very presence of his note metacommunicates that Cobain felt a need to ethically justify his suicide. He also had a need to help others to understand it, perhaps in the hope that it would somehow lessen the painful impact of his suicide. From the amount of space given to the topic in the note, apparently one of the most problematic ethical dilemmas for Cobain was his feeling that he had become a hypocrite, for he no longer was called to the mission of his music. His anguish resonates in this passage:

> I haven't felt the excitement of listening to as well as creating music along with reading and writing for too many years now. I feel guilty beyond words about these things. . . . The fact is, I can't fool you, any of you. It simply isn't fair to you or me. The worst crime I can think of would be to rip people off by faking it and pretending as if I'm having 100% fun.

Inherent in these words is the seductive whisper of death that is heard when one has lost face or failed. Yukio Mishima heard that whisper when he placed the tip of his ritual knife to his abdomen.

Another major ethical plank in Cobain's framework for meaning was his deep and genuine love for his wife and his daughter, reflected by his concern for their future without him. Often, a strong family allegiance is the one lifeline that prevents people from killing themselves. In Cobain's note, this lifeline is abruptly snapped by a simple yet lethal rationalization, some of the very last words he put to paper referring to his daughter Frances: "for her life will be so much happier without me." This rationalization highlights an important fact that assessment clinicians should remember. Even when patients have compelling ethical reasons not to kill themselves—for example, the welfare of their children—their emotional pain is sometimes too great to bear. Their anguish simply overwhelms their ethical stance. The answer to the first question of suicide, which deals with relief from unrelenting pain, becomes more compelling than the answer to the second question, which deals with moral rectitude.

From Cobain's suicide note, we see that when he faced these two core ethical dilemmas, his internal debate led to the decision that ending his life was the "right thing to do." In answer to the second question of suicide, each individual will arrive at unique and sometimes idiosyncratic rationalizations that support the eventual decision. Here are some of the more common ethical rationalizations for suicide:

1. I have shamed myself or failed to accomplish my mission and the honorable thing to do is end my life. (as with Yukio Mishima and Admiral Inman)
2. People will be better off without me and all the problems I cause them. (as with Kurt Cobain)
3. The dignity of life is ethically more important than the mere presence of life. (as with Bruno Bettelheim)
4. My illness is bankrupting my family, and they will be better off without my costs. (as seen in patients with severely debilitating illnesses that are poorly covered by insurance, such as schizophrenia and bipolar disorder)
5. I may physically hurt someone if I do not kill myself. (as with driving while intoxicated, or assaulting people during a manic/psychotic episode)
6. God wants me to sacrifice myself. (as seen with psychotic states, including delusions and command hallucinations)
7. I do not deserve to live. (as seen with survivor guilt after causing another person's death, as in a car accident; impulsive acts such as crimes of passion; shame-producing acts such as child molestation; and psychotic self-denigrations)

There is a final lesson to be learned from Cobain's note. It is not so much what he wrote, rather it is the type of cognitive processing that he must have exhibited in order to arrive at what he wrote. If there is a cognitive style that predisposes clients toward suicide, then perhaps we can learn to spot it and even transform it.

## COGNITIVE STYLES COMMON TO THE DEVELOPMENT OF BOTH DEPRESSION AND SUICIDAL IDEATION

We have discovered that when any stressors are present, their impact is determined more by a client's interpretation of them than by the nature of the stressor. The same holds true for internal cognitions. It is not so much what information is summoned from the client's conscious and unconscious processes, but how the client interprets this information that determines its ultimate impact. Kurt Cobain exhibited four cognitive distortions: (1) overgeneralization, (2) catastrophization, (3) self-denigration, and (4) a black-or-white view of the world. These four cognitive traps are commonly seen in depressive states, with or without suicidal ideation. They may have contributed to the generation of some of the ethical dilemmas Cobain wrestled with in his last days.

Although some speculation will be inevitable, let us try to reconstruct some of the unconscious cognitive processes that may have led Cobain to a decision he could not escape. More specifically, his cognitive distortions seem to have constructed a world that demanded he fit his experience of "not feeling dedicated to his music" into one of two boxes. Thus "lack of dedication" was interpreted as being evidence that Cobain was either a "good" musician who had a mission, or he was a "bad" musician who did not. If he fit the latter category, then he was a hypocrite as well. There was no in-between. Much like a young child, Cobain may not have had the ability to see gray. If he had possessed that cognitive skill, he might have interpreted his experience of not feeling dedicated to his music as evidence that he was a very good musician who just happened to be burned out, as opposed to a bad musician who had become a hypocrite. This more realistic cognitive belief would not have demanded suicide as a solution.

The cognitive process that drove Cobain toward such a punishing ethical stance may have been further accelerated by the simultaneous actions of another cognitive distortion: overgeneralization. In an unconscious fashion, dictated by his tendency for overgeneralization, the above statement could have been malignantly transformed into: "You are not only a bad musician, but you are also a bad person." This life-denying conclusion may have been reinforced by wave after wave of confirmatory self-condemnations resulting from the machinations of yet another form of cognitive distortion—self-denigration. The net result may have been that Cobain's internal reality was insidiously transformed into a false reality in which suicide became a logical solution to a painful ethical dilemma. Taking his own life could end the hypocrisy. He saw no other viable or ethical method to end the charade. Indeed, at least with suicide as a solution, some honor could be regained.

Another cognitive factor, consistent both with people who are depressed and with people contemplating suicide, is a perception that they have no control. They experience the unsettling sensation that they are at the mercy of life, of other people, and of their own urges. Such a sensation is both unpleasant and humiliating, but there remains one aspect of life over which they can maintain total control: They can decide whether they live or die. The choice for suicide thus provides a chance for dignity via the conduit of self-determination. On an individual level, this attitude toward suicide was elegantly stated by the surrealist poet Antonin Artaud:

> If I commit suicide, it will not be to destroy myself but to put myself back together again. Suicide will be for me only one means of violently reconquering myself, of brutally invading my being, of anticipating the unpredictable approaches of God. By suicide, I reintroduce my design in nature, I shall for the first time give things the shape of my will.[13]

This use of suicide as a method of regaining a sense of control in an otherwise uncontrollable world can establish itself as a unifying hallmark of an entire subculture. For example, in reference to a spate of adolescent suicides on a Native American reservation, a pastor described suicide as a way for bringing order to a society where "everything is basically out of control. . . . It's a tiny fraction of dignity in a world that doesn't make sense."

A cognitive style may very well have played a significant role in Kurt Cobain's slide both into depression and into suicide. The question now arises: Are there specific cognitive styles common to most people who develop suicidal ideation? The answer seems to be Yes and No. On one hand, not everyone who becomes suicidal does so with the same set of cognitive distortions at work. On the other hand, some groups of suicidal people seem to share remarkably similar cognitive styles. If these distinctive styles of cognitive processing can be delineated, perhaps the clinician can more readily spot serious suicidal intent, and, more importantly, transform it.

Two relevant cognitive styles are germane to our discussion. There are probably other clusters as well, but these two will give us a good start: (1) the cognitive styles commonly seen in suicidal patients who have severe characterological damage, and (2) the cognitive styles of suicidal patients who have relatively normal characterological development. Clients within each of these groups have the potential to use quite different cognitive styles as they interpret and process suicidal ideation—or, indeed, the world at large. As we shall soon see, in addition to their cognitive styles, people within each of these two groups may share other personality traits and propensities.

This grouping includes people who are dealing with the following personality disorders: borderline personality disorder, histrionic personality disorder, and poorly compensated narcissistic personality disorder. People suffering from severe drug and alcohol abuse frequently share these same characteristics. Indeed, chronic substance abuse can lead to what is sometimes referred to as an "acquired personality disorder." Such people may have shown normal personality development as children and adolescents, but after years of addiction, they function as if they have severe personality disorders.

Several therapeutic innovators have focused on the use of cognitive interventions in the assessment and management of suicidal ideation with this particularly challenging group of clients. In this discussion, I shall borrow heavily from the pioneering work of Marsha Linehan, the developer of Dialectical Behavior Therapy (DBT),[14] and from the cogent insights of Chiles and Strosahl.[15]

People with severe personality dysfunction and/or severe substance abuse often display some of the cognitive distortions that were evident in the suicide note of Kurt Cobain. Indeed, Kurt Cobain was suffering from a severe substance abuse problem. They tend to display extreme forms of overgeneralization, catastrophization, self-denigration, and black-or-white thinking. In addition, they have a peculiar tendency to "forget" the significance of people's past behaviors toward them; they judge people on the basis of immediate impressions. For instance, a person suffering with a borderline personality disorder might abruptly declare that a clinician who has been a trusted therapist for years is an unreliable "son of a bitch" merely for arriving twenty minutes late for a therapy session.

Patients with borderline structure, as well as people with other severe character pathologies or substance abuse, also demonstrate a maladaptive approach to problem solving. They tend to: generate few alternative solutions to new problems, prematurely reject potentially viable alternatives, depend on others for answers, and show little tenacity for following through with the work needed to solve a problem.

All of these cognitive markers are imbedded in an emotional and volatile matrix. These patients tend to tolerate stress poorly and often have difficulty modulating their affects and moods secondary to the distorting actions of their cognitive mechanisms. In addition, patients with severe personality dysfunction may act impulsively to alleviate these distressing mood states. To make matters worse, although they are already bad enough, they also tend to tolerate emotional pain poorly. A feeling of mild rejection or disappointment may be perceived as unbearable, much to the surprise of friends and family. Their poor toleration for emotional pain proves to be quite problematic because the cognitive distortions listed above may precipitate an unusually high number of painful interactions with others and disappointing results with tasks. Consequently, the common vicissitudes of daily living may present these clients with a bewildering array of unbearable pains.

Ultimately, patients with these characteristics find themselves in painful emotional states much more frequently than is normal. Because they have poor problem-solving skills and little toleration for emotional pain, they quickly find that their intense pain is intolerable, interminable, and inescapable. Suicide then becomes a viable solution.

As noted earlier, these traits are also common in people with long-term substance abuse. Add the immediately disinhibiting effects of alcohol and/or drug ingestion, and such patients can become acutely suicidal or self-destructive (cutting, burning, or head banging) with remarkable rapidity. Equally striking is the speed with which such patients can drop suicidal ideation. Factors as diverse as pleasant interpersonal encounters, skilled cognitive therapy interventions, and the removal of the acute ingestion of alcohol can result in a surprisingly rapid loss of suicidal intent.

This roller-coaster ride is complicated by the fact that the secondary gains associated with a failed suicide attempt or gesture can be both impressive and seductive. The patient's suicidal pain, their most immediate problem, is solved by the interpersonal nurturance, time out from stress, and relief from responsibilities that often follow in the wake of a suicide attempt. These secondary gains are epitomized by the potentially nurturing atmosphere of a hospital. The end result is that acts of attempted suicide or self-mutilation become learned solutions to emotional pain.

An example from my clinical practice will illustrate the manner in which these cognitive styles and emotional characteristics can precipitously slide a client into a suicidal crisis.

---

## ANNA: A CASE STUDY

Years ago, I was working with a woman whom we shall call Anna. Anna was packaged in a short frame that held more than its fair share of weight. Her brownish hair was closely bobbed. Her attire was usually a pair of jeans and a solid-color shirt. Anna had a bit of a dowdy look. But there was nothing dowdy about her smile. It was crisp, quick, and genuine.

Behind the bright smile and the quickness of her eyes lay a long string of empty pill boxes, a few episodes of self-cutting, and numerous pieces of broken furniture, including a picnic table tossed artfully through a picture window. Although almost desperately drawn to people, Anna had a knack for scaring them off. She also had a severe problem with overdependence on previous clinicians, as evidenced by the fact that the police had to escort her out of her last therapist's office during the termination session. It will come as no surprise that she had a history of being abused. Previous clinicians had made the appropriate diagnosis of borderline personality disorder.

I was using a form of cognitive behavioral therapy designed to be given in bursts of weekly series. Consecutive series were separated by periods of no therapy, during which Anna was to practice the techniques she had learned. During our absences, she was able to attend a support group. The approach, which was designed to minimize overdependence and maximize concrete learning of new and more useful cognitive styles, was proving to be quite powerful for Anna. Because of her genuine motivation and quick intelligence, Anna's psychological growth had been rather remarkable.

We were somewhere in the third year of therapy. She had become quite proficient in catching her cognitive distortions and using cognitive restructuring to transform them into less threatening perceptions—a process she liked to call "thought repair." There had been no suicidal actions in over a year. I decided to give her the assignment of writing down the five goals that she had achieved in therapy. The completed list was to be prominently placed on her refrigerator door as a reminder of her progress. I wanted to make sure Anna was creating the list for herself and not to please me. Consequently, I asked her to remember, as she wrote it, that she was making the list for herself. Anna was excited about the project. The past several months had been especially good.

The session in question was going very well. Anna was in high spirits and proud of her progress. As I reviewed her list, her eyes were riveted on my face. A broad smile erupted as I complimented her work:

DR. SHEA:   Well, you've really done a great job here.

ANNA:   Well, you deserve the credit.

DR. SHEA:   I'm willing to accept a small part of the credit. But you are the person who is doing all the hard work. You're the person who is willing to make the changes, and you should be proud. You deserve most of the credit. And I grant you, we've been a good therapeutic team.

ANNA:   Thanks.

During previous sessions, before returning Anna's homework assignments, I routinely made a photocopy for our chart to mark her progress "officially," an idea that she liked. But on this day, I wanted to emphasize that she had done this work for herself and was not doing it to please me. Consequently, I decided to give her list back to her so that she could immediately place it back on her refrigerator door. We then continued with the session.

In the next few minutes, Anna's expression became subdued. She started to cast her eyes downward toward the piece of paper in her lap. Then she became restless. She began to fidget in her seat and looked about the room as if bored.

Plowing right ahead with my behavioral spiel, it took me a while to realize that something was awry. When I did recognize that there was a problem, I grossly underestimated the power of the maelstrom that Anna had slipped into—a maelstrom whose waters I had inadvertently stirred.

DR. SHEA:   Anna, you look sort of upset. Is there anything wrong?

ANNA:   You don't give a damn, do you? [venomous look] You just don't give a damn, do you?

DR. SHEA:   [truly dumb-struck; I suspect my jaw was dropping down in some inelegant fashion] I . . . I . . . I'm not certain I know what you mean. What's wrong?

ANNA:   You could give a shit about me. [pause, chin quivering] If you cared about me, you would have made a copy of my list. [pause] But you just don't care.

DR. SHEA:  Anna, I'm truly puzzled. Obviously, I didn't explain why I didn't make a copy and I should have; let me . . . [Anna cuts me off].

ANNA:  You don't have to explain anything, Dr. Shea. [pause] You know what I was going to do? I was going to tell you I needed to go to the bathroom. And then I wasn't going to come back. And I just might have gone home to take a few pills, if you know what I mean.

Within the span of five minutes, Anna went from feeling wonderful to feeling suicidal. That's how quickly such a descent into a suicidal maelstrom can occur when fed by a borderline rage created from a bevy of cognitive distortions.

From a psychodynamic standpoint, I had missed the significance of the act of photocopying Anna's homework assignments. A healthy parental reassurance inherent in this act was important to Anna and was not to be trifled with lightly. Anna's tendency to black-or-white experiences had abruptly transformed my oversight into a major declaration of abandonment. She probably felt that I hated her. Furthermore, she suddenly and categorically lost sight of the years of caring interaction she had experienced with me, which, if they had been remembered, would have pointed Anna toward a different conclusion. Instead, it was as if none of our previous interactions had occurred.

When the emotional storm took over, she lost her more mature cognitive moorings. Because she lacked the interpersonal skills to ask why I had not done what I had always done before, she was stuck with her projections. Anna's lack of an ability to tolerate emotional pain told her that she had to get out of the room. Overwhelmed with rejection and feelings of inferiority alternating with rage, she needed a solution fast. And at this point of intense emotional pain and confusion, Anna reverted to a solution she had learned to use over the course of many years: suicide.

The trick here, once I regained my composure, was to spot the "cornerstone cognitive distortion" that began the entire cascade. After apologizing for not explaining my change in behavioral routine, I pointed out that I thought perhaps we were seeing her tendency "to lose sight of the past," a distorting mechanism she had worked hard on minimizing in the therapy. She agreed to review our relationship step by step, looking for evidence that I cared for her or did not care for her. We agreed that, depending on her findings, she would be free to leave the session or not. As we performed this step-by-step inventory of our past interactions, her affect changed markedly. Her anger slipped away. By the end of the session, she felt fine. The suicidal crisis had been transformed into a mere footnote in a borderline short story.

This incident illustrates the etiologic role cognitive distortions can play in precipitating suicidal ideation in people with severe character pathology. Understanding the above principles highlights two practical lessons for assessment clinicians:

1. With such patients, it is always wise to maintain a healthy respect for how rapidly they can move in and out of a suicidal frame of mind.
2. When determining a safe disposition, it is critical to assess the interpersonal situation that these patients will be returning to following their interviews, for such patients are exquisitely sensitive to the nuances of interpersonal support or rejection.

The rapidity of their descent into suicidal ideation is the downside of working with these patients. The upside is the fact that they can respond equally rapidly to effective cognitive/behavioral interventions, which can add a powerful tool to the assessment package.

There are some distinctive patterns to the cognitive and emotional fashions in which suicidal ideation is born and processed by people with severe character pathology and/or chronic substance abuse. But what happens when clients who have more stable and mature defense mechanisms contemplate suicide? Do they also share a unique set of cognitive characteristics with each other?

## COGNITIVE STYLES, ASSOCIATED WITH SUICIDAL IDEATION, IN CLIENTS WITH RELATIVELY MATURE CHARACTER STRUCTURES

Although people with more primitive personality structures such as borderline personality disorder are at a high relative risk for suicide, many people who attempt suicide have relatively mature character structures. These people attempt suicide in response to intense environmental or interpersonal stresses and/or to the direct impact of serious psychiatric disturbances such as major depression, bipolar disorder, schizophrenia, panic disorder, obsessive–compulsive disorder, and post-traumatic stress disorder. The more typical cognitive characteristics associated with these patients' suicidal ideation were discussed earlier in this chapter. They are the characteristic cognitive responses when people are genuinely attempting to find answers to the "two questions of suicide."

In my opinion, the single most definitive distinction between patients with relatively mature personality function and patients with primitive personality structures is the relative lack of impulsivity in suicidal action within the more mature group. For them, the time required to answer the two questions of suicide tends to prevent highly impulsive action. In contrast, clients with severe characterological dysfunction can precipitously develop suicidal ideation and action, as we saw with Anna, without giving thought to either of the two questions. Lack of attention to the two questions of suicide, which can result in impulsive suicidal action, can happen among people with more mature defenses, but, in my experience, it occurs far less frequently in this group. On the other hand, there can be a surprising amount of overlapping qualities to the cognitive worlds of the two groups, especially with regard to the cognitive distortions commonly seen during depression. The similarities and the differences of these groups, as they move into suicidal thought, will be the focus of this section, for these similarities and differences can have important implications in predicting acute suicide risk.

As depression begins to invade the everyday experience of people with mature characterological structures, they experience a peculiar phenomenon. Their cognitive processing begins to insidiously retreat into a more and more primitive process. People who, before the onset of their depressions, tended to look carefully for the "gray" in debates and behaviors, begin to see things as black or white. People who were able to see the individual nuances of human experience now can see only generalities and stereotypes. People who were able to judge others' behaviors in the light of their histories and interpersonal "track records" begin to impulsively judge people solely by their immediate actions. In short, many of the cognitive distorting mechanisms typically seen in people with primitive personalities now emerge. Overgeneralization, catastrophization, self-denigration, and black-or-white thought processes are the stuff of depressive experience even in people with mature personality structures. These cognitive gremlins can guide any client inexorably into the maelstrom of hopelessness.

We shall see in this chapter that there is fascinating evidence that some of these cognitive changes may be directly caused by biochemical alterations of the brain during biologically induced depressive states. In addition, there is convincing evidence that once these cognitive distorting mechanisms appear, they can themselves create or greatly intensify depressive mood, hence the wonderful abilities of cognitive therapies to transform depression.

On a superficial level, it is easy to think that these depressed patients who began with mature defenses have now developed the exact same cognitive style as people with more primitive personality structures. It might even be argued that we have stumbled upon the cognitive processes common to "suicidal patients" in general. But a closer look demonstrates that this is not the case. The difference lies in the fact that there is a pattern to the loss of the mature defenses and the appearance of the primitive ones.

As a client with mature defenses is engulfed by a major depression, the protective walls created by those defenses begin to give way. The defenses do not go down without a fight, and they do not disappear overnight. Destroyed one day, they may be rebuilt the next. New mature defenses may be suddenly mobilized or emphasized. Friends and family may contradict the overgeneralizations and other cognitive distortions fostered by the depression. Eventually, the walls go down once too often. The mature defenses slip away beneath the morass of depressive tide.

As the depressed patient succumbs to this tide, his or her interpretations of other people, current stresses, the future, the past, and even the chance for help can fall beneath the black waves of depressive cognition. But something quite remarkable is sometimes in play as well. Not always, but often, despite the onrushing depression, one of the last topics toward which these patients can still muster a surprisingly mature cognitive attitude is the very topic of committing suicide itself. Exactly with the topic of suicide, where people with severe personality disorders are most apt to use primitive process, people with mature egos are most apt to fight its use. The last remnants of their mature defenses seem to pitch a furious battle against the idea of self-destruction.

Let me contrast the two groups of clients more specifically. People with mature personalities, despite their slide into the use of primitive cognitive distortions, tend to look at the act of suicide with surprisingly diverse lenses. Unlike people with borderline processes, they are more apt to find shades of gray. The pros and cons of suicide are often meticulously debated and reviewed. High-level problem-solving tools such as detached observation and abstraction are used by patients with more mature defenses to foresee the possible consequences of their suicidal action. Empathic concern turns toward those who are potentially left behind. Concerns such as the financial and psychological impact of the suicide on survivors are carefully digested; topics range from who will find the body to who will provide future parenting for abandoned children. And these people, unlike those with primitive processes, often show outstanding and sometimes courageous impulse control. They tolerate high levels of emotional pain for long periods of time, deferring the suicidal act until the two questions of suicide are answered to their satisfaction. I have seen people with high-level defenses control the impulse to kill themselves for month after painful month, and sometimes for years. For such people, suicide is not a learned solution to which they frequently turn. It is an alien solution to be avoided if at all possible.

However, once a person with high-level defenses decides that suicide is the correct choice, he or she can move with startling speed to implement the plan successfully. This process is sometimes mistakenly labeled as *impulsive* by the stunned clinicians left behind. But the patient has not acted impulsively; the patient has acted decisively, and this decisiveness has caught the clinician off guard. A lethal trap was camouflaged by the effectiveness of the individual's high-functioning defenses. Adeptly and cleverly, the person "put on a front," especially in situations in which it was important to maintain appearances. They have learned to hide their pain from fellow workers and family members. And they know how to hide their pain from a therapist as well. One day, a patient may look like he or she is responding well to cognitive therapeutic interventions. The next day, the patient is found to have committed suicide.

In ongoing therapy with clients who have mature developmental defenses and are expressing suicidal ideation, this fatal trap can often be avoided by keeping the patient open to the intimate process of expressing suicidal ideation. Once the window into the patient's world of suicidal ideation has been effectively opened, don't close it until you no longer need it. No matter how well the therapy is progressing or how well the patient looks, as long as the client is having *any* suicidal ideation, inquire about it during every session. It will soon be a natural aspect of the therapy, and that stance can often short-circuit the potentially deadly chain of events described above.

Experienced clinicians are often aware of an irony here. At some level, it is almost easier to predict suicidal action with people who clearly are impulsive, such as clients with borderline personality disorders, than it can be with high-functioning individuals who are decisive. This paradox exists because there is a "predictable unpredictability" in people with borderline structures, once the clinician understands the cognitive roots of their suicidal ideation.

Borderline suicidal crises are often triggered by the sharp darts of interpersonal conflict or a patient's erroneous perception that such a dart has been fired. Impressions of rejection or disappointment can quickly propel patients into the hostile back-alley ways of their past, abruptly triggering a learned adaptive solution to such interpersonal stress: an act of suicide or self-mutilation. After sketching out a "road map" of the unique cognitive templates of each specific patient, the therapist can often predict which circumstances will trigger this vicious cycle in particular patients. Indeed, much of the therapy consists of helping patients to make this prediction themselves. When these situations are recognized beforehand, or as they are unfolding, a patient has a fighting chance of employing adaptive cognitive skills that may derail a reflexive suicidal response. Such was the process that helped Anna to transform her rage toward me.

The cognitive processes surrounding suicidal ideation, whether in people with severe personality disorders or people with normal personality structure, have traps that can lead to "unexpected" suicide attempts. Our understanding of these processes can keep us from being caught off guard and remind us to be aware of imminent risk.

We have now studied external stressors and internal conflict as major etiologic factors in the genesis of suicidal ideation. It is time to look at our third and last etiologic category: the biology of the brain.

## PART III: THE ROLE OF BRAIN PATHOPHYSIOLOGY IN THE ETIOLOGY OF SUICIDAL IDEATION

Humans like to espouse a holistic perspective on life, the universe, and everything in it, but the truth is that most humans are reductionists.

Depending on where we were trained, who trained us, and what books we like to read, we tend, not infrequently, to see the world through lenses that give us limited perspectives. Conflicting data are simply shunted aside. Never has this process been more apparent than in descriptions of the role of the brain in the etiology of human thought and behavior. In explanations of abnormal behavior, historically the role of brain pathophysiology has been minimized compared to the roles of external stressors and internal conflicts as etiologic agents.

For centuries, the etiology of problematic behaviors, including suicide, has generally been rapidly and adamantly ascribed to one of the two etiologic regions discussed earlier in this chapter. From this perspective, abnormal behavior, including suicidal thought, is the direct result of environmental stresses (death of a loved one, poverty, loss of job, divorce) or psychological conflicts (cognitive distortions, conflicts between unconscious structures or warring archetypes, spiritual crises, lack of psychological strength, demonic possession). Such a non-holistic oversimplification continues to result in a cruel stigmatization of people who are diagnosed as having schizophrenia, bipolar disorder, and obsessive–compulsive disorder (e.g., many insurance companies still refuse to reimburse the expense of these illnesses as they would any other neurologic disease).

On the other hand, some current thinkers tend to overzealously emphasize the role of the brain in the creation of thought and emotion. These biologic reductionists tremble at the suggested use of psychotherapy as a major treatment modality, and shudder at the mention of the word *soul*. A synthesis of these viewpoints is needed. The world of human thought and behavior is an enigmatic interlocking of diverse processes—environmental, psychological/spiritual, and biological. In this worldview, people are not so much stagnant things as they are transforming processes defined by the interaction of these volatile and ever changing fields.

With these ideas in mind, we come to two questions:

1. Can the biochemistry of the brain directly cause major psychiatric symptoms such as depression, delusions, and hallucinations?
2. If so, and of immediate importance to the study of suicide, can the biochemistry of the brain directly cause suicidal ideation?

The answer to the second question can have important ramifications for assessment clinicians; it can rapidly move us from philosophical musings to practical clinical decisions. Note that the question is not whether pathophysiology can lead to a depressive state that subsequently yields to suicidal ideation. It is much more provocative: Can neuropathophysiology directly cause a human to have suicidal thoughts?

## THE ROLE OF THE BRAIN: THE FIRST QUESTION

Can malfunction in the biochemistry of the brain directly cause major psychiatric symptoms? The complexity of the brain is a good topic for launching this inquiry. The typical human brain, a gelatinous mass that roughly houses an astounding 100 billion neurons, weighs about 3.5 pounds. One brain may hold nearly as many neurons as the universe holds stars. If one considers the almost innumerable interconnections among these 100 billion neurons, it can be argued that the human brain may be the most complex 3.5-pound gelatinous mass in the universe.

In the brain, as in every other organ in the human body, problems arise. Malfunction in the neural centers that cause movement can result in tremor or paralysis; malfunction in the centers for visual processing can cause double vision or blindness; malfunction across large masses of neurons can result in seizures. It follows, then, that malfunctions in the centers involving mood regulation should cause some type of disturbance in mood; severe depressions and manias result. Malfunctions in the areas integrating thought process should cause problems with thought production (loosening of associations) and content (delusions). We call these resulting problems "psychosis." To argue that there are no mental illnesses, one would have to argue the untenable position that the parts of the brain that regulate these abilities always function normally in all people at all times.

More convincing than the logical conclusions of the above arguments is Nature's own conclusive evidence that some very severe mental symptoms, including the development of specific abnormal ideas, are caused directly by pathophysiology. This compelling evidence, so vital

to our understanding of how pathophysiology may directly create suicidal ideas, is well worth a brief historical side trip.

We are back in the Victorian era of Elizabeth Siddal and the Pre-
Raphaelite Brotherhood, but we are on the Continent. In Paris, the
compassionate care of people suffering from severe mental illnesses
was still in its infancy. Dedicated and courageous people such as
Philippe Pinel and Esquirol had broken the superstitions of demonic
possession and the chains of imprisonment as a form of treatment, but
little was known about the etiology of any of the major mental illnesses. Most of the insane asylums remained truly frightening places
filled with ignorance and fear.

If we were to walk within the halls of these asylums, we would be
confronted by the ravages of unfettered madness. In particular, the
wards were littered with people suffering from a singular form of insanity that is seldom seen today. In fact, in my entire career as a psychiatrist, I have never had to treat this specific mental illness. As a
physician in a Parisian insane asylum, helping such patients would
have been the focus of much of my day.

These patients were often late middle-aged, and they frequently
showed decline in their intellectual functioning, a condition we now
know as dementia. In addition, they demonstrated a host of even more
classic signs of mental illness—signs quite similar to the symptoms in
patients struggling with the brain disease of schizophrenia today.
Many of these patients would have demonstrated bizarrely illogical
thought patterns and idiosyncratic ways of viewing the world. Vivid
hallucinations would have tormented them with malicious regularity.
As they walked about the cold and damp halls of the asylum, they
would find themselves aglow with Napoleonic grandeur or aghast with
persecutory anguish. The majority of the patients were not quite this
dramatic in presentation, but all were ultimately devastated by the dementia and/or psychotic processes inherent in the disorder.

At the time, those of psychiatric and psychological bent had all sorts
of ideas as to what caused this syndrome. For theoreticians who were
partial to the concept of external stress as the cause of mental illness,
it was easy to point to the extreme social injustices of the time—
poverty, debtors' prisons, hunger, crime, and political instability. Bi-
ographers of famous people who succumbed to this puzzling disorder
always seemed to have an inside track on the exact marital failure,

career debacle, financial catastrophe, or public humiliation that had proven to have been "too much" and pushed the celebrity to the brink of insanity.

On the other hand, those theoreticians who preferred a psychological explanation for etiology had a different list of devils—religious doubts wrought by the pens of Charles Darwin and positivist philosophers; the machinations of the unconscious; losing God or finding God; standing face-to-face with failure or, equally frightening, standing face-to-face with success. Perhaps the psychological turmoil was somehow created by lunar tides or corsets bound too tightly. Although multiple theories abounded, there was universal agreement that some hideous external stressor or malignant psychological failing would have been required to break people down into these psychotic parodies of their former selves.

However, these social and psychological theories were wrong. The illogical thoughts, grandiose delusions, and bizarre perceptions of these patients had absolutely nothing to do with stress or psychological conflict, and everything to do with damage to the brain and its resulting pathophysiology. The brain damage that produced these bizarre delusions and dementias was, strangely enough, the work of a large pack of very small animals.

The beasts in question, *Treponema pallidum,* are delicate organisms whose thin bodies are composed of 6 to 14 spirals that end in a wispy taper. Being microorganisms, they are a minuscule 6 to 15 microns in length and only 0.2 micron in width. They enter the human body during sexual activity, and it was tertiary syphilis or syphilis of the brain, that was directly causing the strange behaviors and thoughts of the patients who filled the asylums of nineteenth-century Europe. Every symptom, every specific delusion, every bit of illogical thought was the direct result of neurosyphilis.

Frequently, a good twenty years would pass before these patients started to show the symptoms of neurosyphilis (also called general paresis), for it often took this long for the microorganisms to invade brain tissue. As neuronal cells were destroyed, pathophysiology erupted. The delicate molecular balance of the brain was lost, as was the veil of reason. Thus, there should be no debate about whether pathophysiology can directly create bizarre thought, illogical reasoning, or even hallucinations.

Our first question is answered. Neuronal pathophysiology can directly cause major psychiatric symptoms and even specific ideas such as delusions of grandeur or persecution. In retrospect, it seems obvious for it is continuously affirmed by daily experience. Any person who has worked in an inner-city emergency room will attest to the direct changes that occur in thinking and perception when the brain's chemistry is disturbed by cocaine or LSD. Chronic use of speed can create persecutory delusions that are essentially indistinguishable from those found in schizophrenia. The entire personality of a human can be changed by pathophysiology as anyone can attest who has seen a patient's personality deteriorate during the pathophysiologic onslaught of Alzheimer's disease or a frontal lobe cancer. Like *Treponema pallidum*, Alzheimer's and brain cancer destroy the delicate latticework of neuronal architecture. Today, we are well aware that abnormal biochemistry of the brain can directly cause the odd thoughts and damaging mood states of diseases such as schizophrenia and bipolar disorder.

## THE ROLE OF THE BRAIN: THE SECOND QUESTION

Can the brain, when it is malfunctioning, literally create a suicidal thought? A spin-off question would be: Can a malfunctioning brain intensify or increase the frequency of suicidal ideations that were originally spawned by external stress and/or internal conflict? To answer these questions, two case examples offer some intriguing clues.

---

### STEVE: A CASE STUDY

In the early 1980s, late at night, in a nondescript hotel room near a small hospital in a small steel town southeast of Pittsburgh, Pennsylvania, I was awakened by a call from a crisis clinician. At the time I was on call as a moonlighter for the local emergency room. The clock said 1:00 A.M., and it was apparently time for me to earn my pay. The patient, Steve, was a young man of about thirty-five years, who looked to be in good physical condition. He presented in a red plaid shirt and old blue jeans. His hair was a bit unkempt, in keeping with a week of restless nights. As I sat down with Steve, his eyes had an intensely troubled and puzzled look.

The crisis worker had commented that she was worried about suicide potential, but she added, "There's something really strange here; something is not right." Given the presence of suicidal ideation, I naively assumed that Mr. Jackson was depressed. Our conversation sounded like this:

DR. SHEA:   I see, Mr. Jackson, from the crisis worker's note, that you are depressed. Is that right?

MR. JACKSON:   Is that what she wrote? [frowns]

DR. SHEA:   Well, not exactly. She wrote you were having suicidal ideation.

MR. JACKSON:   [nodding an affirmative] Yea, that's what I said. I'm suicidal, but I'm not depressed.

DR. SHEA:   How do you mean?

MR. JACKSON:   Doctor, you aren't going to believe this. I'm not going crazy. I don't know, maybe I am. [pause] I got a good life. I have a great wife, two great kids, and I'm a lucky guy. I got a good job after Bethlehem closed down. I got no reason to be depressed. [pause] And I'm not. That's what is so damn strange.

DR. SHEA:   How do you mean strange?

MR. JACKSON:   About a month ago, I started having thoughts about killing myself. It's really wild. I don't have any reason to want to kill myself. But they are there. [pause] They are scary thoughts. Dark thoughts.

DR. SHEA:   What ways have you thought about?

MR. JACKSON:   Shooting myself, I don't know, overdosing. I don't usually think about the way, but they are getting worse. I just don't know what to do. It is so weird. You can ask my wife, she came down with me; I'm never like this.

Naturally, I proceeded to do a careful suicide assessment. I also carefully explored for the neurovegetative symptoms of depression and the atypical symptoms of depression. Sometimes people are actually unaware that they are depressed because they are not accustomed to applying the label to themselves or because they worry that the label will be viewed as an admission of weakness or defeat. As I proceeded with my inquiries, things became, as Alice would say in Wonderland, curiouser and curiouser. Mr. Jackson had a few symptoms of depression. His sleep was getting rattled and his concentration and energy were flagging, but these depressive symptoms all seemed to be in direct response to his worries about his unexpected and unexplainable onset of suicidal ideation.

I wondered whether he was developing a form of obsessive-compulsive disorder. However, after further questioning, I dismissed that idea. He just didn't have the distinctive phenomenology associated with obsessive-compulsive disorder. Most puzzling was his own puzzlement. It was so genuine, so intense, that it was disturbing. Our conversation continued later, as I tried to round out my database with his medical history:

DR. SHEA:   Mr. Jackson, you said earlier that you are as fit as a horse. Do you have any medications you take for any ongoing medical problems?

MR. JACKSON:   No way. [reflective pause]

DR. SHEA:   Yes?

MR. JACKSON:   Well, I take something, but not because I have a chronic problem or anything.

DR. SHEA:   What are you taking? Do you remember its name?

MR. JACKSON:   I think its called amanarine or something.

DR. SHEA:   Amantadine?

MR. JACKSON:   Yea, that's it.

DR. SHEA:   Do you remember what you are on amantadine for?

MR. JACKSON:   My doctor thinks it might help prevent the flu.

DR. SHEA:   Yes. It's sometimes used that way. [pause] When did you start it?

MR. JACKSON:   About two months ago. Do you think that could have anything to do with this [with a look of hopeful incredulity]?

DR. SHEA:   Not really. But I'll check and see if it is ever associated with depression. I'll be right back.

Amantadine is much more commonly used to help relieve the horrible stiffening of Parkinson's disease than as a deterrent to a flu virus. In this capacity, it has brought tremendous relief to many people. I doubted it was the problem, but it was worth checking out. I went back to the nurses' station and consulted the *Physician's Desk Reference* (PDR). As I was skimming the section on the side effects of amantadine, a phrase caught my eye. It was benignly sitting at the very end of the listing of neuropsychiatric side effects, relatively unheralded, probably because it was seldom reported. When I returned to the room, I said four words to Steve: "Stop the amantadine, tonight."

If you refer to amantadine in a PDR today, you'll find a warning following a bold heading about a side effect. The warning is even more explicit than I remember reading that night back with Steve, undoubtedly reflecting its confirmed reappearance over the years:

**Suicide Attempts:** Suicide attempts, some of which have been fatal, have been reported in patients treated with Symmetrel (Amantadine), many of whom received short courses for influenza treatment or prophylaxis. The incidence of suicide attempts is not known and the pathophysiologic mechanism is not understood. Suicide attempts and suicidal ideation have been reported in patients with and without prior history of psychiatric illness.[16]

Amantadine, like a number of other medications, can, on relatively rare occasions, create a depressive state, but that depressive state is not the topic of this warning. The warning does not state that amantadine can cause a depressive state in response to which the patient might develop suicidal ideation. It states that amantadine, itself, can create suicidal ideation. We just don't know how. The answer to our second question—Can the brain create suicidal ideation?—is an unqualified Yes. Like a bevy of spirochetes triggering a specific persecutory delusion in a patient with neurosyphilis, it would appear that, in rare instances, amantadine can, at a biochemical level, trigger the circuits that tell a human to end his or her life.

With amantadine we have an example of how an exogenous substance placed into the brain can occasionally result in pathophysiology. This particular abnormality somehow triggers suicidal ideation. In some respects, this news is not overly surprising. Suicidal ideation was relatively common in patients with general paresis where spirochetes were at work, and LSD, another exogenous substance, has been documented to trigger suicidal ideation in patients without a history of suicidal thought.

On the other hand, the phenomenon at work with amantadine raises another haunting question: If an exogenous substance can clearly create suicidal ideation, is it possible that an endogenous substance could create suicidal ideation? Put differently, is it possible that a spontaneous disruption of neuronal firing, as seems to occur in some biologic depressions, could result in the direct creation of suicidal ideation? Suicidal ideation, in this instance, would not be a psychological response to the severe onslaught of depressive symptoms. It would be a stand-alone symptom of depression, directly caused by biochemical dysfunction and not necessarily related to environmental stress nor caused by psychological conflict.

## PAT: A SECOND CASE STUDY

Several years after my experience with Mr. Jackson in the emergency room, I had completed my residency at Western Psychiatric Institute and Clinic and had remained there as a faculty member. It was 3:00 P.M., and I was expecting to see one of my outpatients, whom I had been following for several years. The patient, Pat, had responded well to both an antidepressant medication and a mixture of cognitive and psychodynamic therapies.

Pat was a pleasant, middle-age woman who had a style of demeaning her importance that really didn't do her justice. It also served as a bit of a defensive refuge from her own passive anger toward others, including her husband and her children. For the past couple of years, she had experienced a severe major depression with suicidal ideation. Pat had required hospitalization for several months. The inpatient clinicians had had a rough time finding a suitable antidepressant for her. Six different agents had been utilized; all of them failed. Finally, number seven proved to be lucky. Pat responded extremely well to Parnate, a specialized antidepressant belonging to a class called monoamine oxidase inhibitors. The results were stunning. Pat had a new life. It was a life sans suicidal ideation.

I functioned as her outpatient psychotherapist and the guardian of the Parnate. Pat did fairly well with therapy over the next year and a half. She had been without any depressive symptoms for about seven months. She was eager to try a med-free period. I approved. We were both hoping that the Parnate(SmithKline Beecham) had somehow had a lasting effect on the way that her brain produced and processed the neurotransmitter serotonin, which is often low in people experiencing depressive states.

Off the medication, things went well for about four months. Then, one day, Pat entered my office with a sort of chagrined look. I hadn't seen her for a couple of weeks. The depressive symptoms had come back. She was even experiencing some early suicidal ideation. Curious to me was the fact that I could tell that she was getting depressed after listening to her for several minutes; some of her old cognitive distortions, such as overgeneralization, had returned. She restarted her Parnate regimen. The depression was completely gone within three weeks. Even her cognitive distortions vanished as if a button had been pushed. The link between her biochemistry and the production of her cognitive distortions fascinated me. Absolutely nothing had changed with regard to the stresses in her life or the psychotherapy itself.

About a year later, we tried coming off the medicine again, hoping that somehow the many months of high functioning on the Parnate had "locked in" the biochemical changes and returned the chemical balance of her brain to normal. We had high hopes. It had been a good year.

This time, Pat was off the Parnate for almost five months. As she entered my office, I saw the chagrined smile:

PAT:   Well, it's starting up.
DR. SHEA:   I'm sorry to hear that.
PAT:   Yea, me too. It's not bad at all. But I can feel it. It's not a big deal.
DR. SHEA:   Yea, but it is frustrating. [pause] What are you noticing?
PAT:   Not much, really. But I feel my energy going down a little. My concentration is starting to go. But I'm not real depressed yet. I'm really not. I'm still an eight out of ten on my mood scale, but it's just coming back. I can sense it. [pause] That's the funny thing.
DR. SHEA:   How do you mean?
PAT:   I'm getting suicidal.
DR. SHEA:   What? [said with a bit of a startle]
PAT:   Oh don't worry [she smiles], I'm not going to hurt myself. It's just so strange, Dr. Shea. I'm not really very depressed at all, but I'm having pretty strong suicidal ideation. Plans and all. The thoughts just come, just like they did when I was very depressed and in the hospital. Spooky. But I'm not going to do it. I don't want to do it. It's just there. I think we should start the Parnate back up.
DR. SHEA:   You don't have to convince me [we both laughed].

It is important to note that, similar to the first time we stopped the Parnate, there had been no new environmental stressors, and no new psychological conflicts had arisen. In fact, Pat had been doing even better with her cognitive therapy. We resumed the Parnate and within ten days, all suicidal ideation had vanished. *Poof!* Like magic. Pat did quite well on long-term maintenance with Parnate. The pathophysiology of her brain had directly created the thoughts that could have led to its own self-destruction.

---

Interestingly, there is growing scientific evidence to support this clinical supposition. Of particular note are the various studies of the concentration of the neurotransmitter, serotonin, one of the main messenger molecules between the neurons of the brain. This particular neurotransmitter is increased by many of the antidepressants, including such well known medications as Prozac (Eli Lilly), Paxil (Smith-Kline Beecham), and Zoloft (Pfizer). All three seem to increase the relative amount of serotonin sitting free within synaptic clefts. After the serotonin is released into the synaptic cleft, its reuptake into its "parent" cell is slowed or relatively blocked by the medication.

The association between blocking serotonin reuptake (thus indirectly increasing serotonin concentration) and improved mood has led theoreticians to postulate that depression may be partially explained by too low a level of serotonin in the brains of some depressed patients.

After serotonin is used by neurons, it is ultimately broken down into a metabolite, 5-hydroxyindoleacetic acid (5-HIAA). This metabolite will appear in the cerebrospinal fluids of patients. The higher the concentration in the cerebrospinal fluid, the more serotonin is being processed by the brain. Thus, one would expect depressed patients, in whom it is postulated there is too little serotonin to start with, to reflect this low level of serotonin with lower cerebrospinal fluid levels of 5-HIAA, which they do. Even more interesting is the finding that depressed patients who attempt suicide have even lower levels of 5-HIAA in their cerebrospinal fluids. This unusually low level is particularly common among patients who try violent means of suicide, such as hanging, drowning, shooting, and deep cutting, as opposed to nonviolent techniques, such as overdosing.[17, 18]

Where does all this knowledge leave us? We gain a sense of wonderment and a better understanding of the interplay among environment, internal cognitive functioning, and biology. It is quite possible that spontaneous fluxes in the level of neurotransmitters could actually create or at least predispose an individual to certain types of thinking, such as the cognitive distortions seen in depression. It is certain, in my opinion, that dysfunctional biochemistry can create suicidal ideation in some individuals, as I have seen with Steve Jackson and Pat.

Not only can biochemistry affect cognition, but there is growing evidence that cognitive therapies can actually correct the physiology of the brain. For instance, current research is demonstrating that brain imaging abnormalities shown on PET (positron-emission tomography) scans in people suffering from severe obsessive–compulsive disorder actually disappeared after successful treatment consisting of cognitive behavioral treatments without medications.[19]

Long-term exposure to environmental stresses, if perceived by the patient as severe, probably can also change brain biochemistry—this time, for the worse. Thus, we might theorize that Elizabeth Siddal, following her stillbirth, may have acquired an endogenous biologic depression as well as her reactive depression to the external stress. This biologic depression could have initiated her suicidal ideation or intensified a suicidal ideation that was already present. This vicious depressive cycle could have been further exacerbated by a severe propensity for the development of the type of cognitive distortions commonly seen in depressed and suicidal patients. The presence of such maladaptive cognitive distortions could only have worsened her depression and her sense of hopelessness.

All three of the etiologic factors described in this chapter are capable of producing suicidal ideation and may be at work in any individual. For instance, all three factors may have played a role in the death of Kurt Cobain, our prototype for an individual in whom internal conflict/cognitive distortion was viewed as the main etiologic force behind suicide. Biology may also have played a role; his long-term drug abuse could have contributed to his depression and may have even triggered an endogenous biologic depression, further amplifying the intensity of his suicidal ideation. All of these factors may have made it more difficult for Cobain to handle the myriad of stresses around him—growing fame, hectic touring and recording demands, and strained relations with his wife.

In summary, the pathophysiology of the brain can theoretically increase suicide risk in the following five ways:

1. The patient reactively develops suicidal ideation in response to the severe depressive symptoms caused by a spontaneously arising endogenous depression (probably the most common circumstance).
2. The pathophysiology of an endogenous depression directly creates suicidal ideation (as seen with Pat).
3. External stressors or psychological conflicts/cognitive distortions trigger a biological depression, which then increases the intensity and/or frequency of the suicidal ideation primarily caused by the external stressors and/or psychological conflicts (as seen with Elizabeth Siddal and Kurt Cobain).
4. Pathophysiology caused by exogenous sources (street drugs, medications, toxins) causes a depression that the patient psychologically responds to with the development of suicidal ideation. (This may have been a factor with Elizabeth Siddal's chronic use of laudanum.)

5. Pathophysiology caused by exogenous sources (street drugs, medications, toxins) creates suicidal ideation directly or intensifies the suicidal ideation caused by external stressors and/or psychological conflicts (as seen with Steve Jackson and amantadine).

These five concepts lead to several practical clinical considerations. Never underestimate the possible role of biology as an etiologic force toward suicide. It is always easy to see supposed environmental and psychological reasons for the development of suicidal ideation, just as it was always easy for the Victorian experts to create convincing yet invalid social and psychological reasons for the insanity caused by neurosyphilis.

In depression, one can seldom be entirely sure whether biology is or is not playing a role. If you have a patient who has developed suicidal ideation that is more than fleeting in nature, I believe that the patient should be assessed for the potential use of an antidepressant. Even if a clear-cut stressor can be identified, such as the death of a child or spouse, it does not rule out the possibility that the patient may have also developed a biologic depression, perhaps triggered by the severe stressor. This biologic depression may now be creating and/or intensifying the patient's suicidal ideation. By returning the patient's serotonin to a normal level through the effective use of an antidepressant, the clinician could be saving the patient's life. In a similar light, any person who has a sustained depression should be referred for a physical examination and an evaluation of thyroid functioning. Many physical diseases can present with depression or anxiety, including cancer and various hormonal disturbances.

Despite apparent improvements in both environmental stressors and cognitive distortions, a patient's biologic milieu may still be pushing the patient toward suicide. This possibility reemphasizes the point already made: Continue to monitor suicidal ideation at every session, no matter how well the therapy appears to be progressing, until it is clear that the patient is no longer having any suicidal ideation.

## THE ASCENT FROM THE MAELSTROM: CONCLUDING COMMENTS

As the protagonist in Poe's tale descends into the maelstrom, he encounters a horrifying world of tattered sails and splintered masts. He has no doubt that all is lost—death is at hand. He experiences the same hopelessness as those who have become acutely suicidal. Then, deep within the roar of the maelstrom, Poe's sailor happens upon a new emotion: "It was not a new terror that thus affected me, but the dawn of a more exciting hope. This hope arose partly from memory, and partly from present observation."[20] The sailor regains both his desire and his ability to be a problem solver. The solution to his dilemma comes from his remembering the "floating properties" characteristic of certain shapes. He consequently straps himself to a nearby wooden cask that he observes passing on the frothing wall of the maelstrom and rises to the surface.

It is our job to help our clients find "floating casks" and other creative alternatives to suicide. Like the protagonist in Poe's story, our clients' hopes come partly from the work of their own memories. In this case it is the reawakening of memories of previous successes, of past moments in which they overcame great odds. We are there to rekindle these memories, to point our patients toward this life-sustaining sense of mastery that is the seed of hope.

As with Poe's protagonist, this emergent hope is then given full birth by the revitalization of our clients' problem-solving abilities. They find new solutions to old problems—solutions that are both more practical and, ultimately, less costly than suicide. In the last analysis, we are less intrigued by the idea that Poe's sailor descended into a maelstrom than by the fact that he managed to ascend out of one. That ascent serves to remind us of the mystery of our work.

## NOTES

1. Poe, E.A.: *Tales of Edgar Allan Poe.* Franklin Center, Pennsylvania, The Franklin Library, 1974.

2. Daly, G.: *Pre-Raphaelites in Love.* New York, Ticknor & Fields, 1989, pp. 100–101.

3. Weintraub, S.: *Four Rossettis.* New York, Weybright and Talley, 1977, p. 117.

4. Weintraub, S., 1977, p. 117.

5. Weintraub, S., 1977, p. 121.

6. Weintraub, S., 1977, p. 122.

7. Fremon, C.: Love and death. In *Suicide: Right or Wrong, 2nd Edition,* edited by J. Donnelly. Amherst, New York, Prometheus Books, 1998, p. 77.

8. Stokes, H.S.: *The Life and Death of Yukio Mishima, Revised Edition.* The Noonday Press, 1995, pp. 9–34.

9. Website [http://ourworld.compuserve.com/homepages/gracefyr/greatone.htm], 1/13/98.

10. Beck, A.: Hopelessness and suicidal behavior. *Journal of the American Medical Association* 234: 1146-1149, 1975.

11. Chiles, J.A. and Strosahl, K.D.: *The Suicidal Patient: Principles of Assessment, Treatment, and Case Management.* Washington, DC, American Psychiatric Press, Inc., 1995, p. 60.

12. Frankl, V.W.: *The Doctor and the Soul.* New York, Vintage Books, 1973.

13. Alvarez, A., 1971, p. 131.

14. Linehan, M.: *Cognitive-Behavioral Treatment of Borderline Personality Disorder.* New York, Guilford Press, 1993.

15. Chiles, J.A. and Strosahl, K.D., 1995.

16. Physician's Desk Reference (PDR) 51st Edition: Montvale, New Jersey, Medical Economics Company, Inc., 1997, p. 966.

17. Brown, G.L., Ebert, M.H., Boyer, P.F., et al: Aggression, suicide and serotonin: Relationships to CSF amine metabolites. *American Journal of Psychiatry* 139: 741–746, 1982.

18. Traskman-Bendz, L., Alling, C., Oreland, L., et al: Prediction of suicidal behavior from biologic tests. *Journal of Clinical Psychopharmacology (supplement)* 12: 21s–26s, 1992.

19. Baxter, Jr., L.R.: Positron emission tomography studies of cerebral glucose metabolism in obsessive-compulsive disorder. *Journal of Clinical Psychiatry (supplement)* 55: 54–59, 1994.

20. Poe, E.A., 1974, p. 40.

# CHAPTER 3

# Risk Factors: Harbingers of Death

Cases of suicide occur at all ages of life, even among mere children. We have already seen that it is frequently hereditary, and that it may alternate with other forms of insanity in different generations. It is about three times more frequent among males than females. The most recent and reliable statistics would seem to indicate that it is increasing in frequency at a most astounding and, so to speak, progressive rate.

W. Griesinger, M.D., University of Berlin, 1882[1]

## INTRODUCTION

IT IS important to understand the distinction between "risk factors" and "risk predictors." A risk factor is a characteristic of a large sample of people who have committed suicide, that appears to be statistically more common than would be expected. In contrast, a risk predictor is a characteristic of a specific living person that indicates the likelihood of imminent suicide for that individual. Risk factors often include demographics (such as age or sex), living circumstances (such as the presence of a severe stressor or the lack of a significant other), historical associations (a family member has committed suicide or the client has a previous history of attempting suicide), and clinical condition (such as the presence of acute alcohol intoxication or psychosis).

It has always been hoped that risk factors, if studied collectively in a specific client, would also serve as reliable risk predictors alerting the clinician to an immediate danger of suicide. Such is not the case. Not a single piece of research has shown that the presence of any collection of risk factors can accurately predict the imminent dangerousness of a client.

An example can help to illustrate this dilemma. Let us rate a client's dangerousness using the SAD PERSONS Scale,[2] a ten-point risk-factor scale that we will make use of later in this chapter. It consists of ten risk factors. The presence of each factor is allotted a point value of 1. The closer one approaches to ten points, the more dangerous the person is supposed to be. But is this true?

Let us look at a middle-aged woman who has the following characteristics: she is not particularly depressed, has never attempted suicide, does not drink alcohol or use drugs, has a loving nuclear family (including two healthy parents and three loving brothers living nearby), has a wonderful spouse, has no organized suicide plan, and has no chronic illnesses. She lacks nine of the ten risk factors on the SAD PERSONS Scale. The very highest she could score is one point out of ten (if she has the last risk factor). Using this scale, the clinician would rate the client's immediate risk as quite low.

The last risk factor rated on the scale is the presence of psychotic process. Our hypothetical client is unfortunately in the throes of a post-partum psychosis. She is convinced that demons have entered her daughter and are torturing her relentlessly. The voice of the main demon, who, she believes, is Satan himself, is hounding her minute by minute. He harangues, "You must pay for your sins. Kill yourself *now* or we will torture your daughter forever." The woman turns to the clinician and begs frantically, "*Do* something. You've got to stop them. I can't let them do this to her. You've got to stop them."

Rather dramatically, our scale has failed us as a predictive instrument. The client, despite a very low risk rating on the SAD PERSONS Scale, is potentially at very high risk. She is perhaps best served by acute hospitalization.

If risk factors are not necessarily good risk predictors, one might wonder why we study them at all. The answer lies in the utility of risk factors to alert the clinician not to the fact that the client *is* at higher risk but that there is good reason to suspect that the client *may be* at higher risk. Such situations often require particular tenacity in the clinician's approach. It may even signal one of the most dangerous of situations, a client who has truly decided to kill himself or herself and is intent on hiding this information. The presence of a large number of risk factors may also suggest that corroborative sources should be interviewed. They may provide a picture of the client's suicidal intent that is markedly different from the patient's self-report. In short, the elicitation of numerous risk factors may trigger both analytic and intuitive suspicions that all is not as it appears to be.

The search for risk factors provides other benefits as well; sometimes, it suggests specific lines of questioning. Psychotic process may indicate the need for quite specific lines of questioning, such as inquiries about the presence of command hallucinations, which proved to be so telling with the hypothetical middle-aged woman described above. Consistent elicitation and formulation of risk factors serve yet one more practical function: conditioning the clinician to consider suicide risk with every client. Such a clinical habit can only prove to be beneficial over time. It will prompt careful suicidal formulation even when the clinician is feeling pressured, weary, or harried, or is simply having an "off day."

Two clinical case studies will launch our inquiry into risk factor analysis. With these studies, we will attempt to accomplish the following goals:

1. Introduce the commonly cited risk factors associated with suicide.
2. Demonstrate specific questions for effectively eliciting these factors.
3. Illustrate the use of specialized interview strategies indicated by the presence of specific risk factors (such as questions to ask psychotic patients).
4. Briefly introduce the formulation of acute versus chronic risk, based on the presence or absence of specific risk factors.

---

### CASE PRESENTATION ONE:
### MR. FREDERICKS

Mr. Fredericks, a 21-year-old male, presents to the emergency room on a Sunday afternoon at around 3:00 P.M. He prefers being called

"Jimmy" and quickly hastens to say, "I'm not here for an emergency. I can come back at another time if you're busy. I just need some help with my stress. I'm really stressed out." Jimmy is a junior at a prestigious university where he sports a rather remarkable 3.8 grade-point average. He is well on his way to a career in dental school, much to his parents' pride.

Jimmy is spending the summer at school. He is working in a nearby dental lab in an effort to bolster his already bulging list of extracurricular accomplishments. His light red T-shirt and Bermuda shorts hang on a thin frame—a frame that has been toughened by a demanding jogging schedule. His hair, dark and trimmed short, complements a lightly tanned and freshly shaven face. His face is somewhat curious, less for what it shows than for what it doesn't show. Jimmy has a restricted affect although he manages to push out a sheepish but somehow winning smile, especially in moments when he feels self-conscious. Such moments are not uncommon in the interview. Despite all of his academic accomplishments, Jimmy is refreshingly unassuming. He is also quite troubled.

His main complaint is: "I'm just really stressed out, I can't stop being anxious. I just can never relax." He ascribes this situation to his intensely competitive nature, "It's like there's a man in my head, always pushing me. I always feel I'm not good enough. A 92% on a final is not enough, I need to get a 100%." This last statement tails off into one of his embarrassed smiles. "I know I shouldn't talk like this. It sounds like I'm complimenting myself. But this is what I'm feeling." Jimmy pauses and then repeats, "I know I shouldn't talk like this."

He denies feeling depressed, and he reports few neurovegetative symptoms of depression except for a sleep disturbance. The discussion of his sleep problems draws another sheepish smile. He comments that he has been taking some "pep" pills to key him up for some upcoming tests. "I know that's not right. And I'm not going to do it anymore." Jimmy's need to please the interviewer is painfully tangible. The interviewer almost feels as if he is hearing a confession. Further inquiry reveals only a handful of occasions of pill popping. Adolescents are notorious for minimizing drug use, but one gets the feeling that Jimmy is telling the truth. Jimmy denies the use of alcohol, LSD, crack, marijuana, or any other street drugs.

When asked about whether he wants to kill himself, Jimmy comments, "Not really. But sometimes I feel pressure to do that. But I know it's wrong." Asked to elaborate, Jimmy's smile returns, and he quickly changes the topic. "I'm not going to kill myself. That's why I'm here. I think I need therapy. Something is not right. Life can't be this stressful.

You know, at midnight on a Saturday I still feel like I should be in the library studying. Now that's not right."

By the end of the interview, Jimmy is well engaged and very comfortable with the idea of outpatient counseling. The interviewer is not equally comfortable. Perhaps an examination of some of Jimmy's risk factors may help explain the clinician's unsettled feelings.

---

Jimmy's sex and age are consistent with an increased suicide risk. With regard to sex, males more frequently successfully commit suicide at a three-to-one ratio when compared to females. On the other hand, females *attempt* suicide three times more frequently than males.[3] Perhaps this increased "suicide efficiency" in males relates to the choice of the means of suicide. Males more frequently choose guns and other violent methods that provide a surer means of death.

With regard to age, in general, suicide risk is greater for both sexes with increasing age. In women, the suicide rate increases until midlife, after which it tends to plateau. In men, the suicide rate increases precipitously with advancing age; the highest rate is in white males 70 years and older. But the suicide curve for all males is complicated by a bimodal tendency. A second peak occurs in late adolescence,[4] a point of special significance with regard to Jimmy.

Unfortunately, in recent years, there has been a marked rise in the frequency of adolescents' attempting suicide; suicide now represents the third highest cause of death among teenagers. Although white males traditionally are at highest risk, there has been a disturbing increase in adolescent suicides in both African American and Native Americans.[5] Between 1952 and 1992, the rate of suicide tripled in the age group of 15 to 24 years.[6] It has been estimated that a staggering half-million adolescents and young adults perform suicide gestures or attempts each year.[7] Moreover, a clinician should always keep in mind that even though young children are much less likely to commit suicide, they still do. As mentioned in Chapter 1, this fact is driven home by the knowledge that 330 children, ages 10 to 14, killed themselves in 1995.[8]

Jimmy's age points toward another important risk factor: use of alcohol and/or street drugs. His admission that he used "uppers" was at first disturbing and suggested a possible reason for both his anxiety and his sleep problem. But if he is telling the truth, his small dose of amphetamine is unlikely to be a causative agent for this amount of distress.

Chronic alcohol abuse or other drug abuse is a significant risk factor because these agents may decrease impulse control or precipitate psychotic process. But, beyond poor impulse control, alcohol also appears to cause long-term problems with suicidal ideation. It has been shown that people who have a chronic depression directly caused by alcohol abuse are at a significantly higher risk of making a serious suicide attempt.[9]

An acutely intoxicated patient presents a particular problem because, in two ways, the intoxication predisposes the patient toward a suicide attempt. First, the person's impulse control may be significantly lowered. Second, because of cognitive impairment, the patient may inadvertently commit suicide—for example, by forgetting that a large number of pills were taken earlier in an evening and subsequently proceeding to ingest "just a few more." Such miscalculations can result in a fatal overdose. Because of these dangers even chronic emergency-room abusers who present with serious suicidal ideation while acutely intoxicated should be observed until they sober up. Frequently, as the alcohol wears off, the suicidal ideation disappears and may not even be remembered.

There was more to worry about with Jimmy than the implications of his sex and age. The interviewer left the encounter feeling there was something slightly "odd" about Jimmy's presentation. His affect was restricted, he appeared unusually intense, and he displayed a powerful need to please the interviewer. More puzzling were his references to "the man in my head," which he described as being only a metaphor but almost sounded drawn from experience. The clinician doubted Jimmy was psychotic, but he was upset that he had not explored psychotic process in more detail.

## EXPLORING DANGEROUS PSYCHOTIC PROCESS

Psychosis should be considered a potentially major suicide risk factor because rational thought often acts as the final obstacle to self-destruction. In particular, three disturbing processes that could possibly push a patient toward violence to self (or to others, for that matter) should be carefully evaluated when the clinician is suspicious of psychotic process: (1) command hallucinations, (2) feelings of alien control, and (3) religious preoccupation.

Command hallucinations are auditory commands to perform specific acts. Such commands may be egging on patients to harm themselves or others. Their presence, in some instances, should strongly lean the evaluator toward the patient's immediate hospitalization. Because they are often not volunteered by the psychotic patient, they require active inquiry by the clinician.

During an inquiry into command hallucinations, several phenomenological considerations merit the attention of the clinician. Command hallucinations are not black-or-white phenomena in the sense that the patient either has them or does not. Command hallucinations can vary in numerous ways. Among their defining characteristics are: emotional impact on the patient, loudness, frequency, duration, content, degree of hostility, and degree to which the patient feels driven to follow them.

Command hallucinations can vary from relatively innocuous phenomena that are infrequent and have little impact on the patient to dangerous phenomena in which the voices incessantly hammer at the patient in an effort to provoke violence. Some people suffering with chronic schizophrenia have adapted to their voices and pay them little heed. This level of command hallucination is probably of minimal concern. At the other end of the continuum, command hallucinations can become acutely harassing, loud, and insistent. In such cases, the clinician should always ask to what degree the patient feels in control. Some patients may feel unable to resist soft yet persistent voices. These types of acutely dystonic command hallucinations generally indicate the need for acute hospitalization. To determine the dangerousness of the command hallucinations, the clinician must take the time to explore these phenomenologic variables.

Over the years, a variety of papers have purported that there is little or no statistical correlation between command hallucinations and suicide or violence.[10-14] But, from a close look at these papers, it becomes evident that none of the research carefully categorized the hallucinations along the critical phenomenological variables listed above. The research is generally based on hospital charts, which are notorious for poor reporting of the nuances of patient phenomenology. In this research, it is unclear whether the voices were at one end or the other end of the continuum of dangerousness. Consequently, the statistical analyses are difficult to interpret.

A paper by Junginger, published in 1990, utilized direct interviews of patients who had recently experienced command hallucinations.[15] Although this study was not prospective in nature, the results are worth noting. Of the twenty patients who had experienced dangerous command hallucinations, eight had acted on them. These results are more consistent with the observations of experienced clinicians, and the paper represents a first step toward a more rigorous study of the phenomena of command hallucinations.

Nevertheless, to date, I have not seen a prospective study that carefully operationalized the phenomenological data in such a way that the data are appropriate for statistical analysis. Until such a study exists, clinicians must remember that some patients do act violently in response to command hallucinations.

In a similar sense, alien control, as evidenced by the feeling that one is being controlled by an outside agent, is a second dangerous psychotic process if this "other agent" becomes suicidally or homicidally oriented. It is not uncommon for a patient to battle off such potentially lethal urges on a minute-by-minute basis. The most common reputed agents of alien control are devils, but one can also feel that an evil persecutory figure has taken control of one's mind. In our high-tech society, it has also become more common for patients to feel that they are being controlled by radio waves, satellites, television celebrities, and computers.

A third significant concern arises when a patient exhibits a specific type of excessive religious preoccupation. This type of rumination centers on ideas that God wants the patient to perform certain acts to prove his or her love for God or to carry out an act of atonement. These acts may include suicide, homicide, or self-mutilation. Such concerns can be associated with command hallucinations, as described above, except that the commands originate from figures as ultimately persuasive as God. Patients may feel that their faith is being tested. They may compare themselves with Abraham, who was commanded by God to sacrifice his only son, Isaac. This "Abraham Syndrome" can prove fatal. Some patients may feel that Satan is pushing them toward violence.

At this juncture, a direct transcript from an interview I performed with another adolescent male may bring to life the peculiar hyperreligiosity that sometimes can be a true harbinger of imminent dangerousness. It also highlights a specific aspect of this hyperreligiosity, about which the clinician should directly inquire if the client appears to be psychotic. The patient, who unfortunately suffers from schizophrenia, was being assessed in our emergency room after a recent suicide attempt.

CLINICIAN: You had mentioned a little bit earlier, Dan, that you had felt guilty and that you needed to get back at yourself for doing something. What were you referring to?

PATIENT: I was [pause] I called it chastising myself back then. Like my right hand [patient rubs his right wrist with his left hand], I'd cut off circulation to my right hand.

CLINICIAN: [pointing to patient's right hand] Is that what that scar is? It looks like an older scar.

PATIENT: Yea. I took a steak knife and cut it. I was feeling angry with myself at the time. [pause] I was also into the Bible. You know, where it says, "If thy right hand offends thee, cast it off." I took that too literally.

CLINICIAN: And what did you think that meant?

PATIENT: I thought it meant to actually cut your right hand off.

CLINICIAN: So what did you do?

PATIENT: I cut it. I almost cut into the main ligament or the main blood vessel, whatever. For some reason I didn't get that far.

CLINICIAN: Thankfully.

PATIENT: [patient nods in agreement] Yea.

CLINICIAN: So that is what that scar is from? [points toward wrist]

PATIENT: Yea.

CLINICIAN: So when you were cutting at your wrist, when was that, Dan?

PATIENT: That was back in 1994. I think I was only 15 at the time.

CLINICIAN: Now how long had you been thinking about that Bible verse, when you did that back then?

PATIENT: When I got to that Bible verse is when I cut my hand. There wasn't no long period to it.

CLINICIAN: From the time you read it in the Bible till you cut yourself, how long had elapsed?

PATIENT: Well, about a month, I think.

CLINICIAN: From the time you read about it, it took a month before you actually cut?

PATIENT: No. [pause] I cut my right hand when I was reading the Bible. I had the Bible up in my foster Dad's station wagon. And I was reading a verse, and I had the steak knife, and I was going at it as I read the verse that day.

CLINICIAN:   So you were aware of that verse before, but you came upon it again?

PATIENT:   Yea.

CLINICIAN:   In the days right before you cut yourself, had you been thinking about that Bible verse?

PATIENT:   No. I was thinking about what my right hand was doing, though. And I wanted to stop what it was doing.

CLINICIAN:   And your right hand at that time was doing what?

PATIENT:   [pause] Masturbation.

This excerpt highlights the fact that some patients may be preoccupied with specific verses from the Bible that suggest violent action. In this case, the biblical injunction that prompted the patient's attempt at self-mutilation is from Matthew 5:29, where lustful wanderings of the eye are handled in a rather absolute fashion:

> So if thy right eye is an occasion of sin to thee, pluck it out and cast it from thee; for it is better for thee that one of thy members should perish than that thy whole body should be thrown into hell. And if thy right hand is an occasion of sin to thee, cut it off and cast it from thee; for it is better for thee that one of thy members should be lost than that thy whole body should go into hell.[16]

Bizarre methods of self-mutilation, such as autocastration and removal of the tongue, may result when verses such as this one are twisted by psychotic thought.[17] If religious preoccupation is found, simple questions can help to uncover dangerousness: "Are there parts of the Bible that seem particularly important to you?" or "Are there parts of the Bible that you feel are directing you to do something?"

Although we have been focusing on some of the common ways in which psychotic process can lead to self-harm, it is important to remember that the most dangerous times for most people with long-term psychotic disorders are not during phases of acute psychotic process. Patients with diseases such as schizophrenia and schizoaffective disorder more frequently attempt suicide, not in relation to active psychotic processes, but in relation to the devastating demoralization—resulting from years of pain, frustration, and low-self esteem—caused by the disease process itself.[18-20]

Schizophrenia rapes the soul of the patient, robbing an individual of the chance to pursue the dreams that motivate all of us. The core pains of losing a sense of internal control, and, subsequently, a loss of meaning in life can prove unbearable even for the most courageous of people. As people suffering from schizophrenia perceive themselves to be hopelessly damaged, their reasons for living are gradually extinguished. It has been postulated that patients with the following characteristics may be most at risk: young age, chronic relapses, good educational background, high performance expectations, painful awareness of the illness, fear of further mental deterioration, suicidal ideation or threat, and hopelessness.[21]

A psychotic process not yet described, delirium, is one of the most commonly encountered psychotic states. Delirial states, whether caused by street drugs, medications, or metabolic imbalances, can precipitate serious impairments in sensorium and/or confusional states. During these periods of confusion and psychotic process, patients may be at increased risk for self-harm. Any fluctuation in the level of consciousness or the presence of impaired concentration warrants careful attention during the interview, a more formal cognitive mental status and a close exploration for the presence of hallucinations and delusions.

---

### CASE PRESENTATION ONE: NEW INFORMATION

Returning now to our case study, the clinician was considering reinterviewing Jimmy in an effort to uncover any evidence of psychotic dangerousness. He then noticed that someone displaying a mildly annoyed air was talking with Jimmy in the waiting room in an animated fashion. The visitor would prove to be Jimmy's roommate at college. Here was a chance for some fresh information.

With Jimmy's readily granted approval, the roommate was interviewed. When the interviewer began, "Well, it's very nice of one of Jimmy's friends to come down with him," the roommate was quick to answer, "I'm not exactly a friend, more of a roommate. I don't think Jimmy has too many friends. He's a bit of a geek [smiles], but an okay geek, don't get me wrong. [pause] To tell you the truth, I'm a little worried about him. I think he's taking this school thing a little too seriously, if you know what I mean."

Jimmy's roommate proceeded to validate Jimmy's self-report of a proclivity for late nights at the library. He added that Jimmy had not seemed himself for almost two months. About two months before, he had received a B-minus on a political science exam, his lowest score since entering college. He really seemed "bent out of shape" about this grade and hadn't seemed the same since. The interview, as reconstructed, proceeded as follows:

CLINICIAN:   When you say he hasn't been the same since, how do you mean?

ROOMMATE:   I don't know. Sort of . . . I don't know. He's just sort of spooking me.

CLINICIAN:   In what sense?

ROOMMATE:   He gets up a lot at night. Not every night; about a couple times a week maybe. And he's really uptight. He sometimes seems sort of angry. He's always pacing around. It's driving me nuts!

CLINICIAN:   What else have you noticed?

ROOMMATE:   Nothing really. He's just got to "cool down," that's all.

CLINICIAN:   When you say he was sort of spooking you, has he done anything that you feel is sort of strange?

ROOMMATE:   Not really.

CLINICIAN:   Anything?

ROOMMATE:   I don't want to get him into trouble or anything, and I don't want you to think he's wacko or something, 'cause he's not, but [pauses]. . . .

CLINICIAN:   But?

ROOMMATE:   I think he's talking to himself a lot. It's sort of weird. But I catch him sort of mumbling to himself, like he's angry with himself. He doesn't do it a lot, but sometimes at night he does it and that's what spooks me the most. [pause] Oh yea, I remember something else sort of weird. About a week ago, while we were eating dinner, he asked me if I believed in demons. After the look I gave him, he changed the subject and laughed, saying that he didn't either. But that was sort of weird.

CLINICIAN:   Is Jimmy pretty religious?

ROOMMATE:   [shaking his head negatively] Not that I know of.

CLINICIAN:   You know, sometimes when people are stressed out, they have thoughts of killing themselves. Has Jimmy ever said anything about that?

ROOMMATE:   Nope. If he has, he didn't say it to me.

CLINICIAN:   You'd mentioned that he was angry a lot. Has he said anything about a specific person or talked about hurting anybody?

ROOMMATE:   Jimmy? [looking skeptical] No way.
CLINICIAN:   Did you ever see Jimmy harm himself or anything like that?
ROOMMATE:   No way. [long pause] Hmm.
CLINICIAN:   You look like you're remembering something.
ROOMMATE:   Well, you know, there is something.
CLINICIAN:   And what's that?
ROOMMATE:   I saw a pack of razors in our bathroom a couple of weeks ago.
CLINICIAN:   Is that strange?
ROOMMATE:   It is, if both of us use electric razors.

The evidence was building rapidly that some type of psychotic process was brewing. Delusional thoughts and fears are often viewed as very intimate material by patients. Perhaps Jimmy just didn't feel comfortable enough to share these experiences in detail during his first meeting with the clinician. Who knows, perhaps Jimmy's open willingness to have his roommate interviewed was an unconscious wish that some of this material would somehow surface. Regardless of how the information was gained, it was definitely time for a second interview with Jimmy. But before we study the transcript, it will be informative to look at some of the implications of our new information with regard to risk factors.

---

One cause for concern regarding the newly gleaned information was the presence of intense anxiety in Jimmy. Recent research has suggested that increased anxiety, especially if acute and intense, may play a role in impulsive suicide attempts. On inpatient units, there is evidence that patients with high levels of anxiety and agitation are more prone to kill themselves.[22] Jimmy's anxiety could be related to a variety of factors. At first glance, it sounded like the prototypic anxiety of a "pre-dent" college kid on superego overdrive. But the input from his roommate suggested that a more worrisome process might be at work, and its etiology could be caused by, among other things: intense generalized anxiety; the anxiety seen with panic disorder or obsessive compulsive disorder; the anxiety seen with substance abuse/withdrawal; or, more ominously, the anxiety seen with emerging psychotic process. Jimmy's roommate, upon further questioning, denied that Jimmy used drugs other than "a rare tab of speed the night before a test. He hardly ever uses drugs. He's squeaky clean, trust me."

The above data, culled from a corroborative source, illustrate the important principle of interviewing appropriate friends or family members when assessing suicide potential. In an emergency room situation, it is often critical to talk with significant others before making a decision on safety. If there are serious concerns about safety, they outweigh confidentiality. At times, it is necessary to contact relatives against a person's will. These contacts should be made after consulting with a supervisor or colleague, and clearly stated on the patient's chart should be the reason for choosing to break confidentiality and the role of the consultation.

In general, corroborative sources should be asked whether they have seen anything that suggests possible suicide intent. After such a general inquiry, specific questions such as the following may be useful:

Has he made any comments about being "better off dead?"
Has he joked about killing himself?
Have there been any statements about "things being better soon?"
Does he have any potential weapons available, such as guns or knives?
Has he ever tried to hurt himself before, even in small ways like taking
     a few pills too many?
Has he appeared depressed or tearful?
Is he spending more time alone than usual?

In this type of questioning, besides determining lethality, the clinician is searching for information that would fulfill involuntary commitment criteria. Specifically, using New Hampshire criteria (criteria differ from state to state), one checks to see whether the patient has participated in behavior that is a clear danger to self or others. The criteria are also met if the patient has expressed a desire to harm self or others while taking some steps (such as purchasing a weapon) to fulfill this desire. Jimmy's roommate knew of no such behavior but was wary of the purchase of the razor blades. We do not know for a fact that the razor blades were bought for the purpose of self-harm (thus, committable grounds are not yet present), but knowledge of the purchase of the razor blades allows a much more powerful window for inquiry when Jimmy is reinterviewed. With adolescents, the most common method of suicide is shooting, distantly followed by hanging.[23]

A corroborative interview also provides a chance to determine stressors and social supports. With regard to stress, the clinician should search for situations such as unemployment, family disruption, rejection by a significant other, abrupt changes in career responsibilities, or a recent catastrophic stress. Although there is no typical catastrophic stress in Jimmy's recent life, one wonders whether the impact of the "low" test score was psychologically catastrophic to this relatively frail college student. A lack of friends, family, or societal supports such as church organizations has often been reported as a risk factor. In particular, the clinician should be looking for evidence of recent losses.

In their practical primer on the assessment and treatment of suicidal patients, Fremouw, de Perczel, and Ellis[24] point out that one of the more striking statistical correlations with suicide is the increased risk associated with the absence of a spouse. The highest risk is among couples who are separated. Divorced people have the next highest risk, and those who have lost their spouse to death follow. People who have never been married are next in order of risk, and happily married couples are at least risk.

Regarding the risk factor of social isolation, Jimmy is a cause for concern. His roommate paints a picture of an isolated individual more at home with the silence of a library than the confidences of a friend. During the social history, Jimmy related that he had never dated. He was an only child but had distanced himself from loving but overbearing parents. It was no coincidence that Jimmy was attending college on the East Coast and his parents lived in California.

Determining the quality of immediately available supports is of particular importance if an emergency room clinician has decided to release a somewhat tentative patient who has agreed to come for reassessment the next day. If friends or family members can stay with the patient until the scheduled appointment, then such a plan may be more feasible.

In such cases, it is critical that the family members thoroughly understand that the patient is not to be alone. I generally find it useful to have a discussion with the patient and the family together, talking openly about suicidal concerns and the design of the safety plan. Such a procedure helps to teach the patient and his or her family members that it is both safe and appropriate to discuss suicidal ideation frankly. Suicidal ideation *not* talked about may prove deadly.

Although not immediately obvious, one other support system should always be considered in a suicide assessment: the quality of the mental health system itself. Considerations include: outpatient "waiting list" time, availability of twenty-four-hour crisis support, presence of crisis support groups, and a frank analysis of the quality of the clinicians available. Not all clinicians are comfortable with helping clients who have significant suicidal ideation. Such a lack of outpatient expertise can suggest the wisdom of briefly admitting a somewhat tenuous patient who otherwise might have been referred for outpatient services. Jimmy's catchment center had an excellent crisis team as well as an ongoing crisis group staffed by talented clinicians.

At this point, despite some growing concerns that Jimmy had some psychotic process and that other significant risk factors were identifiable, it remained unclear how lethal a risk Jimmy presented. It must be remembered that he denied suicidal intent, albeit in a somewhat quizzical fashion, and grounds for commitment were lacking.

As noted earlier, it is sometimes expedient to reinterview a patient, especially in emergency room settings. Coupled with knowledge garnered from corroborative sources as well as the improved engagement secured from the first interview (in essence, the client is no longer talking with a stranger), the reinterview results are sometimes rather startling.

In the second encounter with Jimmy, the interviewer will make an even more concerted effort to bring psychotic ideation to the surface while persistently listening for adequate grounds for commitment. After carefully bridging the topic of school stress, the clinician has decided to once again visit Jimmy's comments that it sometimes feels "like there is a man in my head," for these feelings may be the outward manifestation of his psychotic process. As we will see in the following direct transcript, this time around, Jimmy will prove to be more forthcoming:

---

CLINICIAN: Now you had mentioned something about the guy inside you. Tell me a little bit more about that. What's that like?

PATIENT: Well, he doesn't like me at all. No. What he wants is complete control of my body. And that's the way he'd get it.

CLINICIAN: And in what sort of way would he get complete control?

PATIENT: Because once I die [pause] once I die, once I die I wouldn't have any strength to fight him anymore.

CLINICIAN: And then what would probably happen?

PATIENT: Then he'd take completely over.

CLINICIAN: Would he be able to live in your body then?

PATIENT: Yea. No. Well, I think he'd just look for someone else. He'd go on, that was his goal. Unless he has me, he won't like me anymore. You know, he won't be satisfied. He likes the challenge.

CLINICIAN:   The challenge to sort of take over, to win out over someone?

PATIENT:   Yea.

CLINICIAN:   Now when you talk about the guy, do you have a name for him?

PATIENT:   No, I don't have a name for him. [pause] I don't call him by name or any thing. It's just a feeling. That's all it is, it's just a feeling.

CLINICIAN:   How long has he been around?

PATIENT:   As soon as I came to college. Well, I feel he's been a little bit around in high school. But since I came to college, he saw me as a good target.

CLINICIAN:   You said in high school you thought there was a little bit of him. When did you first even get suspicious that there may be this guy?

PATIENT:   Maybe once I realized I was gonna go to college. Well, I knew I was going to go to college. Maybe, I guess it happened in my senior year of high school, when I was filling out all those big long applications.

CLINICIAN:   And what happened?

PATIENT:   That could have been when it started, it's hard to remember, it's hard to remember the exact time. It's not like I have it or I don't have it. But I feel that that is when it could have started to happen.

We are entering a strange world indeed. Perhaps what is most striking is the markedly increased openness of Jimmy during the second interview. The "guy" in his head is discussed much more as an entity, not a metaphor. It appears from the new interview material that, at times, Jimmy is intermittently psychotic. As we now recall the words of his roommate ("But I catch him sort of mumbling to himself, like he's angry with himself"), we realize that it is not himself he had been engaging in conversation. It was the man inside himself.

Through some deft interviewing, which occurred only because of the clinician's wise decision to perform a corroborative interview and to subsequently reinterview Jimmy, a much more accurate picture of Jimmy's state of mind is unfolding. Having pinpointed the presence of psychotic process, the interviewer will now probe for the specific areas of psychotic dangerousness discussed earlier: alien control, command hallucinations, and hyperreligiosity. Note the way in which the interviewer explored this material with a nonjudgmental and matter-of-fact approach. It would prove to be one of the keys to his success in interviewing Jimmy.

CLINICIAN:   Do you ever feel like, literally, that you have an alien force in you?

PATIENT:    Well, I do feel that this thing, that this thing, we'll call it a thing, we'll call it a guy, that this guy, he's not human. So I feel, I do feel like, he came from, well, I'm religious, and I do feel like he came from Hell. [said softly]

CLINICIAN:    In the sense of a demon?

PATIENT:    Yea.

CLINICIAN:    Do you know which demon in your mind?

PATIENT:    Not an exact demon, no, but a demon, yea.

[The interviewer briefly explores Jimmy's views of the demon and then proceeds as follows, in an effort to further pin down Jimmy's acute dangerousness.]

CLINICIAN:    To me it sounds like a very frightening type of experience to feel like there is this thing inside you.

PATIENT:    Yea, it is. [pause] I feel sorry for other people having him too.

CLINICIAN:    Do you ever hear his voice?

PATIENT:    I don't actually hear it, well, I don't actually hear it in my ears, but somehow I hear it.

CLINICIAN:    When you are having that experience, does it sound exactly like your normal thoughts, or are you quite aware that there is something different happening, and you are hearing his voice.

PATIENT:    It's a feeling. It sounds like my thoughts, but they are a little bit different, the way that I can hear them.

CLINICIAN:    And how do you hear them?

PATIENT:    They just seem to come to me. [pause, then speaking very softly, almost in a whisper] They just seem to come to me.

CLINICIAN:    Does the voice ever tell you to hurt yourself?

PATIENT:    Yea. That's what he's telling me.

CLINICIAN:    What exactly will it say?

PATIENT:    He'll say. He'll find another way to do it. Like, he'll say, "Don't study, do bad on the test." And that's his way of saying to hurt myself. And once I do bad on the test, then it will be easy for him to talk to me. [pause] It will be hard not to listen to him.

CLINICIAN:    It changes if you feel you failed on some level?

PATIENT:    I can hear him louder.

CLINICIAN:    Does he ever tell you to cut yourself or to take pills, anything like that?

PATIENT:    He tells me a little bit, and he makes me feel that way also. He'll hint sort of. He'll tell me. [pause] He'll tell me.

CLINICIAN:    What will he say?

PATIENT:    He'll say, "Just do it." He'll say, "Do it." [pause] It's scary.

CLINICIAN:    I'm sure it is. [patient smiles and nods agreement]

The clinician's graceful structuring of Jimmy into the regions of psychosis that are associated with suicide risk is paying off. The roommate's reflections on the razor blade now appear more ominous. A simple question such as, "Jimmy, I'm wondering, if in response to the voices, you ever got a razor blade or knife out with thoughts of cutting yourself?" could quickly uncover grounds for involuntary commitment. Further interviewing will help clarify the imminent dangerousness of Jimmy, but hospitalization may be indicated.

---

Notice the clinician's adept interplay between the use of open-ended and closed-ended inquiries. Whenever a potentially psychotic patient is vague, it is often useful for the interviewer to try to enter the patient's world through an open-ended inquiry, especially if the patient has shown intense affect around a topic. For instance, when Jimmy began to describe his voices as, "It's a feeling. It sounds like my thoughts, but they are a little bit different, the way that I can hear them," the interviewer queried, "And how do you hear them?" Jimmy replied with a peculiar affect that further betrayed the presence of his underlying psychosis: "They just seem to come to me. [pause, then speaking very softly, almost in a whisper] They just seem to come to me." This exchange created a "spooked" sensation in the clinician, similar to the response Jimmy had created in his roommate back in the dormitory.

On the other hand, the clinician directly utilized many closed-ended questions, as he attempted to address the specific areas of dangerousness associated with Jimmy's psychotic process. No room for miscommunication here. A series of closed-ended questions followed, phrased in a nonjudgmental way and with a genuine sense of curiosity: "Does the voice ever tell you to hurt yourself?" "What exactly will he say?" and "Does he ever tell you to cut yourself or to take pills, anything like that?"

As we end our discussion of our first case illustration, a review of some basic principles highlighted by Jimmy's presentation may be of value:

1. A relatively small but significant number of people who attempt suicide are actively psychotic.
2. Any evidence of psychosis warrants a thorough evaluation of lethality.

3. Command hallucinations, feelings of alien control, and hyperreligiosity are particularly dangerous areas of psychotic process. These areas should be actively probed by the interviewer if not elicited spontaneously.

4. Recent evidence suggests that many suicides in schizophrenia occur in response to depressive episodes and/or episodes of intense demoralization while the patient is relatively nonpsychotic.

5. Demographic material such as age, sex, and marital status may indicate risk factors for suicide.

6. Recent losses and poor social support systems are prominent risk factors for suicide.

7. Alcohol, drugs, or any physiologic insult to the central nervous system, as seen with delirium, may increase the likelihood of suicide or homicide.

8. When evaluating systems of immediate outpatient support, clinicians should carefully consider whether the mental health system itself is prepared to offer adequate support.

9. Interviews with corroborative informants may yield valuable information.

10. Clinicians should not be hesitant about reinterviewing a client.

---

## CASE PRESENTATION TWO:
## MRS. KELLY FLANNIGAN

Mrs. Kelly Flannigan is a 40-year-old mother of two, and owner of a local coffeehouse called The Morning Stop. A one-time graphics artist, she turned entrepreneur roughly seven years ago, after leaving New York City to gain a slower pace of life in the hills of New Hampshire. She presents today for an initial assessment at a busy community mental health center. She was discharged two weeks ago from a psychiatric unit, secondary to an overdose of fifteen Tylenol pills.

When the hospital referred her, the chief social worker had commented, "Kelly is a class act—a little zany, mind you—but a class act. We all liked her. She's just beat-up. I don't mean *by* anyone. I mean beat-up by life and by her disease. Her husband is not exactly a charmer either, I can tell you that."

"Kell," as she likes to be called, is blessed with a winning smile. Her cat-green eyes peer from beneath a disobedient mane of red hair. She has the delightful ability to make people feel special, a trait that has drawn customers to the steps of The Morning Stop every hour of the day and night. The café has been a big success. Her multiple sclerosis struck about four years ago, with devastating fury. Her husband began having affairs about two years ago, with disturbing frequency. The panic attacks began a year ago. The drinking is still going on.

She arrived five minutes late for the appointment and had Jennie and Julie, her 8- and 12-year-old daughters, in tow. "I'm sorry I brought the kids but my baby sitter panned out on me." She managed a bit of a coy smile, "Sorry. Is this okay?"

Although feeling much better than before her hospitalization, she still acknowledges being quite depressed. She complains of many of the neurovegetative symptoms of depression. She manages to smile intermittently, but she moves with a halting quality and sometimes slurs her speech, not from the effects of alcohol, but from the remnants of her most recent exacerbation of multiple sclerosis.

Just as the chief social worker had suggested, there is something immediately engaging about Kell that's hard to put into words. This day, she looks weary, her speech punctuated with depressive sighs. When discussing the impending necessity of selling The Morning Stop, because she simply can't keep up the pace required of an effective owner, she begins to cry. Unlike Jimmy, she has no evidence of psychotic process. Her intellectual and cognitive functioning is fine.

When asked about suicide, she openly discusses her recent suicide attempt emphasizing, "I didn't really want to kill myself, you know, I stopped myself. Nobody else stopped me." She denies any specific suicidal ideation or plans since her discharge, other than, "Sometimes I wish I was dead, but I've got to go on."

---

Kell raises concerns different from those encountered with Jimmy. First, she presents with a depressed affect and reports numerous depressive symptoms consistent with the *DSM-IV* criteria for a major depression. In addition, she presents with multiple psychiatric diagnoses. In addition to her depression, she has a panic disorder and was also felt to meet the criteria for alcohol abuse. As one would expect, the presence of depression represents a significant risk factor for suicide. In addition to the classical presentation of depression, which Kell illustrates, the clinician must also keep in mind the possibility of atypical depressions.

A presenting depression may also represent a secondary response to an even more problematic primary diagnosis, whose symptoms the patient is hesitant to talk about for fear of embarrassment. It is very common for patients with disorders such as Obsessive Compulsive Disorder (OCD) and Posttraumatic Stress Disorder (PTSD) to hide their underlying symptoms or problems while presenting with depressive complaints. One study demonstrated that the average number of years before a patient with OCD seeks help is 16.[25] This is particularly disturbing when one realizes that it has been estimated that people suffering from OCD represent nearly 2% of all suicides in the United States annually.[26] Somatoform disorders, such as psychogenic pain syndrome and hypochondriasis (which probably represents a variation of OCD), may also present with comorbid depressions. It is critical to search for such comorbid disorders. If untreated, they can greatly increase the risk of suicide.

The presence of a severe psychiatric disorder such as a major depression is probably the single most robust statistical correlate with suicide risk. In response to the question, "What is one of your best tips for predicting long-term suicide potential?" I often reply, "Begin with a good diagnostic assessment." Reviews of completed suicides have shown that as high as 95% of all suicides, including both adolescents and adults, occur in people suffering with a psychiatric disturbance.[27] Major depression leads the pack. It is followed by alcoholism, schizophrenia, bipolar disorder, and people coping with a severe borderline personality disorder.[28]

The intensity of Kell's anxiety was disturbing, for there is increasing evidence that people experiencing frequent panic attacks are at a higher risk for suicide. If the panic attacks occur in conjunction with a severe depression, as with Kell, then a "red flag" should go up. In a study of nearly 1,000 patients with a mood disorder, Fawcett found that depressed patients who also experienced panic attacks demonstrated three times the suicide rate of other patients and accounted for nearly two-thirds of the suicides in the first year of the study.[29, 30] Other research has supported the idea that patients with panic attacks show an increase in suicidal ideation, but whether this translates into a definitely higher rate of suicide attempts is unclear.[31]

In Chapter 2 and in the discussion of Jimmy's case, we described the importance of stressors and loss as risk factors for suicide. Unlike Jimmy, Kell has had several devastating stressors: the loss of her health, the deterioration of her marriage, the loss of her ability to function effectively at work (she finds the slurring of her speech to be particularly disturbing and feels it "makes me look like I'm drunk"). In the near future, she faces the impending loss of her café. This formidable list of stressors substantially increases her chronic suicide risk.

The presence of a severe and debilitating illness, such as Kell's multiple sclerosis, is one of the highest factors associated with completed suicide. Particular attention should be given to illnesses that result in decreased mobility, disfigurement, chronic pain, or loss of functionality, exactly the types of losses we saw in Chapter 2 that prompted Bruno Bettelheim to commit suicide. Kell's multiple sclerosis markedly changed her life and resulted in fluctuating periods of paresis, slurred speech, urinary incontinence, and severe vision problems. An interviewer should note the impact of any illnesses in which the patient anticipates an unavoidable loss of function or projects a horrifying demise. Such illnesses as Amyotrophic Lateral Sclerosis (Lou Gehrig's Disease), Huntington's chorea, Alzheimer's disease, severe diabetes, severe chronic obstructive pulmonary disease, and paralysis may present more suffering than some individuals can face or would choose to accept.

The interaction of the patient's medical illnesses with the patient's underlying personality structure also warrants attention. Some people, when locked into damaging structures such as narcissistic, histrionic, or borderline personalities, may have an inordinate amount of difficulty dealing with disease processes that others can handle better because they are lucky enough to have more mature coping skills.

Along these lines, Leonard has described three personality types that may be predisposed to suicide when severely stressed.[32] The first type is a controlling personality. These patients tend to constantly manipulate their environment. They are often hard-driven and feel a need to be "on top of things." They frequently pilot their way into roles of power and authority. When such people are suddenly struck by the loss of control caused by a crippling illness, they may attempt escape through death.

A second personality type at risk is characterized by a dependent/dissatisfied approach to life—a common trait of people suffering with borderline personality disorders, narcissistic personality disorders, and passive-aggressive structures. Such people often leave a long line of exasperated care providers in their wake. When the last source of interpersonal support finally closes the door, these people are suddenly without any means of emotional support. Suicide may loom as the only viable option.

A third predisposing characterological type is found in people who have evolved a truly symbiotic relationship with a significant other. These people are at high risk if their sustaining support dies or abandons them.

All of these examples reemphasize one of the most important hallmarks of suicide described in Chapter 2. Suicide is often an interpersonal phenomenon. As we saw with Jimmy, an evaluation of suicide risk involves not only consideration of the identified client but also assessment of the people surrounding the identified client. At times, as we saw with Jimmy, this evaluation proceeds through the use of corroborative interviews. When corroborative sources are not available, the interviewer must depend solely on information provided by the patient. In either case, a careful consideration of interpersonal factors is warranted. A brief look at some of Kell's reconstructed dialogue may provide some insight into the importance of these interpersonal considerations.

---

CLINICIAN:  You had mentioned that you felt you wouldn't kill yourself because you felt you had to go on. I'm wondering what it is that compels you to go on.

KELL:  [points toward the door] Them.

CLINICIAN:  Your children?

KELL:  Absolutely. I couldn't do that to them. Julie in particular would never recover. Just not fair. [pause] I'll tell you. If they were not in the picture, I'd be gone by now. That simple.

CLINICIAN:  What about your husband? Do you feel he needs you?

KELL:  [raises her eyebrows and smiles] Let me put it to you this way, Doc. About a month ago, I turned to Kevin and told him he might be more sorry than he thinks if I killed myself. You know what he said?

CLINICIAN:  What?

KELL:  Nothing. [pause] Absolutely nothing. He rolled his eyes, shook his head, and walked right out of the room. [pause] Oh yea, he did say something as he strutted out.

CLINICIAN:  What was that?

KELL:  "You're fucking crazy."

CLINICIAN:  You tried to kill yourself shortly after that, didn't you? Do you think that exchange was the trigger?

KELL:  I don't know. [shakes her head from side to side] What do you think?

CLINICIAN:  I don't know either. You just sort of look like you're feeling angry and demoralized about things right now, understandably so.

KELL: Yea. I am. I really am. Both of those things. [pause] You think it's okay to feel both those things?

CLINICIAN: Sure do.

KELL: [nods head up and down ever so slightly] Hmmm.

CLINICIAN: Do you see any hope for the future?

KELL: If you mean do I see hope that I'll get through all this and help my kids to grow up with a reasonably okay childhood? Yea. I'll do that. I have to, if the MS doesn't kill me first. But if you mean do I feel hope that I'll ever be happy again, [pause, then leans forward in chair] no way. You know and I know this disease will get worse. You know and I know I'll probably end up wheelchair bound or worse. I don't think that picture fills one with hope, do you?

---

This pointed dialogue illustrates the importance of determining whether the patient is returning to a supportive or a hostile environment. If the patient's family and/or friends provide a caring milieu, this fact bodes well for the patient, but a paradoxical problem can still arise if the patient begins to feel guilty about "being a burden to everyone." There was little doubt that Kell faced a hostile environment. Her husband's affairs and acerbic comments suggest that he has already "moved out" in a psychological sense, leaving Kell alone with her growing fears and disabilities. One can sometimes tap the interpersonal tensions surrounding the client and his or her thoughts of suicide with questions such as the following:

1. If you were to kill yourself, how do you think that would affect your family?
2. How do you think your spouse would feel if you killed yourself?
3. What are your thoughts about your responsibilities to your family and children if you kill yourself?[33]

Such questioning may uncover evidence of an interpersonal maelstrom or of reasons for life, such as Kell's need to care for her children. On the darker side, the interviewer seeks clues indicating that a supposed support system actually wishes that the patient were dead. The death wish may be unconscious or conscious, innocuous or sinister. The clinician's recognition of such a death wish is not a moral judgment passed upon a potential support system but rather an attempt to see the potentially lethal ramifications stemming from such a situation. Premature dismissal of such factors may represent a dangerous naïveté on the part of the interviewer. In Kell's case, one wonders to what degree the marital alliance has been irrevocably destroyed. At some level, does Kevin Flannigan "want out"?

An unconscious death wish may show itself in a family's lax attitude toward appropriate precautions against suicide. The clinician may discover that the safety suggestions of previous mental health professionals, such as removing a firearm from the home, have not been followed by the family. On another plane, there may be resistance to hospitalizing a seriously lethal patient. Considering the perspective of psychological defense mechanisms, family members may see a falsely rosy picture because of denial or repression.

At a more disturbing level, clinicians will undoubtedly encounter a death wish laced with true malice. Perhaps a spouse has long been denied a divorce, or a battered significant other has been unable to retaliate. These family members, rightly or wrongly, may consciously wish the patient dead. It is not known how many people have waited a few hours before contacting help when they have happened upon a "sleeping" family member surrounded by empty pill bottles.

I remember one patient I hospitalized from the emergency room. During our interview her spouse literally yelled at her, "Why don't you just take the damn pills? In fact, I'll stuff them down your throat and, trust me, I won't call a soul." Such vicious interaction should serve as a warning to the clinician. It may mean hospitalizing a patient who otherwise might have been perfectly safe if discharge to a more supportive environment were possible.

In another aspect of hostile environments, the client may be equally angry with family members. With revenge in mind, clients may kill themselves hoping "to show them, they'll be sorry when I'm gone." Responses to questions such as "What have you pictured your funeral being like?" may provide revealing insights into the client's motive for suicide. Some clients answer with variations of "They'll be devastated once they realize what they've done to me." In a similar vein, some authors have viewed suicide as the result of a murderous impulse turned inward—symbolic murder with an ironic satisfaction.[34]

Another aspect of anger, for which experienced assessment clinicians should be watchful, may surface in the denouement of a suicidal act. Suicide engenders anger in those left behind. In some instances, it is a justified anger for they were meant to be hurt.

Returning for a moment to Kurt Cobain's suicide note (see Chapter 2), we see some of this process. In a subtle way, Cobain's letter seems to demonstrate the passive-aggressive flavor that is not uncommon in a suicidal matrix. This undercurrent of passive aggression shows itself in the very first line of the letter, paradoxically, through Cobain's heavy-handed use of his own self-denigrations. When one rereads them—"Speaking from the tongue of an experienced simpleton who obviously would rather be an emasculated, infantile complainee."—it is apparent that the self-denigrations of his letter are dramatic or even, arguably, overly dramatic. They leave no room for significant others to express their anger toward him, for he has already belittled himself to the ultimate degree. In fact, his self-denigrating exhortations place a subtle pressure on significant others to refute their truth—in essence, to pull him back up. If a person is angry with someone who has just been deliberately hurtful, this pressure to say something soothing is frankly annoying, even posthumously.

A further complication is the disturbing psychological bind that the act of suicide places on those left behind, the bind of having to continue the struggle of life alone. An almost galling quality is perceived by some survivors when a suicide note is filled with new demands on the living. Cobain's dying command to his wife, "Please keep going Courtney, for Frances," is a double-edged sword. The remaining parent, greatly traumatized by the role of single parenthood and by intense grief, must now go on alone with life's many struggles while the person committing suicide has "ducked out." The topper to this phenomenon is that survivors, after having recognized this anger, often feel guilt for having it. A clinician can use this understanding to greatly help survivors in the emotional aftermath of a completed suicide.

Of more importance to our goals is the fact that an understanding of these dynamics can be of immediate value in risk assessment itself. The same feelings of resentment and betrayal often occur in friends and family members, albeit to a lesser degree, after a failed suicide attempt. Indeed, repetitious attempts can engender an insidiously growing anger toward the patient in the very people who may be of vital importance to the clinician in safe discharge planning. This process is already well underway between Kell and her husband, as evidenced by his response to her veiled threat that he may be more sorry than he thinks if she kills herself: "You're fucking nuts."

In sharp contrast to the suicidal dynamic engendered by hatred is the equally powerful suicidal dynamic engendered by compassion. Some people kill themselves to help others. As discussed in Chapter 2, the more apparent relief the suicide will bring to those left behind, the more concerned the interviewer should become. It is particularly ominous when the patient perceives suicide as "the only way I can really help my family. My schizophrenia is ruining us. We can't pay for these hospitalizations. And I can't let my kids see me this way. They need a better dad."

Returning to the specific world of Kell, several indicators appear to suggest lowered suicide risk. First, Kell denies immediate hopelessness, albeit in a somewhat unconvincing fashion. In Chapter 2, I noted that Aaron Beck's work has suggested that the presence of hopelessness may be an ominous sign. In fact, hopelessness may even be a more reliable indicator of lethality than the severity of depressive mood over time.[35] Viewed from a logical perspective, suicide usually represents a last option taken when no other alternatives are apparent to the patient. Moreover, a sense of helplessness is often coupled to this state of despair. Patients generally kill themselves for one major reason—to escape from unbearable pain that appears inescapable.

Further inquiry revealed that Kell was a devout Catholic. Believing suicide to be a mortal sin, she felt its end-result would be eternal damnation. At this intensity, religion is probably acting as a major framework for meaning that precludes the suicide option. But our interview excerpt provides a window into an even more powerful framework for meaning for Kell, a framework that, in my opinion, represents her strongest tie to the world of the living: the welfare of her children. Other patients may have different frameworks for meaning, such as caring for elderly parents, community projects, religious/spiritual beliefs, patriotism, or ties with specific subcultures such as the biking culture, sports, or AA. The clinician should seek out evidence of such powerful deterrents as part of every suicide assessment.

Although they often represent a powerful set of deterrents to suicide, ties to one's children can take a paradoxically dangerous turn if the client begins to feel that the child would be better off with the parent dead. Kurt Cobain stated this plainly in his suicide note. A revealing question can be: "What do you foresee for your children in the future, if, indeed, you were dead?"

A peculiar and unsettling twist can enter the picture with regards to children in this light. A suicidal parent may decide that his or her children would be even worse off after the parent's suicide. For instance, the spouse who would survive may have alcoholism and/or an active history of physically and sexually abusing the children. The suicidal parent may then contemplate taking the lives of the children before killing himself or herself. Although rare, one only needs to read the newspaper in order to learn about such tragedies. If such an outcome is suspected, the clinician should ask directly whether such thoughts are harbored. There are many ways of sensitively broaching such a potentially charged topic. If considerable anger is present, this anger can be used as a gateway into an exploration of violent impulses, which, in turn, can gracefully tie into thoughts of taking the lives of one's children. Here is a possible sequence for these sensitive topics:

CLIENT:   I am a total failure, at least that's what my husband says. And he says it every minute of every day.

CLINICIAN:   It sounds like a lot of anger has built up over the years between the two of you.

CLIENT:   You better believe it. I can safely say I hate the abusing son of a bitch. But he'll be sorry when I'm dead.

CLINICIAN:   You mean after you kill yourself?

CLIENT:   Yea. That's what I mean. [pause] Maybe I won't kill myself. I don't know. I just don't know anymore.

CLINICIAN:   With all your anger toward him, have you had any thoughts of killing him?

CLIENT:   No. I'd just end up in jail. And then what's going to happen to my kids? Who is going to take care of them?

CLINICIAN:   In that line of thinking, you had mentioned the negative impact on your husband if you kill yourself. What do you think the impact would be on your children?

CLIENT:   [long pause] Horrible. [pause] I can't imagine what it would be like. I can't picture leaving them with him. That wouldn't be right. He's a monster, he really is.

CLINICIAN:  As difficult as the thought might be, do you ever have the thought, even fleeting, of killing your children first before taking your own life?

CLIENT:   [long pause, client begins to sob] I've thought of it. But it's a horrible thought. I just don't know what to do anymore. I just want it to all end. That's all. To end.

CLINICIAN:   I'm sure that's a terribly painful thought to have for you. I know you adore your children. I'm sure those thoughts come from your pain. Tell me, if you can, exactly what you've thought about doing.

CLIENT:   [client sighs] It's hard for me to say this, but I thought about overdosing them. Just briefly. A couple of weeks ago. [sighs again] But that's not an answer. I know that now.

At other times, the following type of approach is useful. The clinician broaches the topic by inquiring directly about the patient's prediction of the children's future after his or her suicide:

CLIENT:   My husband will never change. He likes to hurt us. We have no future and I now realize that suicide is my only option.

CLINICIAN:   You mentioned "we." What do you think is going to happen to your children after you kill yourself?

CLIENT:   [long pause] I don't really know. Nothing good.

CLINICIAN:   Sometimes, parents consider taking the lives of their children. Has that thought ever crossed your mind?

CLIENT:   Yes, it has . . . it's a terrible thought, but it has.

CLINICIAN:   What exactly have you thought of doing?

Returning to Kell, there is another positive note in her presentation: the lack of an abrupt change in her clinical condition in either direction. A sudden onset of severe sleeplessness, agitation, or marked dysphoria may indicate that patients are rapidly approaching a pain level they cannot tolerate. On the other hand, one sometimes hears the often quoted clinical observation, noted at the beginning of Chapter 2, that an unexpected improvement in clinical condition may be masking a sinister outcome. The patient's peace may be secondary to the patient's decision to commit suicide. Suddenly, the patient senses a perceivable end to the suffering. The most momentous decision of the patient's life has been made.

Another curious problem is the propensity of some seriously depressed patients to attempt suicide as they begin to improve. Suicide is less common while they are in the troughs of their depression. This finding is probably related to the fact that, as they initially improve, they regain initiative and energy while still suffering from an intensely dysphoric mood. The clinician should keep this fact in mind when encountering a patient recently started on an antidepressant.

Further interviewing revealed that Kell had no immediate models for suicide. No friends or family members had ever attempted suicide. A legacy of suicide in a family tree should arouse concern. A particular threat arises when clients see themselves as being similar to someone dear who has committed suicide, as in this response: "Yea. My Aunt Jackie killed herself when she turned thirty. She was my favorite aunt. My mom has always chided me for being just like her. [pause] Maybe I am." As mentioned in Chapter 2, especially with adolescents, one should be on the lookout for suicide compacts or copycat suicides following the suicide of a fellow student or a celebrity. Adolescents should be routinely asked, "Has anybody in your school or have any of your friends attempted suicide?" If the news media are focusing on a student or celebrity suicide, the clinician should explore an adolescent patient's thoughts on the specific suicide in question.

This summary of issues raised in our discussion of Kell may reinforce some key principles:

1. The presence of medical illnesses such as severe diabetes, rheumatoid arthritis, and multiple sclerosis may increase suicide risk, especially if it leads to immobility, disfigurement, loss of functioning/livelihood, or chronic pain.
2. The interviewer should routinely search for evidence of hopelessness by directly asking about it if it is not spontaneously described by the client.
3. A hostile interpersonal environment may substantially increase suicide risk, and some members of the patient's family and/or friends may consciously or unconsciously undercut plans for safety.
4. A strong framework for meaning, such as deeply held religious convictions or commitments to one's children, may decrease risk. The clinician should ask direct questions that will uncover such convictions.
5. Abrupt and unexpected positive or negative changes in clinical condition, including a sudden and unexpected increase or drop in anxiety, may indicate an increased risk.
6. Rational excuses based on a sense of helping others or lessening the burden on others—"They'd be better off with me dead. Honestly, they would"—should be carefully evaluated.

7. The presence of a positive family history of suicide, as well as copycat suicides among adolescents, should be actively looked into by the clinician.

8. Suicide assessment should always include a search for major psychiatric disorders such as major depression, alcohol/street drug abuse, schizophrenia, schizoaffective disorder, bipolar disorder, obsessive–compulsive disorder, posttraumatic stress disorder, panic disorder, and severe character disorders such as borderline personality disorder.

## STATISTICAL AND CLINICAL RISK FACTORS: A QUICK SUMMARY

When pressured by time constraints, clinical demands, and the other everyday pressures of being a mental health professional, substance abuse counselor, or school counselor, it is sometimes difficult to remember all of the risk factors discussed above. Two acronyms can facilitate their recall. The SAD PERSONS Scale, developed by Patterson, Dohn, Bird, and Patterson,[36] serves as a useful checklist of pertinent risk factors. The NO HOPE Scale, developed by the author,[37] adds further depth to the evaluation of suicide potential by emphasizing the need to inquire about feelings of hopelessness and other important risk factors.

| The SAD PERSONS Scale | The NO HOPE Scale |
|---|---|
| Sex | No framework for meaning |
| Age | Overt change in clinical condition |
| Depression | |
| Previous attempt | Hostile interpersonal environment |
| Ethanol abuse | Out of hospital recently |
| Rational thought loss | Predisposing personality factors |
| Social supports lacking | Excuses for dying to help others |
| Organized plan | |
| No spouse | |
| Sickness | |

If clinicians routinely explore the ramifications of these risk factors and the others described in this chapter, they can be assured they are utilizing a sound knowledge base. Moreover, the presence of a large number of these factors should increase clinicians' suspicions of suicide potential.

As we looked at the risk factors present with Jimmy and Kell, we discussed some of their implications for suggesting a chronic risk for suicide. But the question remains for a clinician who must decide what to do with other Jimmys or Kells: How immediately dangerous are they? Do they require hospitalization?

## CHRONIC VERSUS IMMEDIATE RISK OF SUICIDE: THE TRIAD OF LETHALITY

Let us begin with Kell. Perhaps the most important indicator that Kell is probably not imminently suicidal is the fact that she denies current suicidal intent and has no organized plan to harm herself. She also spontaneously expresses an extremely strong rationale for living—the need to be there for her children Jennie and Julie. Still, Kell represents a long-term risk for suicide. This point illustrates the usefulness of distinguishing between chronic suicide potential and immediate suicide potential. If a patient presents with numerous risk factors over a long period of time, that patient may be at chronic risk for suicide, and the clinician will need to periodically check that patient for the appearance of suicidal ideation. Such is the case with Kell, who presents with the following risk factors: presence of a major psychiatric disorder (major depression, panic disorder, and alcohol abuse), numerous major life stresses, loss of functioning, debilitating illness (multiple sclerosis), a tendency toward hopelessness/demoralization, a history of a suicide attempt, recent discharge from a hospital, and a strained marital alliance that may actually represent a hostile environment.

But the presence of numerous risk factors does not necessarily indicate an immediate risk of suicide. By way of example, Kell could probably be safely treated as an outpatient, despite her long list of risk factors. Thus, the pressing question facing the assessment clinician is: What factors would have suggested that Kell was in more immediate danger of committing suicide?

In my opinion, the three most useful indicators—a lethal triad of sorts—are:

1. The patient presents immediately after attempting a serious suicidal act.
2. The patient presents with a dangerous display of the psychotic processes suggestive of lethality.
3. The patient shares suicidal planning or intent in the interview, suggesting that he or she is seriously planning imminent suicide (or corroborative sources supply information suggestive of such planning).

The presence of any element of this triad should alert the clinician that suicide may be imminent. In such instances, with respect to triage, the clinician should strongly consider hospitalization even if opposed by the patient. In my opinion, the last element of the triad, which is primarily dependent on the clinician's interviewing skills, is the single most important indicator of suicide potential. So important is this interviewing process that Part Two of this book is entirely devoted to exploring its subtleties.

In the meantime, as we look at the first element of the triad of lethality—the patient presents immediately after attempting a serious suicidal act—certain points are of practical clinical relevance. First, the clinician wants to determine the potential dangerousness of the method used. Impulsively downing a few extra aspirin is a great deal less disconcerting than shooting oneself or ingesting lye. A threat of an overdose made by a physician who understands the lethal nature of specific medications and has the wherewithal to procure them is more worrisome than the same threat made by a nonphysician.

Second, the clinician wants to determine whether the patient appeared to really want to die. In other words, did the patient leave much room for rescue? The interviewer should search for these and similar factors: Did the patient choose a "death spot" where he or she could easily be discovered? Did the patient choose a spot where help was nearby? Did the patient leave any hints of suicidal intention that could have brought help, such as an easily accessible suicide note? Did the patient contact someone after the suicide attempt?[38] Answers to these questions may provide pivotal evidence as to imminent dangerousness. The significance of these questions will be explored in more detail in Chapter 6.

Note that Kell lacks all three elements of the triad of lethality. Although she presents with a relatively recent suicide attempt, it was not a serious one. She ingested a low number of pills, stopped herself, and feels regret at the attempt. Concerning the second and third elements of the triad, Kell shows no evidence of psychosis, and she denies current ideation or intent. Her immediate safety is further bolstered by the strong framework for meaning provided by her children and her religious beliefs. Despite her numerous risk factors, Kell is probably not in immediate danger, although she will certainly require close follow-up.

Jimmy is considerably trickier. He falls closer to the other end of the continuum—away from chronic risk and toward more acute risk. His risk factors include his adolescent age, his sex, and the fact that, from a psychological perspective, the "low" grade on his test may actually represent a catastrophic stressor to him. Yet, curiously, compared to Kell, he seems to have far fewer risk factors. And he certainly has far less intense stressors, by any objective measure of absolute stress. Unlike Kell, he has not had a recent suicide attempt nor has he recently been hospitalized. Yet he feels more dangerous.

It is the presence in Jimmy of the second element in the triad of lethality, his psychotic process, that is most disturbing. And it is the artful fashion in which the clinician is asking about Jimmy's specific suicidal thoughts and plans, the third element in the triad of lethality, that is bringing dangerous material to the surface. More detailed interviewing about his suicidal planning and his ability to refrain from acting on it will be necessary to determine his immediate dangerousness. For instance, it may be uncovered that the razor blades were bought for the purpose of self-harm. Perhaps a suicide gesture has actually already occurred. Further interviewing may show that Jimmy is less distanced from recent suicidal planning than he intimated thus far in the interview. Hospitalization, even involuntary in nature, may prove to be necessary to ensure safety.

In this sense, Jimmy represents an example of the fact that the number of risk factors present does not necessarily provide an adequate picture of dangerousness. It is necessary to enter the part of the client's interior world where the most intimate details of suicidal thought and intent lay buried. It is here, in the patient's concrete world of suicidal planning that the true harbingers of death can be heard. The practical art of eliciting this suicidal ideation is the topic of Part Two.

## NOTES

1. Griesinger, W.: *Mental Pathology and Therapeutics, 2nd Edition,* 1882 (from the series "The Classics of Psychiatry & Behavioral Sciences

Library" edited by E. T. Carlson). Birmingham, Alabama, Gryphon Editions, Inc., 1990, p. 178.

2. Patterson, W.M., Dohn, H.H., Bird, J., and Patterson, G.: Evaluation of suicidal patients: The SAD PERSONS scale. *Psychosomatics* 24: 343–349, 1983.

3. Patterson, W.M., 1983, 343–349.

4. Conwell, Y. and Duberstein, P.R.: Suicide among older people: A problem for primary care. *Primary Psychiatry* 3: 41–44, 1996.

5. Centers for Disease Control and Prevention—National Center for Prevention and Control (Violence): Suicide in the United States, CDC Website, April 1999.

6. Hirschfeld, R.M.A.: Algorithms for the evaluation and treatment of suicidal patients. *Primary Psychiatry* 3: 26–29. 1996.

7. Husain, S.A.: Current perspectives on the role of psychosocial factors in adolescent suicide. *Psychiatric Annals* 20: 122–127, 1990.

8. Centers for Disease Control and Prevention: Suicide Deaths and Rates per 100,000 (based on 1995 statistics), CDC Website, April 1999.

9. Elliott, A.J., Pages, K.P., Russo, J., Wilson, L.G., and Roy-Byrne, P.P.: A profile of medically serious suicide attempts. *The Journal of Clinical Psychiatry* 57: 567–571, 1996.

10. Roy, A.: Depression, attempted suicide, and suicide in patients with chronic schizophrenia. *Psychiatric Clinics of North America* 9: 193–206, 1986.

11. Wilkinson, G., and Bacon, N.A.: A clinical and epidemiological survey of parasuicide and suicide in Edinburgh schizophrenics. *Psychological Medicine* 14: 899–912, 1984.

12. Breier, A., and Astrachan, B.M.: Characterization of schizophrenic patients who commit suicide. *American Journal of Psychiatry* 141: 206–209, 1984.

13. Drake, R.E., Gates, C., Cotton, P.G., and Whitaker, A.: Suicide among schizophrenics: Who is at risk? *The Journal of Nervous and Mental Disease* 172: 613–617,1984.

14. Hellerstein, D., Frosch, W., and Koenigsberg, H.W.: The clinical significance of command hallucinations. *American Journal of Psychiatry* 144 (2): 219–221, 1987.

15. Junginger, J.: Predicting compliance with command hallucinations. *American Journal of Psychiatry* 147 (2): 245–247, 1990.

16. *The Holy Bible, Revised Standard Version.* New York, Thomas Nelson, Inc., 1971.

17. Lion, J.R., and Conn, L.M.: Self-mutilation: Pathology and treatment. *Psychiatric Annals* 12: 782–787, 1982.

18. Roy, A., 1986, 193–206.

19. Drake, R.E. et al., 1984. pp. 613–617.

20. Amador, X.F., Friedman, J.H., Kasapis, C., Yale, S.A., Flaum, M. and Gorman, J.M.: Suicidal behavior in schizophrenia and its relationship to awareness of illness. *American Journal of Psychiatry* 153: 1185-1188, 1996.

21. Drake, R.E. et al., 1984, p. 617.

22. Busch, K.A., Clark, D.C., Fawcett, J., and Kravitz, H.M.: Clinical features of inpatient suicide. *Psychiatric Annals* 23: 256–262, 1993.

23. Clark, D.C.: Suicidal behavior in childhood and adolescence: Recent studies and clinical implications. *Psychiatric Annals* 23: 271–283, 1993.

24. Fremouw, W.J., de Perczel, M., and Ellis, T.E.: *Suicide Risk: Assessment and Response Guidelines.* New York, Pergamon Press, 1990.

25. Hollander, E., Kwon, J.H., Stein, D.J., Broatch, J., Rowland, C.T., and Himelein, C.A.: Obsessive-compulsive and spectrum disorders: Overview and quality of life issues. *Journal of Clinical Psychiatry (supplement 8)* 57: 3–6, 1996.

26. Dupont, R., Rice, D., Shiraki, S., et al.: Economic costs of obsessive-compulsive disorder. *Pharmacoeconomics* April: 102–109, 1995.

27. Callahan, J.: Blueprint for an adolescent suicidal crisis. *Psychiatric Annals* 23: 263–270, 1993.

28. Fawcett, J., Clark, D.C., and Busch, K.A.: Assessing and treating the patient at risk for suicide. *Psychiatric Annals* 23: 245–255, 1993.

29. Fawcett, J., Scheftner, W.A., Fogg, L., Clark, D.C., Young, M.A., Hedeker, D., and Gibbons, R.: Time-Related predictors of suicide in major affective disorder. *American Journal of Psychiatry* 147: 1189–1194.

30. Fawcett, J., Clark, D.C., et al., 1993, pp. 247–249.

31. Cox, B.J., Direnfeld, D.M., Swinson, R.P., and Norton, G.R.: Suicidal ideation and suicide attempts in panic disorder and social phobia. *American Journal of Psychiatry* 151: 882–887.

32. Fawcett, J.: Saving the suicidal patient—The state of the art. In *Mood Disorders: The World's Major Public Health Problem,* edited by F. Ayd. Ayd Communication Publication, 1978.

33. Fremouw, W.J. et al., 1990, p. 44.

34. Everstine, D.S., and Everstine, L.: *People in Crisis: Strategic Therapeutic Interventions.* New York, Brunner/Mazel, 1983.

35. Beck, A.: Hopelessness and suicidal behavior. *Journal of the American Medical Association* 234: 1146-1149, 1975.

36. Patterson, W.M. et al., 1983, pp. 343–349.

37. Shea, S.C.: *Psychiatric Interviewing: The Art of Understanding.* Philadelphia, W. B. Saunders Company, 1988, p. 426.

38. Weisman, A.D., and Worden, J.M.: Risk-Rescue rating in suicide assessment. *Archives of General Psychiatry* 26: 553–560, 1972.

# PART TWO

# UNCOVERING SUICIDAL IDEATION: PRINCIPLES, TECHNIQUES, AND STRATEGIES

# CHAPTER 4

# Before the Interview Begins: Overcoming the Taboo against Talking about Suicide

The answers you get depend upon the questions you ask.

Thomas Kuhn[1]

## INTRODUCTION TO THE STRUCTURE OF PART TWO

ASKING CLIENTS to openly share their most intimate thoughts concerning their own self-destruction is, at best, a tricky business. In the three chapters of Part Two, we will deal with this often overlooked art. Chapter 5, "Validity Techniques," will look at methods of phrasing questions that enhance the likelihood of receiving valid answers while exploring any type of sensitive material. Chapter 6, "Uncovering Suicidal Intent," builds on these generic validity techniques to introduce an easily mastered interview strategy, the Chronological Assessment of Suicide Events (CASE Approach), which is designed specifically to elicit suicidal ideation itself.

Chapters 5 and 6 deal directly with the practical specifics of phrasing and sequencing questions. In contrast, this chapter addresses the area of eliciting suicidal ideation through a more indirect door. We will explore some of the common resistances, in both the client and the interviewer, that can disrupt the effective use of the strategies described in the subsequent two chapters before they are even utilized.

## MYTHS, RESISTANCES, TRAPS, AND ROADBLOCKS

The subject of suicide raises many confusing factors pertaining to complex issues such as nonverbal communication, client resistance, cultural bias, and countertransference. It is also surrounded with common myths that can function as traps for the unwary clinician if not safely tripped before the interview begins. Before we can study the methods by which a clinician can effectively ask questions about suicide, we must first make sure that the clinician, both consciously and unconsciously, wants to ask them. As Kuhn suggests in the opening epigram, truth is not determined so much by the answers given as by the questions asked.

Perhaps the most important myth to address, for it has a certain logic, is the natural fear that asking about suicidal plans will somehow "give the patient ideas." In the first place, to my knowledge, there is not a single case example of such a process unfolding. Personally, I have never encountered it in over eighteen years of clinical practice and supervision. Granted, on a few occasions, I have heard a client with a borderline personality disorder comment with a baiting grin, "Now that's a new idea, Doc," but these have always proven to be manipulative responses intended to unnerve the interviewer.

In the second place, the idea of committing suicide is no secret. Reports of suicide vigorously compete with one another in films, television soap operas, video games, and music lyrics. A patient would have to be unusually sheltered to be unaware of suicide and the common methods of committing it. Finally, and probably most importantly, suicide is extremely hard to do. A lot more than a single interviewer's discussion of the topic would be needed to lead someone to make a decision to self-destruct.

To the contrary, the clinician's ability to calmly and matter-of-factly explore suicidal thought often provides a platform from which the patient's long endured silence about suicide can be broken. The resulting experience of openly discussing the topic of suicide hints that help may be only a spoken word away. Suddenly, suicidal ideation is no longer a sin to be hidden; it is a problem to be solved.

Having addressed the first myth, we can begin to examine the processes utilized to explore our clients' inner world of suicidal planning without a fear that we will somehow spur this planning forward. At this point, a second myth must be addressed. It is a potentially dangerous myth for it consists of the false belief that, in the interview, truly suicidal patients will "give off" hints that they are at risk. One could call this the "leakage myth" for it is based on the spurious belief that a person who is in enough pain to kill himself or herself will somehow "leak" evidence of his or her underlying distress either verbally or nonverbally. Many do. Some don't.

To their loved ones, work colleagues, and even their therapists, people have looked fine on the day of their suicide. People are capable of "putting on" wonderfully convincing fronts, especially if they feel that their own inner world is unacceptable or somehow tainted. In this regard, few topics are more shame-producing or conversationally taboo than the topic of suicide. An ambivalent patient may give a subtle hint of suicidal intent or even frankly mention thoughts of committing suicide to a friend or family member, but unless the friend or family member immediately inquires further, the subject will often be dropped. Paradoxically, suicide is a culturally hot topic for tabloids and Websites, but, on a personal level, many people keep such thoughts private unless they are prone to dramatic manipulation.

This taboo can be a fatal roadblock. It is well worth examining in detail for it illuminates some of the reasons our clients do not openly answer questions about suicide. Once understood, this roadblock can more effectively be transformed. Our discussion will also lead us to conclude that not all roadblocks are the client's. A clinician may not know the right questions to ask, or, knowing them, may not want to ask them. With these ideas in mind, let's examine some of the resistances to sharing suicidal thought:

1. The client feels that suicide is a sign of weakness and is ashamed.
2. The client feels that suicide is immoral or a sin.

3. The client feels that discussion of suicide is, literally, a taboo subject.
4. The client is worried that the interviewer will perceive the client as crazy.
5. The client fears that he or she will be "locked up" if suicidal ideation is admitted.
6. The client truly wants to die and does not want anyone to know.
7. The client does not think that anyone can help.

This is a formidable list. It highlights the need for clinicians to carefully engage a client before even beginning to approach a topic loaded with so many powerful factors at work in its protection. So important is the ability of the clinician to gracefully open an inquiry about suicide, and to subsequently transform the above resistances, that this set of skills will be the main focus of our attention in Chapters 5 and 6. For now, let's look at "normalization," a simple interviewing technique that can sometimes help to short-circuit the above resistances before they arise.

In this technique, when the clinician first raises the topic of suicide, he or she attempts to prospectively dismantle the client's fears about being perceived as bizarre, weak, or immoral. Normalization can often serve as a gentle lead-in to a discussion of any sensitive topic. It lets the patient know that other people have shared similar thoughts, feelings, or pains. With regard to suicidal ideation, the clinician might say, "When people are feeling extremely upset, they sometimes have thoughts of killing themselves. Have you had any thoughts of wanting to kill yourself?" When asked matter-of-factly and sensitively, such an inquiry can reassure patients that the interviewer does not view them as odd or deviant.

## INTERVIEWER BIASES AND FEARS

Perhaps even more dangerous to the client than his or her own anxieties against talking about suicide are the hidden biases clinicians may unknowingly shelter toward the act of suicide and its discussion. It is critical that such unconscious gremlins not find their way into the therapeutic dialogue. Such anxieties, sometimes rooted in attitudinal biases or countertransference, may be misinterpreted by the client as a forewarning of moral disapproval. If the patient picks up evidence of moral condemnation through tone of voice or body language, the client's secrets will remain just that—secret.

With this problem in mind, it is important for the interviewer to be keenly aware of his or her attitude toward suicide and any counter-transference issues related to the topic. This inner work, done before an interview begins, will determine ultimately whether the interviewer's techniques are a success or a failure. The most critical work of the interview is done before the first word is spoken. This inward exploration is not so much a static awareness to achieve as it is an ongoing process to experience.

A wonderful way to begin this self-exploration is to look at the list of clients' fears of sharing suicidal ideation in a different light. We can ask ourselves if there may well be a good reason for the client to have these fears. In short, "Do I hold and communicate beliefs about suicide that may make a client feel uneasy while talking with me about suicide?" With this new twist in mind, let us revisit our list:

1. Do I feel that suicide is a sign of weakness in which people should feel shame?
2. Do I feel that suicide is immoral or a sin?
3. Do I feel that the topic of suicide is taboo? (Have I ever asked someone I know outside of my professional work, such as a family member or close friend, whether he or she is having suicidal ideation? If the answer is "No," there is a good chance the topic is personally taboo at some level.)
4. Do I feel that suicide is essentially illogical and that someone would have to be pretty crazy to ever consider it seriously?
5. Do I tend to overreact to the conveyance of suicidal ideation? Do I tend to admit such patients to the hospital too quickly? (Has a supervisor ever commented that I admit too readily? Have I ever placed "forensic fears" above patient care?)

As mentioned in Chapter 1, it is important to get a genuine feel for one's own views on suicide and to realize that there is a continuum ranging from "Suicide is wrong" to "Suicide has intrinsic positive worth." Chiles and Strosahl have a nice exercise in the appendix of their book, *The Suicidal Patient: Principles of Assessment, Treatment, and Case Management* in which the clinician reviews many of the differing philosophies of suicide.[2] A review of some of these ideas is well worth our time. As a way of familiarizing ourselves with this philosophical continuum, let's take an example or two from each category exactly as the authors describe them:

 I. Suicide is wrong:
    Suicide does violence to the dignity of life.
    Suicide adversely affects the survivors.
    Suicide is no different than homicide.

 II. Suicide is sometimes permissible:
    Suicide is permissible when, in the individual's view of things, the alternatives are unbearable. An example is extreme and incurable physical pain.

 III. Suicide is not a moral or ethical issue:
    Suicide is a phenomenon of life that is subject to study in the same way that any other phenomenon of life should be studied.

 IV. Suicide is a positive response to certain conditions:
    A person has the innate right to make any decision, provided it is based on rationality and logical thinking. This includes the right to suicide.

 V. Suicide has intrinsic positive value:
    Suicide has a positive value because it is a way in which one can be immediately reunited with valued ancestors and with loved ones.

The above list by Chiles and Strosahl (and the more extensive one in their provocative book) can certainly get one "off and running" into an exploration of one's beliefs. I also advise people to do this exercise first alone and then in a group. The results can be fascinating. Any strong emotions that one feels in such a group are almost bound to be indicators of one's own hotspots and biases.

Five questions that are more directly personal can offer penetrating mirrors into the clinician's own attitudes toward suicide, and I ask you to address them to yourself as you read them:

 1. Have I known anyone in my family or among my friends who has committed suicide? (If so, how did I feel about it when it happened? How do I feel about it now? Do I feel it was the right thing

to do? How does that suicide affect the way I approach the issue in my interviews? When I ask clients about suicidal ideation, do I ever have images of that friend or family member?)

2. Have I ever thought of taking my own life?
3. Under what *exact* circumstances, if any, do I picture myself entertaining suicide as a viable option?
4. If a significant other or one of my children killed himself or herself, how would my life be different?
5. What will I say if a patient asks me, "Do you believe it is okay to kill yourself?"

There is a countertransference issue that many interviewers do not like to admit, but I think it is present in most of us: If we uncover serious suicidal intent, we are potentially creating a mess for ourselves. For instance, if suicidal plans emerge, we may need to greatly prolong our assessment when we are already strapped for time. Family members may need to be involved. We may have to deal with an irate patient or an equally irate family member if we need to proceed with involuntary commitment. Finally, we may have to spend a day in court if commitment occurs. The bottom line is: If we do our job well, we may have to pay a not-so-insignificant price in time. These realistic concerns can definitely emerge as countertransference in the guise of: not even inquiring about suicide; waiting until the end of the interview to ask about it; poorly setting the stage for its discussion; hurrying the assessment; or asking questions in a manner that decreases the likelihood that the patient will share suicidal ideation.

Another unconscious process can cause us to not carefully explore suicidal ideation: As humans, we are programmed to avoid anxiety. When a clinician uncovers serious suicidal ideation, it can have an immediate impact on the quality of his or her life even outside the office. What clinician has not gone home at night worried about the safety of one of his or her patients, or double guessing whether a good decision was made earlier in the day? The truth is that a client who has serious suicidal ideation is an immediate potential stressor for a clinician, both at work and after hours.

Phrased slightly differently, a clinician can strongly wish that a client is not suicidal, not only because of concern for the client but also because of unconscious and sometimes conscious self-centered concerns.

Specifically, the clinician does not wish to be aware of a worrisome situation. I must admit to hoping, during an interview, that I would not find suicidal ideation from a selfish standpoint. Unchecked, such feelings can lead to creative ways of asking about suicidal ideation as demonstrated below:

PATIENT:    Sometimes, things are simply too much. My husband can't stop yelling, the dog is barking, kids screaming—too much, just too much.

CLINICIAN:    You've not thought of hurting yourself, have you? [said with an imploring tone of voice]

PATIENT:    Why no, I haven't thought of that really.

CLINICIAN:    Good.

A leading question as above, characterized by the strategically placed negative—*not*—can suggest to the patient that the interviewer does not morally approve of suicide or may be judgmental if told of suicidal ideation. In reality, it may merely represent the hassled interviewer's unconscious prayer that nothing serious will be revealed. Unfortunately, the interviewee gets a clear message that this clinician wants "No" for an answer, and, as a general rule, interviewees try to please interviewers. Validity then becomes an issue here.

I once watched such an interaction in which the patient denied suicidal ideation to an initial interviewer. A second interviewer reapproached the same patient at the end of the first clinician's interview. This interviewer avoided the question begun with a negative and subsequently discovered that the patient had overdosed on aspirin about five days earlier. Technique counts.

The displeasure of stumbling upon suicidal ideation and the increased clinician anxiety that follows can actually generate feelings of irritation and resentment, or more intense negative reactions. John Maltsberger, in his outstanding book on the psychodynamic aspects of suicide assessment, *Suicide Risk: The Formulation of Clinical Judgment*, points out that people with suicidal ideation, particularly people with borderline personality disorders, narcissistic personality disorders, antisocial personality disorders, and substance abuse, can easily generate anger in clinicians.[3] In its most intense manifestation, true "countertransference hate" can emerge. According to Maltsberger, this hate can be reflected as malice or aversion. Such feelings can occur in all of us, and in all settings, but they are more commonly found on inpatient units and in substance abuse programs, where clinicians undergo prolonged exposure to patients presenting with aversive traits. Another problem can emerge in such closed environments. The pressure cooker atmosphere can foster a mutual promotion of angry "It's-them-against-us" feelings toward problematic patients. Our best defense against such feelings is our acceptance that we are prone to them. Our second best defenses are the twin tools of self-reflection and open discussion with objective colleagues. Vacations help, too.

Another powerful experience can generate significant countertransferential feelings toward people who are expressing suicidal ideation: the earlier loss of one of our own patients to suicide. Perhaps no other experience can create such a profound set of feelings. No matter how dedicated or gifted we are, nor how many books we've read, there is a good chance that, over the course of our career, we will lose one or more of our patients to suicide. This is particularly true if we work with difficult populations such as people suffering from schizophrenia, bipolar disorder, substance abuse disorders, and borderline personality disorders.

If the loss of a patient to suicide is inadequately psychologically processed, the clinician may have lingering and sometimes costly countertransferential demons. These conflicts can precipitate a fascinating array of diverse and counterproductive attitudes toward the process of suicide assessment itself including: overly cautious decision making; an aversion for the process, as shown by brief assessments done sloppily; anger toward patients who express suicidal ideation; nonverbal clues to patients that indicate that the clinician is not comfortable with the topic; and the expression of a flip attitude that, "you can't predict suicide so don't get so bent out of shape about it." Good support from and communication with supervisors and colleagues can go a long way toward preventing these damaging processes. If they do occur, therapy can certainly be of help in their repair.

Within the same line of thinking but one step "closer to home" is the issue of what are we to do, if during the course of our careers, we develop suicidal ideation ourselves? Can a clinician who is wrestling with active suicidal ideation ethically continue to work with patients who are wrestling with the very same demon? It is a testament to the taboo nature of suicide that, in my four years of training at a major psy-chiatric residency, this question was never once broached nor even hinted at as important. This gaping omission in training is rather more remarkable when one considers the increased rate of depression, sub-stance abuse, and suicide among mental health professionals. The ethics of this dilemma, in my opinion, should be as well discussed and delineated as the ethics of what to do if one is beginning to develop a physical attraction to a patient.

Like most ethical questions, this one can trigger intense emotions and differences of opinion. The following thoughts are solely my own, and I do not pretend to have definitive answers. I hope that these thoughts will trigger readers to seek their own answers. I feel that all mental health and substance abuse programs should have a brief course or seminar in which the topic of suicide is explored intimately, from its etiologies to our own biases and beliefs about it. Such a course would directly address complex ethical questions as the one above, as well as discuss in detail specific interviewing techniques and strate-gies for eliciting suicidal ideation. In such a course, trainees would be directly observed eliciting suicidal ideation until the mentors were comfortable that the trainees had mastered these critical interviewing skills.

With these ideas in mind, let's take a look at some of the conse-quences engendered if we should begin contemplating suicide while working with suicidal clients. Because of the nature of our work and the fact that we are all human beings, we are all at risk for depression and/or suicidal thought. When such thoughts first emerge, the thera-pist may feel guilty about them. To avoid the stirring of these guilt feel-ings, the therapist may unconsciously, or even consciously, avoid asking the client about his or her suicidal ideation.

The problem does not stop here. Even if the therapist enters the topic appropriately, the therapist may nonverbally convey an "ill-at-ease" quality that can greatly decrease the client's perception that suicidal ideation is a safe topic to discuss. Even more problematic is the very dangerous possibility that the therapist will unconsciously steer the client toward the therapist's own leanings, whatever they may be, in an effort to validate his or her own decision. The therapist may be uncon-sciously looking for interpersonal validation of his or her own decision to commit suicide or may judgmentally "push" the patient away from the decision in a manner that paradoxically drives the patient *toward* suicide.

If we are having suicidal thoughts, it is highly probable that when the client is discussing his or her own suicidal ideation—a time in which it is critical that the interviewer be 100% attentive to the client—we will become distracted by our own ruminations, pains, and decision-making processes. While listening to the client's own inner debate, a therapist might actually be weighing his or her own pros and cons, in essence, inappropriately using the therapy hour for his or her own decision making. Suddenly, the therapeutic alliance is no longer a safe place for the client, for the therapist is no longer in the room solely to help the client.

With all this in mind, it is important to remember that it is understandable that individual clinicians might sometimes develop suicidal thoughts. We are only human. What is *not* okay is to foolishly think that such thoughts cannot impact on the quality of our work. They can. They do. In my opinion, there is no way to determine subjectively the degree of this impact. An outside, more objective, opinion is needed. Consequently, I feel that two ethical principles emerge if a clinician is developing suicidal ideation. First, the clinician should seek immediate mental health intervention. That step is owed to self and to patients. No clinician, no matter how talented or well trained, can continue to give his or her optimal care while suffering from intense suicidal ideation.

Second, the clinician, even if in private practice, should seek out a weekly supervisor/consultant who can more objectively determine the impact of the clinician's condition on specific ongoing cases. The consultant can also suggest whether certain patients may be best served by a transfer in therapy or whether a medical leave of absence is indicated for the therapist. I believe that it is wise for the clinician's therapist and the clinician's supervisor to be in direct communication. By following these principles, we can better deal with the ramifications of our own mental distress, help ourselves to recover, while also feeling comfortable that we are maximizing our abilities to continue helping our patients. In another light, our openness with both ourselves and our colleagues will help to destigmatize the topic of suicide and further decrease the taboo of talking about it.

We have now traced a variety of myths, biases, and human frailties that "get in the way" of effectively asking about suicidal ideation. With these potential roadblocks addressed, a few general tips, related to transforming or prospectively dismantling resistance, may be of value.

## TIPS FOR DECREASING CLIENT
## RELUCTANCE TO DISCUSS SUICIDE

When asking about lethality, be direct. Use specific wording such as "kill yourself," "commit suicide," or "take your life." I don't think lethality inquiries are any place to risk misunderstandings. The patient needs to know exactly what the clinician is talking about. Such calm frankness on the part of the interviewer provides a powerful metacommunication to the patient—"It is okay to discuss thoughts of suicide with me." In an immediate sense, this implied reassurance may relax the patient and increase his or her sense of safety. In a long-term sense, it may be the single action that brings a potentially suicidal patient back for help. Several months down the road, if the patient becomes seriously suicidal, he or she may remember that there was one place where the patient's "horrible secret" could be shared. That recollection could literally save a life.

A trainee related to me a relevant vignette concerning the importance of the choice of words used during a suicide inquiry. The interviewer had asked an adolescent girl, "Have you had any thoughts of wanting to hurt yourself?" The girl assuredly answered, "No." Because a large number of suicide risk factors were present, the clinician readdressed the issue later: "Have you had any thoughts of wanting to kill yourself?" To the clinician's surprise, the girl matter-of-factly responded, "Oh yes, I've thought about it a lot. I've stored up a lot of pills, and I may really try it someday." When the puzzled clinician asked the girl why she had denied suicide earlier, she replied, "You didn't ask me about suicide. You asked if I wanted to hurt myself, and I hate pain. Even the method I have chosen for suicide is not going to be painful."

Several other points come to mind concerning lethality questioning. They can be summarized as follows:

1. The least hesitancy of patient response may suggest that the patient has had suicidal thoughts, even if he or she proceeds to deny them.

2. Answers such as "No, not really" usually indicate that there has been some concrete suicidal ideation. Some clients naïvely think that we are not interested in hearing about suicidal ideation unless they are seriously considering taking action on it. The interviewer can often break through such resistance by inquiring, in a gentle tone of voice, "What kind of thoughts have you had, even if just fleeting in nature?"

3. The interviewer should carefully look for any body-language clues that the patient is being deceptive or feels anxious. Increased fidgeting, changes in tone of voice, aversions of the eye, and pursing of the lips can all signal deception or ambivalence. At such points, it is often useful to acknowledge the client's discomfort while simultaneously opening the door for deeper exploration with interventions such as, "It looks like this is difficult to talk about. I'm wondering, what are you feeling right now?"

4. In my opinion, to optimize our ability to spot even the subtlest nonverbal clues of deceit or ambivalence, note taking should be avoided while eliciting suicidal ideation. The clinician wants to be 100% available to the interview process. Such unhindered attention can spark both the engagement process and the intuitive process. If using a clipboard, it is useful to set it aside during the suicide assessment.

5. The clinician should avoid any nonverbal evidence of being uncomfortable with the topic of suicide such as might be shown by an increased looking away from the patient, terseness of voice, or an increase in nervous habits such as twisting a strand of hair or fidgeting with a pen. Videotaping is invaluable in helping a clinician become aware of such unconscious habits.

6. No matter how hectic the clinical environment or how hassled the clinician feels, he or she should make every effort to appear unhurried while eliciting suicidal ideation. If the patient feels he or she is not being listened to, disengagement can occur with a brutal swiftness. This is particularly true if the client is prone to anger. Borderline clients seem to be acutely sensitive to being rushed and are rapidly triggered into an angry withholding of information. Responses such as, "Take your time describing these thoughts. I know it is sometimes difficult to talk about suicidal thoughts, and we want to really sort out what you are feeling,"

can be reassuring to borderline patients. Such a feeling of reassurance will often speed up the assessment by dismantling angry acting out before it happens.

7. The clinician should make it a habit, during the elicitation of suicidal ideation, to self-examine, at least once, by asking two questions: "What am I feeling right now?" and "Is there any part of me that doesn't want to hear the truth right now?" These are wonderful questions for uncovering the countertransference issues discussed above, before they become problematic. They also are useful gateways into one's own intuitive processes.

Another simple but important general principle comes to mind: Do not accept the first "No." I am consistently amazed at how many people flatly deny suicidal ideation when first asked, despite the presence of such ideation. The clinician should seldom, if ever, leave the topic after a single denial. As noted earlier, all sorts of resistance issues may be at work. If the patient flatly denies suicidal ideation when first asked, the clinician can continue with, "Sometimes people have fleeting thoughts of suicide, even if they are not thinking of it seriously. Have you had any such thoughts?" Another useful question is: "During all this stress, have you had any thoughts of just wishing that you were dead or could go to sleep and not wake up?"

At this point, we have completed our survey of the various psychological and interpersonal traps that can undermine the process of uncovering suicidal intent even before the interview begins. It is now time to turn our attention, in more detail, to the actual phrasing and sequencing of our questions. The elicitation of suicidal ideation is an art in which our questions are brushes, our facial expressions are pigments, and our canvas is the relationship we jointly create with our client. What is most remarkable about the end product, the portrait of the client, is the fact that, as is the case with all art, the accuracy of the portrait is determined more by what the artist thinks he or she sees than what, in reality, is actually there. As Kuhn suggested at the beginning of the chapter, the artist's questions will determine what answers find themselves translated onto the canvas. Clients clearly share more with some artists than others. Some artists are allowed to see the soul of the client and the act of suicide that waits there. Others are not. The next two chapters try to show why.

## NOTES

1. Bayles, D. and Orland, T.: *Art & Fear.* Santa Barbara, California, Capra Press, 1993, p. 93.

2. Chiles, J.A. and Strosahl, K.D.: *The Suicidal Patient—Principles of Assessment, Treatment, and Case Management.* Washington, D.C., American Psychiatric Press, Inc., 1995, pp. 245–246.

3. Maltsberger, John T.: *Suicide Risk: The Formulation of Clinical Judgment.* New York, New York University Press, 1986, pp. 134–136.

# CHAPTER 5

# Validity Techniques: Simple Tools for Uncovering Complex Secrets

My reality is constantly blurred by the mists of words.

Oscar Wilde *(Turn of the Century)*[1]

## INTRODUCTION

VALIDITY IS the cornerstone of suicide assessment. Nothing is more important to study. Nothing more directly determines the effectiveness of the interviewer in gathering information that forewarns of imminent suicide. If the client does not invite the clinician into the nitty-gritty details of his or her suicidal planning, the best clinician in the world, armed with the best risk factor analysis available, can only proffer a wild guess as to the client's immediate dangerousness.

As noted earlier, despite the large literature available concerning risk factors and clinical judgment, little has been written about the exact phrasing, ordering, and strategic interplay of clinicians' questions regarding suicidal ideation itself. Yet there remains little doubt that two clinicians can interview the same patient and come away with strikingly different databases regarding suicidal intent, depending on factors such as the degree of their engagement with the client and the style of questioning utilized. This chapter and Chapter 6 attempt to rectify this deficit by introducing and demonstrating techniques for enhancing engagement while peeling away distortion.

Paradoxically, the search for specialized strategies for eliciting suicidal ideation must begin with general interviewing principles that have nothing to do with suicide assessment per se, but everything to do with the clinician's ability to elicit valid information. Consequently, in this chapter, we will explore six validity techniques that are of immediate use in the exploration of sensitive material such as sexual abuse, substance abuse, domestic violence, antisocial behavior, and suicide. These validity techniques are:

1. Behavioral incident.
2. Shame attenuation.
3. Gentle assumption.
4. Symptom amplification.
5. Denial of the specific.
6. Normalization.

In Chapter 6, we will use these validity techniques as the foundation stones for developing a flexible strategy for eliciting suicidal ideation, planning, and intent.

One of the first rude awakenings for a novice clinician coincides with the revelation that interviewers basically function in the dark. We do not know for certain what is going on in our client's mind. We never will. The delicate arabesques of the mind cannot be easily transferred from one person's brain to another's. Even direct conversation is, at best, a second-generation copy of internal experience, brimming with data dropout, distortion, and all of the other problems associated with second-generation copies. As Oscar Wilde intimates in the opening quotation, our clients' words weave only mists.

Deep within the suicidal maelstrom described in Chapter 2, the suicidal patient begins to plan. As his or her pain increases and the potential options for relief disappear, the client's suicidal planning intensifies. A method is chosen. Practical details for its implementation are attended to, and preparatory actions are begun. The intensity and extent of this planning, and the actions taken, may represent the single best indication of a client's immediate dangerousness. The degree to which a client allows us to see the secrets hidden within this intimate world may well represent the limiting factor in our ability to help transform that world into one in which suicide is not the only solution. The problem is that our only access to this world is through the verbal mists cast by the client's words.

In this chapter, we will explore some of the interviewing techniques that experienced clinicians use to cut through these mists. The chapter looks at validity from two perspectives: (1) can we significantly increase the validity of our patient's self-reporting, and (2) if so, what are the specific techniques and strategies that allow us to flexibly alter our interviewing styles so as to enhance this effect.

It is important to remember that the validity techniques were developed over the past two decades as methods for enhancing validity related not just to suicidal ideation but also to any area sheltering sensitive material. Thus, I hope that readers will find these techniques to be of immediate practical application in many other areas as well as in the exploration of suicidal ideation.

Each of the six validity techniques is presented in the same fashion. First, a concise definition with underlying principles of effective implementation will be given. Second, a series of five examples of each technique will be provided. Each group of questions begins with examples related to the exploration of more generic sensitive topics and ends with examples directly related to suicide assessment. These prototypical questions are intended to provide a useful reference source for modeling. Finally, a third section provides brief clinical caveats to call attention to the potential problems to be avoided while utilizing the technique.

## 1. BEHAVIORAL INCIDENT

Anxiety, embarrassment, protection of family secrets, defense mechanisms such as rationalization and denial, and conscious attempts to deceive are just some of the resistances that may predispose a patient to provide distorted information. These distortions are more likely to appear when a clinician asks for a patient's opinions as opposed to the patient's description of an event or of the exact thoughts that were present at the time.

A behavioral incident is defined as any question in which the clinician asks about concrete behavioral facts or trains of thought.[2] There exist two styles of behavioral incident. In the first style, the clinician asks directly, in a no-nonsense fashion, about specific behavioral details: "Exactly how many pills did you take?" or "When you placed the gun in your mouth, did you take the safety off?" Notice how the information gathered via a behavioral incident may provide much more valid data than a question that depends on the patient's sharing an opinion, such as, "When you took the gun out, were you close to killing yourself?"

In the second style of behavioral incident, the clinician asks the client to describe what happened next ("What did you do then?") or what thought or feeling came next ("What were you thinking at that moment?"). This second approach to a behavioral incident, when utilized sequentially, can help the interviewer to recreate the incident in question, essentially creating a walk-through of the suicide gesture or attempt. Such walk-throughs are remarkably good at triggering forgotten or repressed material. Both types of behavioral incidents—those that ask for direct factual bits of information and those that prompt the client to describe what happened next—provide precise tools for cutting through the client's conscious or unconscious distorting mechanisms.

For instance, if a clinician wanted to determine whether a patient dates frequently, a patient may respond to an opinion-oriented question ("Do you date fairly regularly?") with a simple "Yes," because the patient may be embarrassed to relate a sparse dating pattern. To overcome this problem, the clinician could employ behavioral incidents by asking sensitively about the frequency of dates over the past year. If the clinician finds only several dates spanning twelve months, the relative lack of dating activity will have been discovered without necessarily embarrassing the patient. Gerald Pascal, who delineated the idea of the behavioral incident, states that it is best for clinicians to make their own judgments based on the details of the story itself as opposed to the client's interpretations of the details. It is unwise to assume that any persons, including ourselves, can objectively describe matters that have strong subjective implications.

PROTOTYPES

1. What did your father say then?
2. What happened next?
3. When you say you "threw a fit," what exactly did you do?
4. Did you put the razor blade up to your wrist?
5. In the past two weeks, have you had even a single thought of killing yourself, even for a fleeting moment?

CLINICAL CAVEAT

Behavioral incidents are outstanding methods for uncovering hidden information, but they are very time-consuming. During a suicide assessment, however, this "time cost" is well worth the increase in validity gained via their use. During other interviewing tasks, behavioral incidents must be used sparingly. For instance, the time it would take to do a full initial assessment, only using behavioral incidents as a means of questioning, would be roughly five to seven hours. A marvelous database would result, which one should take particular measures to savor, for it would probably mark the last database you gathered while under the employ of that particular emergency room or managed care clinic. Obviously the clinician must pick and choose when to utilize behavioral incidents, with a selective emphasis while exploring sensitive areas such as lethality, domestic violence, sexual abuse, and suicide.

## 2. SHAME ATTENUATION

Shame attenuation enhances the clinician's ability to noninvasively inquire about behaviors that many patients would be hesitant to discuss because of the shame and guilt attached (e.g., heavy drinking, stealing, violence, suicidal ideation).[3] This inroad is made possible by assuming a stance of unconditional positive regard[4] and by attempting to ask the question in a way that is compatible with the framework in which the patient experienced the behavior. The clinician must understand some of the client's rationalizing filters and then phrase the question so that a positive response by the client does not feel overly self-incriminating.

For example, instead of asking, "Do you have a bad temper and tend to pick fights?" the clinician might broach the topic of fighting by asking,

"Do you find that other men tend to pick fights with you, when you're just trying to enjoy yourself at the bar?" This is a much easier question for the patient to answer with a "Yes." After a positive response, the clinician can use a series of behavioral incidents to flesh out the number of fights the patient has had, while artfully determining the degree to which the client may have played a role in their initiation.

Imagine for a moment that a clinician has become suspicious that a given client may have an antisocial personality. One of the criteria that might shed some light would be the degree to which the client is prone to deceit. The clinician could initiate the inquiry with, "You know, you sort of look like the kind of guy who lies a lot; am I on the mark here?" Besides representing a marvelous way of prompting an assault on one-self, such a track would most likely lead to invalid information, if one were still conscious and could hear it. But how is a clinician supposed to ask a total stranger, in an initial interview, whether he or she lies a lot, and expect to get the truth?

One method is to use shame attenuation as a bridge from the historical database previously gathered in the interview. In the following illustration, let us assume that the client mentioned, earlier in the conversation, a history of severe childhood abuse from his alcoholic father. The clinician proceeds as follows, "You know, Mike, you had told me your father was very abusive, and it sounds like it was horrible back then. I'm wondering if you ever found it was necessary for you to lie to him in order to protect yourself—do you know what I mean?" The gate to a discussion of deceitful behavior has been gracefully opened.

The patient responds, "Oh yea. No shit, man. If I hadn't done my homework and the old man asked whether it was done or not, I'd tell him 'Yes' and get my ass out the door. If I didn't do that, and he found out I'd not done my work, he'd beat the hell out of me. I'm not kidding you." With the topic of lying having now been broached as an okay topic to discuss, the clinician continues with further shame attenuation, "Growing up learning to lie, because you had to, I'm wondering if you are still a pretty good liar, maybe you even do it when you don't want to?" To which the patient says, "I'm a great liar. [smiles] Trust me on that one."

Note that shame attenuation, in the above example, actually consisted of a preliminary statement or two, which gave the actual question a nonaccusatory tone. Whether imbedded within a question or used as a series of preceding statements, shame attenuations can be extremely powerful techniques for uncovering antisocial behavior as well as other sensitive material.

PROTOTYPES

1. With all the tremendous financial stresses you've encountered recently, have you found that you felt a need to steal just to get food on the table?
2. Have you ever found that your bosses were getting on your case and inappropriately chewing you out?
3. Do you find that you have problems holding your liquor, or are you pretty good at holding your liquor?
4. Sometimes drinking can lead people to have thoughts of killing themselves that they normally wouldn't have. Has that ever happened to you?
5. You had told me you were highly opposed to suicide, but I'm wondering, with all the immense stressors you've recently experienced, did you have some thoughts of suicide, even if just fleeting in nature?

CLINICAL CAVEAT

Shame attenuation is not meant to be an endorsement of inappropriate behavior, and the clinician should never cross the line into such a position. If for some reason you feel the patient has misunderstood your own position toward a given behavior, you should immediately correct the misunderstanding. Effective shame attenuation is based upon a genuine attempt to understand the rationalizations that shape how a patient perceives his or her reality not an agreement with those rationalizations nor the resulting reality to which they lead.

## 3. GENTLE ASSUMPTION

Like shame attenuation, this technique is designed to increase the likelihood that sensitive material will be discussed more openly. When using gentle assumption, the clinician assumes that the suspected behavior is occurring and frames a question based on this assumption.[5]

The technique was developed by sex researchers, who discovered that questions such as "How frequently do you find yourself masturbating?" were much more likely to yield valid answers than "Do you masturbate?" If the clinician is concerned that the patient may be "put off" by the assumption, it can be softened by adding the phrase "if at all" as with, "How often do you find yourself masturbating, if at all?" If previous engagement has gone well and the tone of voice used with the gentle assumption is nonjudgmental, patients are seldom bothered by this validity technique.

To clarify this definition through contrast, let us focus for a moment on questions that are not examples of gentle assumption. Any question that asks whether or not a client engages in a given behavior (often beginning with words such as "Have you ever . . . ") is by definition *not* a gentle assumption. For example, after having heard that a client uses marijuana, the clinician would not ask, "Have you ever used any other street drugs?" Instead, the clinician would matter-of-factly inquire, "Jim, what other street drugs have you ever used?" Only the latter type of question demonstrates the technique of a gentle assumption.

## PROTOTYPES

1. How often have you been pulled over by the police for a DWI?
2. How often have you found yourself in a fistfight, if at all?
3. What other types of street drugs do you like to use?
4. How frequently are your wife and yourself arguing?
5. What other ways have you thought of killing yourself?

## CLINICAL CAVEAT

No one knows exactly why gentle assumptions work, but they do. Perhaps they metacommunicate that the clinician is familiar with the area and has seen other people with similar behaviors, indirectly letting the patient feel less odd or less deviant. They also indicate that, at some level, the clinician may be expecting to hear a positive answer. In short, gentle assumptions are powerful examples of leading questions. (Perry Mason would be on his feet objecting to each and every one of them.) Use them with care.

They should not be used with patients who are trying to please you (e.g., a client with a histrionic or markedly dependent personality disorder) or who might feel intimidated by you (a child or client with limited intelligence). With such persons, gentle assumptions could lead to a patient's reporting something that was not true, because he or she feels that the experience or behavior in question was supposed to have happened. In my opinion, gentle assumptions are inappropriate with children when exploring potential abuse issues. In such situations, I believe that gentle assumptions can lead to the production of false memories of abuse.

## 4. SYMPTOM AMPLIFICATION

This technique is based on the observation that patients sometimes downplay the frequency or amount of their disturbing behaviors—the amount of alcohol they drink, or the frequency and amounts with which they gamble. When using symptom amplification, this distorting mechanism can be bypassed by setting the upper limits of the quantity in question at such a high level that, when the patient downplays the amount, the clinician is still aware there is a significant problem.[6] For a question to be viewed as symptom amplification, the clinician must suggest an actual number.

For instance, when a clinician asks, "How much liquor can you hold in a single night—a pint, a fifth?" and the patient responds, "Oh no, not a fifth; I don't know, maybe a pint," the clinician is still alerted that there is a problem, despite the patient's minimizations. The beauty of the technique lies in the fact that it avoids the creation of a confrontative atmosphere, even though the client is patently minimizing behavior. Instead, almost in the same way that a martial artist allows the momentum of his or her sparring partner to drive the partner to the mat, symptom amplification allows the client to continue to fully utilize his or her own natural defense mechanisms—in this case, minimization.

This technique is often of value in obtaining a more valid history of the extent of a perpetrator's violence in situations of domestic or predatory violence. For example, suppose a perpetrator of domestic violence is asked, "How many times have you ever struck your wife?"

After hemming and hawing for a few seconds, a typical response may be, "Not often, I don't know, two or three times maybe." Contrast this database with the one obtained from the very same client when the interviewer uses symptom amplification: "How many times have you ever struck your wife, you know, in any fashion—twenty times, thirty times?" To this question, the same client might state, "Oh my gosh, not thirty times. I don't know. Fifteen times, ten times. I don't know. It's hard to remember."

It is worth repeating that symptom amplification is utilized in an effort to determine an actual quantity. The interviewer always suggests a specific number, set high.

## Prototypes

1. How many physical fights have you had in your whole life—twenty-five, forty, fifty?
2. How many times have you tripped on acid in your whole life—twenty-five, fifty?
3. How many times have you actually struck your father—twenty, thirty?
4. How many times have you actually exposed yourself, even if you weren't caught—forty times?
5. On the days when your thoughts of suicide were most intense, how much of the day did you spend thinking about killing yourself, 50% of the day, 80%, 90%?

## Clinical Caveat

Be sure that you do not set the upper limit at such a high number that it seems absurd or creates the appearance that you don't know what you are talking about. Perhaps the funniest example of this error I've had the fortune (or misfortune) to encounter was when a clinician asked a very street-wise junkie: "When you've used peyote buttons, how many have you used at a time—a hundred, two hundred?" Besides providing an extremely good chuckle for the junkie, who immediately began imagining the single most nauseated human being in recorded history, it also provided the clinician with a mildly uncomfortable moment when the patient queried, "You don't know much about peyote, do you, Doc?"

## 5. DENIAL OF THE SPECIFIC

Even after a patient has denied a generic question such as, "What other street drugs have you used?" it is surprising how many positives will be uncovered if the patient is asked a series of questions about specific entities from a theoretical list of possible actions. This technique appears to jar the memory of the patient. It also appears to be harder to falsely deny a specific as opposed to a generic question (hence the name of the technique).[7] Examples of the use of the denial of the specific technique with regard to street drug abuse would be: "Have you ever tried cocaine?" "Have you ever smoked crack?" "Have you ever used crystal meth?" "Have you ever dropped acid?" Note that each of these questions is also an example of a behavioral incident. When a series of behavioral incidents is used, stemming from a theoretical list of alternative actions, the questions are preferentially viewed as examples of denial of the specific. In this regard, a supervisor would not use the term *denial of the specific* until the clinician used a series of "list" questions (at least three or more).

PROTOTYPES

1. Have you ever thought of jumping off of a bridge or building?
2. Have you ever thought of using carbon monoxide poisoning?
3. Have you thought of shooting yourself?
4. Have you thought of overdosing?
5. Have you thought of hanging yourself?

CLINICAL CAVEAT

It is important to ask each "specific" as a separate question. Allow a clear-cut pause between each unit of inquiry and client response before asking the next question. Do not combine them into a single "cannon question," "Have you thought of shooting yourself, overdosing, or hanging yourself?" Clinicians are tempted to use cannon questions because they think they are getting a chance to screen a lot of areas with a single question. The problem with cannon questions is that they frequently confuse clients; they hear only parts of them, or they choose to respond to only one part. Consequently, the clinician can come away thinking, mistakenly, that the patient has given a negative to all the answers. Bottom line: Avoid them.

## 6. NORMALIZATION

As described in Chapter 4, when patients are anxious or embarrassed about admitting to a symptom, it sometimes helps if the clinician lets them know that others have experienced the same symptom or feeling.[8] This can be smoothly accomplished within the question itself: "Sometimes, when people are feeling very depressed, they will notice that their interest in sex drops off dramatically. Has this happened to you at all?"

A primary care physician, Edward Hamaty, once described to me a variant of normalization that he had found to be useful with his patients suffering from life-threatening illnesses such as cancer or AIDS. Many of his patients had significant degrees of denial. At first, this denial was of use to these patients. Naturally, such denial had to eventually yield so that the patients could understand the need to take medications and to plan appropriately for future difficulties. In patients for whom it became necessary to "break through" some of their denial, this physician often began, "You know, John, we've known each other for a long time, and I think I can share freely with you. If I had learned that I had AIDS, I think it would create a lot of different feelings inside me. After the shock, I think I might feel some anger, or sadness—who knows, maybe fear too. I'm wondering if you've been having any of those feelings." In this instance, the behavior is being normalized, not to other people, but to the physician/interviewer himself. We refer to this technique as "self-normalization." I have found it to be very useful.

PROTOTYPES

1. Sometimes, when people get extremely anxious, their thoughts will become so painful that they sound almost like voices to them. Have you ever experienced that?

2. Sometimes, when people get really angry, they say things they later regret. Has that ever happened to you?

3. Sometimes, when people are really worried about their weight, they will do things to make sure they don't gain weight—like force themselves to vomit after a meal. Have you ever tried that?

4. A fair number of my patients have told me that when they are feeling really depressed, they find themselves crying, or at least feeling like crying. Have you noticed anything like that?

5. Some of my clients tell me that, at times, the pain of their depressions is so great that they have thoughts of wanting to kill themselves. Have you had any thoughts like that?

CLINICAL CAVEAT

If a patient is trying to malinger or exaggerate his or her clinical condition, normalization is counterindicated, for it can cue the patient as to what to say. It can also be a problem with patients who are "eager to please" or unconsciously may have secondary gains for being sick. One way of avoiding this difficulty is to modify normalization by the statement of a range as with, "Sometimes, when people are depressed, they will notice a difference in their appetite, either increased or decreased. Have you noticed any changes?" Because such a range does not tip patients in any specific direction, validity is increased.

## STRATEGIC TIPS

The preceding six validity techniques can be woven into a sensitive and smoothly flowing interview. An example of just such an interview, reconstructed from memory, will close our chapter providing a hands-on view of the validity techniques at work. But before looking at this illustration, it is important to clarify a few points.

The six validity techniques can be nicely distinguished from one another and, with the exception of the behavioral incident, they do not overlap. The behavioral incident frequently overlaps with the other five techniques, as we saw when discussing the technique of denial of the specific. For instance, "What other ways have you thought of killing yourself?" is clearly an example of gentle assumption, but it is also an example of a behavioral incident. For supervision purposes, when a behavioral incident can also be classified as one of the other techniques, it is preferentially called by the name of the more specific technique, to provide more descriptive information. In this case, "What other ways have you thought of killing yourself?" is simply called a gentle assumption.

In the following dialogue, notice that techniques are sometimes powerfully combined as with, "With all those pressures mounting on you at work [shame attenuation], how many times have you called in sick [gentle assumption]?" Notice that this effective combination could even be expanded into the use of three different techniques by simply adding symptom amplification at the end: "With all those pressures mounting on you at work [shame attenuation], how many times have you called in sick [gentle assumption]—you know, ten times, twenty times [symptom amplification]?"

Some students tend to confuse shame attenuation with normalization. Both are based on the principle of unconditional positive regard and on understanding the process of the specific patient's rationalizations. Structurally, however, they are easily distinguished by the base for the rationalizations. In shame attenuation, the rationalization is always cued to the *patients' perceptions of the difficulties* that necessitate their need to do the problematic behavior: "Considering the marked financial disasters you've had over the past year, have you felt a need to be less than truthful on your income tax this year?" Contrast this with the following use of normalization, where the question is *always* related to what *other people sometimes do:* "Sometimes, people tell me that they feel comfortable withholding information on their income tax. Have you sometimes felt that way or even filed a somewhat false report?"

In the following dialogue, note the power of the behavioral incident to not only cut away the patient's distortions but also to effectively cut away the clinician's assumptions and/or projections, which can also cast a mist of distortion on the story we are hearing. In this dialogue this effect is most strikingly displayed when the patient uses the phrase "I lost it on her."

## INTERVIEW ILLUSTRATION

PATIENT:   My wife and I haven't really gotten along well in years. [pause] Last weekend we really went at it.

CLINICIAN: Tell me what happened. [behavioral incident]

PATIENT: Well. . . . She just started on me about needing to get a job; that's her big thing now. She wants me to go down to the unemployment office *today,* not tomorrow. Today. So she starts ragging and yelling and I [pause] I just couldn't take it anymore so I lost it on her.

CLINICIAN: What do you mean, "lost it on her"? [behavioral incident]

PATIENT: I left. Just took off in a fit of rage. I didn't hit her or anything. I just waited till she went out to the kitchen and I went out the back door and I didn't come back for two days. I didn't call her. I didn't look for a job. I just bagged it all. Screw her. [Many a clinician, including myself, would have thought that the phrase "lost it on her" meant physical violence. But the behavioral incident dismantles this assumption and uncovers a much less disturbing behavior, albeit still a pathological one. Interestingly, although this assumption would have been off here, the clinician's intuition of violence is on the mark, as we shall soon see.]

CLINICIAN: Sounds like you two really do go at it. With all the intense emotions that follow for you in an argument with her [shame attenuation], do you ever find you just can't handle your anger and you do hit her?

PATIENT: Not really.

CLINICIAN: What do you mean "not really"? [behavioral incident]

PATIENT: Well, I've never really ever hit her.

CLINICIAN: Well, have you ever struck her in any way whatsoever including slapping? [behavioral incident]

PATIENT: I slapped her a couple of times.

CLINICIAN: Did you ever slap her hard enough that it caused some bruises? [behavioral incident]

PATIENT: Not really. [pause] Maybe a black eye once or twice.

CLINICIAN: How many times do you think you have ever hit her— twenty, thirty times? [symptom amplification]

PATIENT: Hell, not that often. Maybe six, seven times.

CLINICIAN: Has she ever had to get stitches or go to the E.R.? [behavioral incident]

PATIENT: Oh no, shit no, never.

CLINICIAN: Now I know you grew up in a really tough neighborhood where you had to know how to fight just to get by [shame attenuation]. Just how many fights do you think you've ever been in? [gentle assumption]

PATIENT:   Can't really say. A bundle.

CLINICIAN:   Thirty, forty? [symptom amplification]

PATIENT:   [pause, nods head up and down] Hmm. Not quite that many. I don't know—fifteen, twenty.

CLINICIAN:   Ever use a weapon on anybody? [behavioral incident]

PATIENT:   Never.

CLINICIAN:   How about a gun or something? [the beginning of a string of denials of the specific]

PATIENT:   Nope.

CLINICIAN:   How about a club or blackjack? [denial of the specific]

PATIENT:   Never.

CLINICIAN:   How about brass knuckles? [denial of the specific]

PATIENT:   [Patient chuckles] No man, never.

CLINICIAN:   What about a knife—ever use a knife? [denial of the specific]

PATIENT:   Hmmph. Well, I pulled a knife a couple of times.

CLINICIAN:   How many times, if any, did you actually cut the person? [gentle assumption]

PATIENT:   Just once. Not badly.

CLINICIAN:   Stitches? [behavioral incident]

PATIENT:   Yea. Not many.

CLINICIAN:   How many? [behavioral incident. Notice that this is not a symptom amplification. That technique requires that an actual number be suggested by the clinician. No number is offered here.]

PATIENT:   Oh, just six or seven.

CLINICIAN:   Billy, you told me earlier about all the abuse your father did to you, and it sounded really bad. Did you ever find that you had to lie a lot just to protect yourself from him? [shame attenuation]

PATIENT:   Hell, yea. After he'd had a drunk on, you'd tell the old man whatever he wanted to hear and then you got your ass out of Dodge.

CLINICIAN:   Some people with similar histories of abuse tell me they keep on lying even when they are older and even when they don't want to [normalization]. Do you find that about yourself?

PATIENT:   [smiles] Yea, I lie if I need to.

CLINICIAN: Have you become a pretty good liar over the years? [shame attenuation]
PATIENT: [bigger smile] Yea, I guess you could say that.

In this illustration of an interview with a patient displaying many antisocial traits, the strategic use of validity techniques makes it difficult for the interviewee to distort the truth through processes such as the parsing of words or relying upon an idiosyncratic interpretation of a word. The ability of these techniques to dismantle such "Clinton dodges," as I call them, is best highlighted in the preceding dialogue when the client seemed to be suggesting that he never physically hit his wife, a fallacy based on his interpretation that one was not really "hitting" unless one used a fist. The interviewer's savvy use of behavioral incidents short-circuited this dodge.

It is now time to turn to the strategic interweaving of these validity techniques, not with clients who are distorting the truth for manipulative ends, but with clients who are hesitant to share the truth because of shame, fear, and embarrassment. These are the emotions, characteristic of suicidal clients, that most often cast the mist Oscar Wilde described at the beginning of this chapter—the mist that can come between a client who is contemplating suicide and the clinician who is hoping to prevent it.

## NOTES

1. Pearson, H.: *Oscar Wilde, His Life and Wit.* New York, Harper & Brothers Publishers, 1946, p. 129.

2. Pascal, G.R.: *The Practical Art of Diagnostic Interviewing.* Homewood, Illinois, Dow Jones-Irwin, 1983.

3. Shea, S.C.: *Psychiatric Interviewing: the Art of Understanding, 2nd Edition.* Philadelphia, W.B. Saunders Company, 1998, p. 393.

4. Rogers, C.R.: *Client Centered Therapy.* New York, Houghton Mifflin, 1951.

5. Pomeroy, W.B., Flax, C.C., and Wheeler, C.C.: *Taking a Sex History.* New York, The Free Press, 1982.

6. Shea, S.C.: *Psychiatric Interviewing: the Art of Understanding.* Philadelphia, W. B. Saunders, 1988, p. 372.

7. Shea, S.C., 1988, p. 372.

8. Shea, S.C., 1998, p. 402.

CHAPTER 6

# Eliciting Suicidal Ideation: Practical Techniques and Effective Strategies

But suicides have a special language.
Like carpenters they want to know *which tools*.
They never ask *why build*.

Anne Sexton, American poet[1]
(Died by carbon monoxide poisoning, 1973)

## INTRODUCTION

THERE IS much to learn from these brief lines by Anne Sexton about the language of suicide. It is a language defined by specifics. In the last analysis, the final steps toward suicide lie along a common path. The client must choose a method and plan its successful implementation. The degree to which the clinician becomes familiar with this language's nuances and accents is the degree to which the clinician will be granted entrance into the client's world of suicidal thought. Clinicians must become both adept at and comfortable with asking explicit questions about implicit plans. No detail in the planning is too small, for the degree to which the client has thought out the details often reflects the degree to which the client is about to act on them.

The work of a mental health professional or substance abuse counselor is peculiarly stressful. On a daily basis, we are expected to ask people to describe the explicit means by which they intend to end their own lives. Not your typical job description. Before their training, few clinicians have had much, if any, experience in exploring this taboo topic. In contrast, experienced clinicians talk daily with people who have begun the painful slip into the maelstrom of suicidal ideation. If unchecked, suicidal preoccupations can eventually draw a client onto the path toward ending his or her own life. Even more chilling is the fact that, at some point in our career, many of us will be interviewing a client who has definitely decided to commit suicide. The question becomes whether the client will decide to share his or her decision with us.

At such moments, interviewers, acting almost as measuring instruments, should be set to their highest pitch of sensitivity. While exploring a client's intimate world of suicidal reflection, the clinician wants to elicit even the smallest details related to carrying out the act. Such details, insignificant at first glance, may subsequently provide important clues for disposition and treatment. These details may also serve as the portals through which the clinician may gain access to much more dangerous secrets.

This chapter offers various principles that may significantly increase the likelihood that these portals will be uncovered. Building on the six validity techniques described in Chapter 5, a flexible interviewing strategy, the Chronological Assessment of Suicide Events (the CASE Approach), is described here in detail.

Our discussion will be built on a two-stage framework. First, we will discuss methods for naturally and unobtrusively setting the stage for raising the topic of suicide. And second, we will describe, in easy-to-understand terms, the effective utilization of the CASE Approach.

Before either of these stages can begin, the skilled interviewer will have taken great pains, in the earlier sections of the interview, to have established a powerful engagement with the client. The critical "tricks of the trade" employed to accomplish this delicate task of engagement can be found in books much broader in scope than this text. For readers interested in learning more about the pivotal skills required for securing the initial engagement, enhancing the ongoing alliance, and transforming resistances that block the overall interviewing process,

I suggest, among the many excellent general texts on interviewing, Othmer and Othmer's *The Clinical Interview Using DSM-IV: Vol. 1*,[2] Morrison's *The First Interview: Revised for DSM-IV*,[3] Benjamin's *The Helping Interview: With Case Illustrations*,[4] Sommers-Flanagan's *Clinical Interviewing*, 2nd edition,[5] and my own text, *Psychiatric Interviewing: The Art of Understanding*, 2nd edition.[6]

## STAGE ONE: SETTING THE PLATFORM FOR THE SUICIDE INQUIRY

The interviewer wants to create an atmosphere that enhances the likelihood that the client will want to share suicidal planning. The most conducive atmosphere for this type of intimate sharing is probably a rather unusual state. In it, the patient should feel maximally comfortable with the interviewer while being maximally uncomfortable with his or her own pain. Intense pain can propel the patient to share his or her suicidal thoughts in the sometimes desperate hope of gaining relief. The intensity of the patient's pain and emotional upheaval often overcomes the types of conscious and unconscious taboos that would otherwise prevent a patient from sharing suicidal thought.

Patients will sometimes spontaneously enter these areas of intense emotional turmoil. At other times, the interviewer must skillfully lead them there. In Chapter 3, on risk factors, we saw the utility of leading Jimmy Fredericks, the college student with smoldering psychotic process, toward moments of intense affect. The clinician's decision to probe deeply, yet delicately, into the client's world of psychotic imaginings proved pivotal in uncovering dangerousness ideation in this student.

Well-timed explorations of affectively charged material can sometimes lead psychotic patients into mildly dissociated states in which conscious and unconscious defenses fall away. Direct questions may then yield surprisingly direct answers. At these times, potentially dangerous psychotic processes, such as command hallucinations, alien control, and hyperreligiosity, may be described more openly by patients.

But what of the nonpsychotic clients whom the typical clinician encounters much more frequently? Are there similarly useful portals that can provide clinicians with more ready access to suicidal thought? Two such affectively charged portals come to mind: (1) depression and hopelessness and (2) a sense of crisis, anger, anxiety, or confusion. If the client does not spontaneously raise the issue of suicide, the clinician can choose to carefully guide the client toward its discussion via either of these two gateways. When the client becomes more affectively charged, with his or her pain rising closer to the surface, the interviewer can then gracefully cue off of this pain into the realm of suicidal ideation. Great effort is made to avoid "popping" the question of suicide. Having delineated this key principle, let's look at it in practice.

In this illustration, we will picture a client referred for outpatient alcohol counseling. The client is in denial of the consequences of his alcohol abuse, yet is quite aware of the intensity of his own depressive symptoms. Note how the substance abuse counselor skillfully sets the stage for the exploration of suicidal ideation by patiently avoiding an inquiry into this topic until the client's pain is closer to the surface. It is almost as if the interviewer chooses to pluck the bubble of the client's pain, hoping that the onrush of emotion will provide an unshielded view of the underlying suicidal thought.

CLINICIAN:   Mr. Janson, you told me earlier that you didn't think that your drinking was a major problem. Having looked at what is going on at home and at work, what, in your opinion, might be some of the major problems?

CLIENT:   I'm afraid my marriage is falling apart. Don't get me wrong. I play a part there, but it's not all my fault. [pause] And I'm sick of everybody, including therapists, telling me I'm the problem. My wife is part of the problem too, trust me.

CLINICIAN:   Tell me a little bit about that.

CLIENT:   Nothing I ever do is right. Nothing I ever do is enough. She just can't say things like, "You're doing a great job at work. Thank you." Just can't. Always makes me feel small. It's just so depressing. So I get angry. So I drink. Anybody would.

CLINICIAN:   Sounds very difficult. Is it any better at work?

CLIENT:   Not really. Business is going bad. I used to love work. I created something special out of nothing. But now, everybody is a competitor. I can't trust anybody. Contracting is just nuts.

CLINICIAN:   Tell me a little more about how your job has changed for you.

CLIENT:   A good example was this morning. My office manager was supposed to have some bids all set up for an important contract meeting. I walk in and ask where she is. My secretary tells me she called in sick. I asked if she had said anything about where the proposal was. No one knew. Turns out, she didn't even have the stuff photocopied yet. I couldn't believe it. [sounds angry] When I got mad on the phone, she said I needed to realize that she was sick. It's just too much. Nobody takes responsibility anymore. But I'm supposed to. Doesn't matter if it's work or at home. I'm the problem. I'm just sick of it.

CLINICIAN: Do you see a way out of all of this?

CLIENT: No. Not really. She'll never change, because I'm the problem. [said sarcastically] Christ. [shakes his head from side to side and sighs]

CLINICIAN: Looks like it's sort of overwhelming.

CLIENT: It is. [pause, looks sad and subdued] It is.

CLINICIAN: You look really beaten right now, almost ready to cry.

CLIENT: [starts to cry] Christ. There's just no end in sight.

CLINICIAN: Have you had thoughts of bringing on an end, in the sense of killing yourself?

CLIENT: Sometimes I get those thoughts. [pause] I just don't know anymore.

CLINICIAN: You're obviously in a lot of pain. And from what you've told me, that makes a lot of sense. You're under a lot of pressure. Maybe we can get you some help. It's not surprising you've had some thoughts of suicide. What have you thought of doing?

CLIENT: I thought of overdosing. That's the main thing.

CLINICIAN: Have you stored up any pills to do that?

CLIENT: Yea, some. And then we just got a lot of pills in the house.

The clinician has deftly gained entrance into the patient's world of suicidal ideation by keying into the client's sense of feeling overwhelmed and hopeless. The client's affect was carefully brought to the surface via the use of open-ended, nonjudgmental questions accompanied by expressions of empathy. Ironically, part of the clinician's success resulted from what he *didn't* do. Specifically, when the client blamed his drinking on his wife's lack of support ("It's just so depressing. So I get angry. So I drink. Anybody would."), the substance abuse clinician wisely chose not to address the client's alcoholic denial. Such a confrontation might have decreased the engagement before the clinician had had time to adequately explore suicidal thinking, and a drop in engagement could be costly to the ability to gather valid information.

The client did not spontaneously hint at suicidal ideation. Not infrequently, a client will hint at suicidal ideation, and such a hint suggests that the stage may already be set for the elicitation of suicidal ideation. If suicide is raised spontaneously, the clinician should generally pursue it, as illustrated here:

CLIENT:  My life is very different for me now. Over the past several years it seems to have gone empty.

CLINICIAN:  How do you mean?

CLIENT:  After the divorce, I was on automatic pilot, but eventually it all sunk in, it all seemed horribly empty, not worth continuing, much as it seems now. But I have managed, and have had some brighter days.

CLINICIAN:  When you say it seemed not worth continuing, had you thought of ending your life?

CLIENT:  Yes . . . and I still do.

CLINICIAN:  What kinds of things have you thought of doing?

CLIENT:  I thought of taking pills and I did that once. . . .

If the clinician does not pick up on such nuances by referring to them directly, the conversation might quickly move to new topics and the clinician may then have missed the most opportune spot for inquiry. When such thoughts are brought up, the metacommunication of the patient seems to be: "Ask me about suicide." Given such an open gate, a clinician would be unwise to walk by it. If there is no follow-up, the interviewer may discover that, later on, because of an unexpected problem with engagement, the interviewee no longer feels comfortable about sharing. The suicidal ideation will remain silent—a most deadly situation.

Two other technical points bear mentioning. First, if one gate fails, the interviewer can try a different gate. For instance, a psychotic client may deny suicidal ideation when the clinician approaches through the gate of the client's depression. The same client, approached through the gate of his or her unique psychotic process, may share previously withheld suicidal ideation.

Second, some interviewers may initially approach suicidality by asking a mildly ambiguous question, essentially inviting the interviewee to discuss suicidal ideation without spelling it out. If the patient does not follow this type of lead, the clinician should proceed to the direct questioning described earlier. The ambiguous-question technique may be of value when interviewing patients who appear exceptionally anxious about being interviewed. It provides a "back door" through which they might enter a discussion of suicide more comfortably, as follows:

PATIENT:   Nothing seems to matter much anymore and everything seems wrong.
CLINICIAN:   How do you mean?
PATIENT:   I can't sleep, I can't eat, and every minute seems worse than the one before. I'm not kidding when I say I feel miserable.
CLINICIAN:   Have you ever thought of a way of ending your pain?
PATIENT:   Yes, yes I have . . . I thought of blowing my brains out [nervous laughter] but that's a little messy.
CLINICIAN:   Sounds scary.
PATIENT:   Yes it is.
CLINICIAN:   Do you have a gun in the house?
PATIENT:   Yes I do . . . beside my bed.

Once the stage has been set, it is time for the clinician to begin the actual exploration of the patient's suicidal ideation. As Anne Sexton's lines suggest at the beginning of the chapter, in the language of suicide, it is time to find out what tools the carpenter has decided to use.

## STAGE TWO: ELICITING SUICIDAL IDEATION USING THE CASE APPROACH

### THE PROBLEM AND THE CHALLENGE

As clinicians, the practical problems related to uncovering a valid history of suicidal ideation are compounded by the hectic clinical settings in which we find ourselves practicing. The time constraints related to managed care pressures, the downstaffing that causes increased workloads, and our increasingly litigious society put pressures on us when we are already heavily pressured.

Moreover, complicated suicide assessments have a knack for occurring at "wrong" times: in the middle of an extremely hectic clinic day, or in the chaotic environment of a packed emergency room. And the stakes are high. An error can result in not only an unnecessary death—a terrible tragedy—but also in a lawsuit, much less important but very disturbing in its own right. In many suicide assessment scenarios, we find a harried clinician performing a difficult task, under extreme pressure, in an unforgiving environment. No wonder mistakes are made.

Among the more common errors that occur during the elicitation of suicidal ideation are: omissions, distortions, and assumptions—a potentially deadly trio. In my experience, most errors in suicide assessment do not result from a poor clinical decision. They result from a good clinical decision being made from a poor or incomplete database.

The goal has been to create a practical interviewing strategy that can be reliably utilized no matter how tired or overwhelmed the clinician may be or how hectic the clinical environment may have become. To be effective, this interviewing approach should have these traits:

1. The approach should be easily learned.
2. The approach should be easily remembered.
3. The approach should not require written prompts.
4. The approach should help to ensure that the large database regarding suicidal ideation is comprehensively covered (e.g., errors of omission are decreased).
5. The approach should increase the validity of the information elicited from the patient (whether this information is a denial of suicidal ideation or an explication of the extent of ideation and planning).
6. The approach should be easily taught, and the skill level of the clinician should be easily tested.

The CASE Approach is one such method. It is not presented as the "right way" to elicit suicidal ideation. It is presented merely as "a way." Clinicians can directly adopt the entire approach or only those parts they find most useful to their own styles. The approach is not intended to be a "cookbook" way of interviewing. Its purpose is to encourage clinicians to discover their own way of strategically eliciting suicidal ideation. With this in mind, let us turn our attention to some of the solutions suggested by the CASE Approach.

PRINCIPLES AND SOLUTIONS

In Chapter 5, we delineated the six validity techniques that form the foundation for the CASE Approach, and we arrived at methods for decreasing both clients' distortions and clinicians' assumptions. The next step in the development of the CASE Approach consists of answering this two-part question: Why do interviewers frequently miss important data, and is there a way to decrease such errors of omission? The answer to our question lay in a revisiting of a supervision system developed over fifteen years ago at Western Psychiatric Institute and Clinic in Pittsburgh, Pennsylvania. The supervision system, known as *facilics*,[7, 8, 9] unlocks the secrets of how effective clinicians manage to sensitively structure interviews while simultaneously attending to both engagement and time management. The word *facilics* is derived from the Latin root *facilis*, gracefulness of movement.

One of the cornerstone facilic principles is that individual clinicians tend to make errors of omission in proportion to how large and unmanageable a database appears, psychologically, to them. If a clinician feels overwhelmed by the size of a database, the tendency is often to shrug his or her shoulders and "wing it." Numerous errors of omission are the common result.

If the clinician can split the large database into smaller regions of well-defined data requirements, the errors of omission decrease. Using smaller, well-defined data regions, the clinician can more easily recognize when a client is wandering off target, can more easily recognize whether the desired data region has been completed, and does not feel as overwhelmed by the interview process. If the required databases within each region are logically developed, they "make sense" to the interviewer and require little memorization. As one simplified database is finished, the next one is begun, and so on down the line, with each step providing one more piece to the puzzle. Such a simplified interview format is easily learned and hard to forget.

With regard to eliciting suicidal ideation, this facilic principle is applied by organizing the sprawling set of pertinent questions, regarding concrete suicidal planning, into four smaller and more manageable regions. These regions represent four contiguous time frames extending from the distant past to the present. Each region is based on an exploration of the suicidal ideation and actions that were present during that specific time frame—hence the term *chronological*. Regions are thoroughly explored one at a time. The clinician keeps the patient focused on the region at hand and does not follow a patient's ramblings out of that region unless there is a very good reason to do so.

The clinician explores the four regions in this order:

1. The presenting suicidal ideation and behaviors.
2. Any recent suicidal ideation and behaviors (over the preceding eight weeks).
3. Past suicidal ideation and behaviors.
4. Immediate suicidal ideation and future plans for its implementation.

Figure 6.1 represents these events. In the CASE Approach, the term *suicide events* is used in a broad sense to include death wishes, suicidal thoughts or feelings, and actual suicide gestures and attempts.

This sequential pathway seems to flow in a conversational manner for most patients. Naturally, the clinician can (and should) alter it to satisfy the needs of any specific patient, but, in general, if a patient raises the issue of an immediately presenting suicide attempt, it makes sense to explore this attempt in detail. It follows naturally to discuss the most recent suicidal ideation and subsequently more distant past

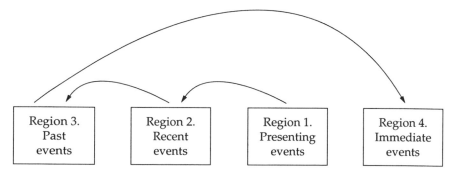

**Figure 6.1**  Chronological Assessment of Suicide Events (CASE) Approach. Adapted from S.C. Shea. *Psychiatric Interviewing: The Art of Understanding*, 2nd Edition, W.B. Saunders Company, Philadelphia, 1998.

ideation. We have found that these joint explorations of the recent and distant past generally improve engagement as the patient learns that it is okay to talk about suicidal ideation. Finally, when trust is maximized, it is useful to explore the region that may provide the most direct clues of acute dangerousness—the patient's immediate plans for suicide. In this region, the subtlest nuances of facial expression or hesitancy of speech may indicate that suicide is imminent.

This chronological approach is very simple and is actually hard to forget. Most clinicians relate that after they have studied it, the CASE Approach naturally pops into their mind as soon as they begin an exploration of suicidal ideation. All that remains is to determine what information is important to explore in each time frame, always attempting to simplify the task by organizing the material into logical miniregions and strategies.

In the next four sections, I will describe the specific strategies utilized in each time frame of the CASE Approach. These strategies will be "brought to life" through a verbatim transcript recorded during an initial session with a client in crisis. Thus, each step of the CASE Approach will be modeled for the reader. As the interview progresses, I will share some of my clinical thoughts and decisions as they actually unfolded in "real time." Vicariously, the reader has a chance to watch a clinician dealing with a complicated suicidal crisis exactly as it presented. The discussion will help bring together many of the factors described in the earlier chapters of the book. It will also function as a bridge to our final chapter, which is devoted to the clinical decision-making process—the third and final component of suicide assessment.

REGION 1: EXPLORATION OF PRESENTING SUICIDE EVENTS

When a client presents with immediately recent suicidal ideation, it is important to uncover the extent of the concrete planning. That information can guide the clinician toward sound decisions as to the frequency of sessions and the possible need for crisis intervention or hospitalization. If a patient presents with an actual suicide attempt or gesture, it becomes even more critical to understand the severity of the event because a serious suicide attempt represents one of the criteria of the triad of lethality described in Chapter 3. A serious attempt usually indicates a need for immediate hospitalization.

What specific information would give the clinician the most accurate picture of the seriousness of a presenting gesture or attempt? What information would alert the clinician that hospitalization might be necessary? The answers seem to lie in the process of entering the client's world at the time of the suicide attempt and understanding how the client feels about the fact that he or she did not die.

1. How did the client try to kill himself or herself? (What method was used?)
2. How serious was the action taken with this method? (If the client overdosed, what pills were taken? How many? If the client cut himself or herself, what body area was cut? Did the cut require stitches? Even if the chosen method proved not to be dangerous, as with an overdose of ampicillin, if the client was under the mistaken impression that the method was lethal, this circumstance is just as ominous as an attempt with a deadly substance.)
3. To what degree did the client intend to die? Did the client tell anyone about the attempt afterward? Did the client hint to anyone beforehand? Did the client try the attempt in an isolated area or in a place where he or she was likely to be found? Did the client write a will, confirm insurance status, write suicide notes, or say good-bye to significant others in the days preceding the event?
4. How does the client feel about the fact that the attempt was not successful? A good question here is to ask, "What are some of your thoughts about the fact that you are still alive now?"
5. How well planned was this attempt, as opposed to an impulsive act?
6. Did alcohol or drugs play a role in the attempt?
7. Did interpersonal factors have a major role in the attempt? Were there feelings of failure ("People would be better off without me") and anger toward people? (Some suicide attempts are undertaken to make others feel guilt.)
8. Did a specific stressor or set of stressors prompt the attempt?
9. At the time of the attempt, how hopeless did the client feel?
10. Why did the attempt fail? How was the client found, and how was help summoned?

Answers to these questions can provide a clear window into the internal world of the client at the time of the attempt. Such a window provides the best information available as to the seriousness of the client's action. As noted earlier, all the statistical risk factors in the world will not tell us whether a specific client intended death. Some clients may accidentally kill themselves during manipulative gestures, but most people kill themselves because they have decided to kill themselves. The information gathered in response to these questions illuminates the shadowy recesses of the client's decision-making process.

At first glance, especially for a clinician in training, this may appear to be an intimidating list of questions to remember. Fortunately, one of the six validity techniques discussed earlier, the behavioral incident, can provide the clinician with a simpler and more logical approach than memorization. A clinician is employing a behavioral incident every time he or she: (1) asks for a specific piece of behavioral data (e.g., "Did you put the gun up to your head?") or (2) asks the client for a sequential description of what happened (e.g., "Tell me what you did next").

In the CASE Approach, the clinician, using a series of behavioral incidents, asks the client to describe the suicide incident from beginning to end. The clinician can begin this process by using a framing comment such as, "Mr. Jones, help me to understand exactly what happened during your overdose. Try to walk me through last night step by step. Let's begin at the point where your suicidal ideation was getting stronger." If a piece of the account is missing, the clinician returns to that area, exploring with a new set of clarifying behavioral incidents until the clinician feels confident that he or she has an accurate picture of what happened. In essence, the client is being asked to produce a step-by-step "verbal videotape." Using such an approach, the clinician will frequently uncover most, if not all, of the material outlined above, in a naturally unfolding dialogue without much need for memorization.

Let's see this strategy at work with a client presenting in crisis. At the time of the interview, I was working in a community mental health center. One of my assignments was to function as the psychiatrist for a crisis group known as Life Management Services (LMS). This crisis group was designed to help prevent hospitalizations and to consolidate the recovery of people who were leaving inpatient units. Each prospective client was initially interviewed by the program director, a gifted clinician named Paul, or by one of his group therapists. Clients who were appropriate for the program were referred to me for a full initial assessment, including biopsychosocial assessment, a *DSM-IV* differential diagnosis, and a medication evaluation. After my session, I would meet with the group therapists and jointly determine the treatment plan.

The crisis group met at two times on every weekday. An attempt was made to tailor the group therapy to the individual needs of each client. Thus, a client with a relatively mild crisis might attend one session on Mondays, Tuesdays, and Fridays for three weeks. A client with a severe crisis and clinical deterioration might be seen twice a day every day for six weeks.

One Monday afternoon, I was asked to see Barbara, who had been interviewed by Paul that morning. At a friend's insistence, Barbara had presented to the emergency room late on Friday night. Earlier that evening, Barbara had shared her serious suicidal plans with her friend. There had not been an actual attempt, but her friend's concern for Barbara's safety was appropriate considering the nature of Barbara's plans as we shall soon see.

Initially, both Barbara's primary care physician and the crisis team clinician felt hospitalization was indicated. But Barbara would have no part of it. The clinicians, who were in agreement that adequate grounds for commitment were present, contemplated involuntary commitment. When they shared their thoughts with Barbara, she maintained that she would refuse hospitalization. If they wanted her in the hospital, they would have to commit her. Period. She stated that she felt better and she could promise she would not hurt herself. She also said she would agree to seek outpatient treatment. Barbara felt hospitalization would be too stigmatizing for her and would prove to be ultimately counterproductive.

The psychiatrist on call was consulted. After much deliberation, the team decided that forcing a commitment with Barbara would, indeed, be counterproductive. Like Barbara, they ultimately concluded that commitment would be unnecessary, for she appeared to have calmed considerably. But it was still a tough call. As the transcript will demonstrate, Barbara's suicidal ruminations were far from fleeting in nature. Among the deciding factors that supported the validity of Barbara's outpatient safety were: the presence of a highly supportive husband who would stay with her over the weekend, her ready agreement to call in regularly over the weekend, and her agreement to attend the LMS group, if deemed appropriate, on Monday.

When Paul dropped off his clinical notes for my perusal before Barbara arrived, he commented, "I think we can manage her in the group, but this is a bit of a 'dicey call.'" He feigned a tight smile and blinked his eyes, providing a sarcastic nonverbal that he was not having a lot of fun this morning. Paul, an experienced clinician, was no stranger to actively suicidal clients. At any given time, one-third of his crisis group could be populated with clients with borderline personalities. He had a cool head when it came to determining suicide potential and hospitalization; in a sense, he made his living helping clients mobilize their resources so as to avoid unnecessary hospitalizations. For Paul to "blink" on Barbara's safety was not a good sign. He subsequently related that he had told Barbara that the final decision, as to whether she could enter the group, would rest with me. If I felt comfortable with her outpatient safety, he wanted me to tell her she was in the group. If I felt uncomfortable, I was to tell her Paul and I would meet first, before making our final decision.

One other detail of the clinical context of this interview should be kept in mind: I was to perform this entire biopsychosocial assessment, differential diagnosis by *DSM-IV* criteria, medication assessment, and determination of outpatient safety within sixty minutes. My astral body was supposed to be writing up the clinical document during this same time frame because a new client would be waiting at my door sixty-one minutes later. It was a typical day at a community mental health center.

When Barbara entered my office, her hesitant "Hello" was promptly punctuated with a quick depressive sigh. She was clearly carrying a heavy load, in the physical sense of being markedly overweight, and in the psychological sense of being markedly overstressed. Her hair, a bit wanting for shampoo, was clipped short about her ears, nicely framing the roundness of her cheeks. She had gone to some pains to apply a light makeup. Although a bit dowdy, her clothes were washed and freshly pressed. As Barbara sat, glancing at the camera, she managed a nervous smile. I could sense that she was straining to present herself as well as she could possibly manage. I liked her immediately. She was clearly one of life's warriors, but the war was not going well.

As the interview proceeded, a bevy of self-denigrations and cognitive distortions hovered about her words, like demons buzzing about a besieged penitent's head. They would prove to be the hallmarks of a moderately severe major depressive episode. Her story was complicated by the presence of a severe panic disorder that had also given birth to an agoraphobic isolation. When she described her struggles to get out to the grocery store and to take her kids to school, she ended with, "I can't do it anymore. My husband has to do it all. I've let them all down." At that point, her shoulders heaved and she could no longer hold back her tears.

All was not bleak. Barbara demonstrated a feisty courage. She could dot her answers with a refreshingly quiet, yet pithy wit. She had a knack for putting her struggles into perspective, and she lacked the bitterness so commonly seen in those who have personalized the inevitable struggles inherent in being alive. About twenty minutes into the interview, the stage had been well set for entering the world of her suicidal ideation. I could sense that Barbara liked me and that the engagement process was unfolding nicely. She once again tearfully raised the issue of her children, commenting on her musings as to whether they might be better off if she were dead. The portal for entering the region of presenting events, utilizing the CASE Approach, had been opened.

Barbara did not have an actual presenting gesture or attempt. On the other hand, she had presented to the emergency room with a disturbing array of suicidal thoughts, which functioned as the presenting suicide "events" to be explored with the CASE Approach. We pick up the conversation at my query about the extent of her crying.

CLINICIAN:   Obviously you have been very depressed. It looks like you have been crying a lot. How frequently do you find yourself crying?

PATIENT:   Umm . . . I just started. For a long time I couldn't cry at all even though I wanted to. You know, I thought maybe if I'd cry I'd feel better.

CLINICIAN:   Okay.

PATIENT:   But for a long time I couldn't cry at all. I couldn't do anything at all.

CLINICIAN:   How about over the past month, how frequently?

PATIENT:   Ummm . . . all the time [patient smiles].

CLINICIAN:   Okay.

PATIENT:   Over everything [looks up sheepishly and lightly laughs].

CLINICIAN:   It sounds like it has gotten worse for you then.

PATIENT:   Yea [nodding yes].

CLINICIAN:   Well, when things were really getting very difficult to cope with, what kinds of thoughts did you have about killing yourself? [gentle assumption]

PATIENT:   Umm . . . I had a plan.

CLINICIAN:   Okay.

PATIENT:   I [pauses] that's what got me here. Umm . . . I had written letters to my family cuz, like, I don't want them to feel guilty. [begins to cry] I want them to know that it was something that I thought I was doing for their best interest. [pauses] Then I was going to . . . you see, they go on vacation . . . my children go on vacation with my parents at the end of June, so I had written letters, and I had started to buy over-the-counter medicines. I was gonna go to my favorite sort of camp in Bennington. It's way out in the woods. And I was gonna swallow the pills to make me drowsy. And then I was going to shoot myself.

CLINICIAN:   Okay. When were you planning on doing this? [behavioral incident]

PATIENT:   While they were gone in June.

CLINICIAN:   In June?

PATIENT:   The last week in June.

CLINICIAN:   What pills did you start to stockpile? [behavioral incident]

PATIENT:   Umm . . . I bought Tylenol with the sleeping med, you know, Tylenol PM, and, umm . . . Benadryl, and umm. . . .

CLINICIAN:   Roughly, how many of these pills did you stock up on? [behavioral incident]

PATIENT:   I've probably got about 20 bottles.

CLINICIAN:   Oh, a lot.

PATIENT:   Yea.

Although there was not a specific presenting suicide gesture, I utilized a series of behavioral incidents to clarify the extent of planning and the action taken on that planning, as illustrated by, "What pills did you start to stockpile?" and "Roughly, how many of these pills did you stock up on?" The answer, ". . . about 20 bottles," was disturbing.

I was concerned, and a bit surprised, by the extent of Barbara's planning. Keeping in mind the risk factors described in Chapter 3, Barbara was beginning to look like a cheat sheet for a clinical skills class in suicide assessment. She had written letters, chosen a well-defined method, and designated an out-of-the-way summer house for implementation. Perhaps even more disturbing was her plan to use two methods, one of which, a gun, seldom fails.

Even this early in the use of the CASE Approach, note how the behavioral incident, when used to delineate sequential details, is a powerful means of uncovering pertinent information. Behavioral incidents function as deftly guided probes that are already distilling unexpected information related to the many areas listed earlier as critical for determining acute dangerousness. Even more remarkable is the fact that the use of the behavioral incidents has already uncovered material that could be used as grounds, albeit a bit shaky, for involuntary commitment. (In New Hampshire, any significant action taken toward self-harm, such as Barbara's meticulous hoarding of pills, can be used as grounds for involuntary commitment.)

The dialogue also contains an easily overlooked but disturbing comment in reference to her children: "I want them to know that it was something that I thought I was doing for their best interest." Here we see a rational reason for Barbara's killing herself: an effort to help others—in this instance, her children. I must admit that, at this point in the interview, Paul's comment about this being a "dicey call" was looking a bit like an understatement. At this juncture watch as I try to create a "verbal videotape" through the consistent use of behavioral incidents. I would have given a more effective display of good technique had I used each behavioral incident separately, waiting for Barbara to reply, as opposed to stringing them together as I did in my first question below. Nevertheless, powerful information was provided.

CLINICIAN:  Now how did this come to light? What brought you here? Did you call Dr. Whalen [patient's therapist]? [set of behavioral incidents]

PATIENT:  No.

CLINICIAN:  How did people discover this? [behavioral incident]

PATIENT:  I made the mistake of telling an acquaintance. She said something about summer and I said, well, don't count me in, or something, and she said, "What?" I told her that I had decided that was the only way I could get over this or to solve this. [begins crying again]

CLINICIAN:   So you shared this with her? [said gently]

PATIENT:   Yea. I don't know why. I've never done that before. I've never talked about my feelings with her or anybody before.

CLINICIAN:   Perhaps it's the part of you that may not want to die and wanted to let someone know. I don't know. There was some reason you shared it. Okay, you've been thinking about taking the pills and shooting yourself. Had you bought a gun or something? [behavioral incident]

PATIENT:   We had a gun.

CLINICIAN:   Did you get the gun out of the house? [behavioral incident]

PATIENT:   No. It's put away where I know where it is. It wouldn't be missed. It's not [pause], I figured, well, while I went to work, I could get it into my parents' car before he knew.

At this point, I was beginning to be less concerned about whether Barbara might be crazy than about whether Paul might be crazy. Handling Barbara as an outpatient seemed beyond "dicey." Note that the behavioral incident technique is nicely demonstrated by the persistent follow-through on whether the client has a gun and what has she done with it. The resulting answers were hardly reassuring. Another easily overlooked comment raised a red flag concerning safety: "I made the mistake of telling an acquaintance." This off-the-cuff comment seems to be hinting that Barbara is dissatisfied that her plan has been disrupted.

As ominous as her answers have been so far, we are seeing some of the first evidence in support of her current safety. The bottom line remains, she did choose to tell somebody. Moreover, if Barbara's description of how her secret came to light is accurate, her friend could hardly be said to have been probing for such a confession. A part of Barbara wanted to share the secret. Her presentation to the emergency room occurred at the end of May, a full month before her planned attempt, further suggesting that Barbara had some significant ambivalence about proceeding with her plan.

I attempted to highlight this ambivalence to her by commenting, "Perhaps it's the part of you that may not want to die and wanted to let someone know. I don't know. There was some reason you shared it." I carefully avoided stating that she definitely did not want to die for such an assertion can strike a client as a confrontation. Instead, I was careful to be vague with my speculation, beginning with the word "Perhaps" and ending with "I don't know." I then stated the one fact that could not be disputed, leaving it to her to contemplate on its significance, "there was some reason you shared it."

At this point, something did not feel right to me. Barbara had not seemed this dangerous to me earlier in the interview, and it was hard for me to believe that the crisis clinician—who, I knew was quite skilled—would have let her go home to a house with a gun in it. I decided to ask for clarification.

CLINICIAN:    Now is the gun still in your house?
PATIENT:    No. My husband removed it this weekend.
CLINICIAN:    I was going to say, I would urge you to get the gun out. I would also urge you to get rid of any of those pills. Are they still there?
PATIENT:    They're still there but I will get rid of them.

The situation looked a bit better. The gun had been removed. Barbara had done exactly what the crisis clinician had suggested—a very good sign. I was also privy to a bit of information, that the reader does not have, that is significant. The crisis clinicians had told Paul that Barbara had followed their crisis support plan perfectly over the weekend. She checked in on time, and she projected an apparent enthusiasm for getting some help. This improvement in her condition, suggesting that the acute suicidal crisis had passed, was verified by her conscientious husband, who felt she *looked* better too. He did not feel she was currently suicidal. With my last question, I brought the exploration of her presenting suicide event to a close and we are ready for a bridge into the next region of the CASE Approach: recent suicidal events.

REGION 2: EXPLORATION OF RECENT SUICIDAL EVENTS

In this region, the clinician will elicit the types of suicidal thoughts and actions that the patient has had during the previous two months, hoping to gain insights into the degree of the patient's suicidal planning and intent. The more concrete and thorough the planning, and the more frequent and intense the ideation, the more concerned the clinician should be about acute suicide risk. This region also provides a wonderful window into the patient's weighing of the pros and cons of suicide, including the patient's thoughts of what death will bring, all of which can provide insight into the patient's immediate risk.

After watching hundreds of clinicians elicit suicide histories, I have become convinced that this two-month time frame is, traditionally, poorly explored, yet I believe it is one of the richest areas for uncovering acute dangerousness. So important is the exploration of this two-month region that it warrants our careful attention.

Earlier in the book, as we explored the phenomenology of suicide, it became apparent that a suicidal person often spends considerable time preparing for its implementation. Suicide is not a simple act. The ethics of the act, the method of its implementation, and the assurance of its fruition must be carefully examined, as is intimated in the lines by Anne Sexton, at the beginning of this chapter.

Some people may be inexorably pulled toward suicide or even fascinated by its prospects, as Anne Sexton may have been, but I believe that most people have more ambivalent feelings. These ambivalent feelings often result in an approach–avoidant relationship with the act itself. To my knowledge, no study has carefully explored this phenomenology, but it seems logical that this approach–avoidant conflict would often play itself out in the months directly before the attempt. Thus, for many people, the intensity of suicidal preoccupation and the power of their determination to kill themselves probably fluctuate in the months directly before they take action (see Figure 6.2).

For some people, progress toward suicide may consistently rise linearly over time, reaching its peak in the act itself. For many other people, as Figure 6.2 illustrates, the line toward death unfolds not so much as a gradually intensifying wave but more as a roller coaster careening on tracks constructed on the vicissitudes of their stresses, their perceptions of alternative solutions, their fears of death, and the rages of their symptoms and/or intoxications from alcohol or street drugs.

Figure 6.2 illustrates the fluctuating course for a hypothetical client who is coping with both alcoholism and suicidal ideation, which are common bedfellows. At point A, our hypothetical client has become acutely suicidal. On this particular night, he had actually loaded a gun

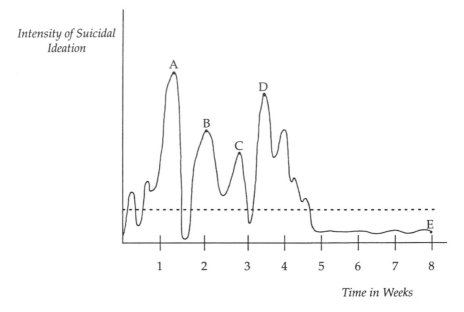

**Figure 6.2** An example of the fluctuations seen with suicidal ideation in the two months before an initial assessment.

and placed it in his mouth. The crisis has been precipitated by his girl-friend's abruptly ending their relationship. The crisis is being intensi-fied by the ingestion of two bottles of wine. Two days later, with the return of his girlfriend and a brief interlude of being dry, there is no suicidal ideation. At points B and C, we are seeing significant returns of suicidal ideation, contingent on increasing arguments and threats of abandonment by his girlfriend. The drinking intensifies and, at point D, following an episode of domestic violence, the client finds himself once more gun in hand, bullets loaded. Three weeks before meeting with the initial interviewer, the situation once again calms dramati-cally. The drinking declines and the couple has temporarily "patched things up." At which point, the client agrees to see a counselor but en-counters a "waiting list."

By the time of the client's initial assessment at the mental health clinic, there will have been no suicidal ideation for three weeks. In-deed, it is not uncommon to find a client who has been free of suicidal ideation for several weeks, who has had a gesture or even made a se-rious attempt during the previous two months. From the history of this client's last two months, we know that he could abruptly become suicidal. For instance, if his girlfriend finally "pulls out" for good or his drinking erupts, suicidal ideation may rapidly reappear. But the question is: Will the clinician be aware of this patient's tumultuous recent history?

Imagine for a moment that the clinician asks our hypothetical client about suicide, employing a phrasing which is commonly used such as, "Have you been having any suicidal thoughts recently?" or "Have you been having any thoughts of killing yourself?" At first glance, the first phrasing seems like a good enough question. It is direct and to the point. But, on second reading, one can see that the question has a built-in communication trap. The clinician and the client may have strikingly different definitions of "recently." In my experience, clients tend to interpret this word as meaning the last two or so weeks. Even with the second question, where no time frame is proffered, I find that many clients assume they are being asked about the recent past, which to them, once again, consists of the last two or three weeks.

Let's look at the impact that such innocent and natural assumptions might have on our hypothetical client. He has reached a decision not to kill himself, for "life is now good." He might answer the two questions above with a convincing and immediate "No." His tone of voice and nonverbals would strongly support the certainty of his current frame of mind. In such a situation, a clinician might easily assume that there has been no significant recent ideation. At which point, the clinician might then ask: "Have you ever tried to kill yourself in the past?" This inquiry, especially if there has been a past attempt, may quickly divert the conversation from the more recent and ominous ideation, and focus it on the enticing facts dealing with past attempts and their resulting hospitalizations. Often, this oversight is never redressed. The clinician could leave the initial interview with no idea that the client had had a loaded gun in his mouth two months ago. Nor would the clinician have a good feel for the volatility and impulsivity of the client's suicidal storms.

With the time pressures of current clinical settings and the complexities of the massive databases required for sound treatment planning in today's clinical work, during direct supervision, I have seen similar scenarios played out time and again. The CASE Approach is specifically designed to avoid such traps. In the CASE Approach, the previous two months, which are rich in potentially vital information, are explored by determining exactly what types of plans for suicide the client has had, and how far the client has acted on them. This firsthand behavioral information, as opposed to a clinician's conjecture, can provide a valid database that is of immediate value in the estimation of lethality. The process unfolds best by determining:

1. The specific plans that have been contemplated.
2. How far the client took actions on these plans.
3. How much of the client's time has been spent on these plans.

The size of this database is formidable, but its value is inestimable. The goal for the frontline clinician is to gather the most valid and comprehensive database that will allow the best educated guess—for it is always a guess—about the patient's lethality potential. But the interviewer wants to guess based on the best information regarding the client's recent state of mind. Fortunately, as with the exploration of Region 1, the tools necessary to do the task engagingly and in minimal time already exist. Once again, the behavioral incident will be of great use, but this time it will be coupled with some of the other validity techniques described earlier including, gentle assumption, denial of the specific, and symptom amplification.

Two different strategies will be described for exploring the region of recent suicide events, but readers should feel free to design new approaches in a flexible fashion as the need arises. There is no "correct" cookbook approach, but I believe an honest attempt at applying the principles described below can enhance the clinician's ability to rapidly and reliably develop a sound database.

The first approach is straightforward (Figure 6.3). After the clinician finishes exploring the region of the presenting event, a gentle assumption ("What other ways have you thought of killing yourself?") is used to delineate the next method of suicide being considered by the patient. The clinician then uses a series of behavioral incidents to establish how far the patient may have acted on this method. If the patient admits to thoughts of using a gun, the series may look something like this:

1. "Do you have a gun in the house?"
2. "Have you ever gotten the gun out with the intention of thinking about using it to kill yourself?"

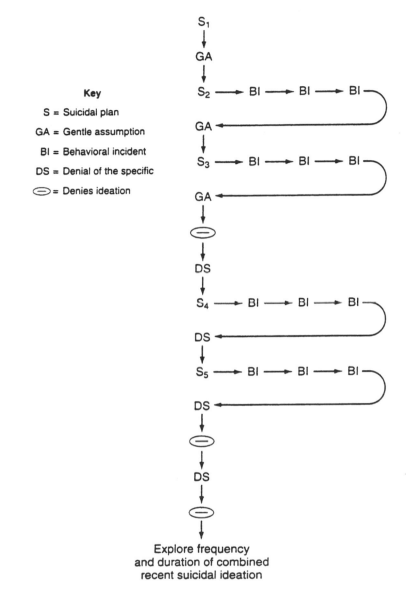

**Figure 6.3** Exploration of recent suicidal ideation. Adapted from S.C. Shea. *Psychiatric Interviewing: The Art of Understanding,* 2nd Edition, W.B. Saunders Company, Philadelphia, 1998.

3. "Have you ever loaded the gun?"
4. "Have you put the gun up to your body or head?"
5. "How long did you hold the gun there?"
6. "Did you take the safety off?"
7. "What stopped you from pulling the trigger?"

Once the clinician knows how close the client came to attempting suicide with this method, the clinician once again uses gentle assumption to establish a third method, if indeed one exists. This method is then explored using behavioral incidents in exactly the same manner. The clinician continues with a series of gentle assumptions, always following up any new method with a series of behavioral incidents that clarify the extent of action taken on the specific method.

When the use of a gentle assumption yields a blanket denial of all other methods, the clinician uses denial of the specific repeatedly. As we saw in Chapter 5, this technique can be surprisingly effective at uncovering previously denied sensitive material. The interviewer doesn't "drive this technique into the ground" by probing a long series of methods. He or she simply asks for any methods that are common to the patient's culture that have not yet been discussed. For example, if the client has talked about overdosing, guns, and driving a car off the road, the clinician may employ this short list of denials of the specific:

1. "Have you thought about cutting or stabbing yourself?"
2. "Have you thought about hanging yourself?"
3. "Have you thought about jumping off a bridge or other high place?"
4. "Have you thought about carbon monoxide?"

Such questions often reveal more ideation, and, in a few instances, recent attempts that were denied earlier may be discovered. As before, if a new method is revealed, the clinician uses a series of behavioral incidents to find out how far the patient took the suicidal action.

After establishing the list of methods the patient considered and the extent of action taken on each method, the clinician hones in on the frequency, duration, and intensity of the suicidal ideation with a question such as: "Over the past six to eight weeks, how much time did you spend, on your bad days, thinking about killing yourself?"

The validity technique of symptom amplification may be added: "You know, 90% of the day, 70% of the day?"

This strategy for exploring the suicidal history of the past two months is easy to learn and simple to remember, and it flows imperceptibly for the client, frequently increasing engagement as the client is pleasantly surprised at how easy it is to talk to the clinician about material that had frequently been shouldered as a topic of shame.

Let's return to Barbara. Could this approach shed new light on her suicide potential? Gentle assumption will be used to enter the region of recent events. Typically this is done by using a gentle assumption that probes for new methods as with, "What other ways have you thought of committing suicide?" On the other hand if the clinician is suspicious that the client may have practiced or attempted the same method recently as had been discussed in the presenting event, then the interviewer may choose to use a gentle assumption focused on that specific method as with, "Barbara, how often in the last two months have you thought of overdosing?" I chose to use this latter approach with Barbara in the excerpt below.

Note that as new methods are uncovered, I use behavioral incidents to create a "verbal videotape" for each method. Sometimes, this careful search for details concerning method yields surprising insights as to whether a client has decided to proceed with suicide. This information may be tremendously significant for the client's immediate safety.

PATIENT:   They're still there but I will get rid of them.

CLINICIAN:   Now, before this time, over the last two months, how often, if ever, have you ever gotten the pills out in your hand, you know, dumped some of them out and thought of overdosing on the spot? [gentle assumption]

PATIENT:   Umm . . . a little while ago I thought I was going to cut my wrists. Umm . . . I was in the bathroom, I had the warm water running, and I knew I had to cut up my arm and not across my arm. And I had the razor out. And I didn't do it. I don't know why.

CLINICIAN:   I was going to say, what do you think stopped you? [behavioral incident]

PATIENT:   I don't know. I wasn't crying or anything. I was home all alone. I just kind of thought about the mess it was going to make and my son would probably be the first one home.

CLINICIAN:    Okay. You didn't want him to see it.

PATIENT:    No.

CLINICIAN:    Now did you actually touch the razor blade up against your wrist? [behavioral incident]

PATIENT:    No. I don't think so. I took it out of the paper, and I set it on the sink.

CLINICIAN:    Okay, how long did you think about this? You know, how long were you sitting there? [behavioral incident]

PATIENT:    I was probably there for a while. Probably a half hour or so. I was thinking, "Is this really worth what I'm going to do to the kids?" You know I don't want anyone else raising my kids.

CLINICIAN:    Right.

PATIENT:    And I've seen a lot of suicides being an EMT, and I've seen what it can do to people and their families and everything. It's so stupid. I don't want to do this.

CLINICIAN:    It is true. It is devastating for those who are left behind. That is an important thing for you to remember. It can help you to not do it. I am just a little bit confused. The knife incident, was it recent, or when was that? [behavioral incident]

PATIENT:    It was about three months ago.

CLINICIAN:    Okay. So the incident that brought you here was the idea of overdosing and shooting yourself and that you shared it with your friend.

PATIENT:    Yea. She must have been. . . .

CLINICIAN:    Have you written letters? [behavioral incident]

PATIENT:    Yes.

CLINICIAN:    Did you work on your will or anything to make sure . . . ? [behavioral incident]

PATIENT:    The will was all up-to-date.

Our strategy is paying off. Important information—some disturbing and some significantly more reassuring—is being uncovered. On the disturbing side, we uncovered a new method, cutting, which was acted on relatively recently. This information could prove to be a pivotal support for involuntary commitment if commitment is deemed necessary. In addition, it is hardly reassuring to learn that Barbara has written suicide notes to friends and has reviewed her will. As was the case with Anne Sexton, suicide has not been merely a passing fancy for

Barbara. Much forethought has been evidenced. As predicted, the CASE Approach is providing more and more of the pieces of the puzzle that are relevant in determining Barbara's immediate safety.

In this regard one of the new pieces has shed a decidedly more reassuring light. As intimated earlier, Barbara's review of her actions with the razor blade has opened a large window into her reasons for not killing herself. Such unexpected portals into clients' decision-making processes are not uncommon with the use of sequential behavioral incidents. The process of clients' replaying their physical actions seems to trigger an associated reliving of their internal thoughts. When these internal thoughts are shared, the clinician is often granted access to an intimate view of the client's personal struggles regarding the pros and cons of suicide and the client's questions concerning the personal ethics of the action. With Barbara, such a view has given us the most telling evidence supportive of her safety to date.

Spontaneously, and with genuine affect, Barbara shared her framework for meaning and her main reason for choosing life, "I was thinking, Is this really worth what I'm going to do to the kids? You know I don't want anyone else raising my kids." Although not evident from a transcript, her affect was intensely genuine. This had obviously been a major turning point in her own deliberations. And although earlier in the interview she had described her pondering of whether her kids would benefit from her death, the intensity of her affect while describing this incident strongly suggested that, for the time being, she deeply felt they needed her. I took that opportunity to reinforce her conviction with, "It is true. It is devastating for those who are left behind. That is an important thing for you to remember. It can help you to not do it." Note that I am not trying to convince her not to kill herself; I am merely reinforcing a conclusion she had arrived at herself.

It was now time to continue our search for other methods of suicide. Gentle assumption will be used to uncover each method, until she denies any other methods. Each method, in sequence, will be carefully explored with behavioral incidents.

CLINICIAN: Now, let's talk a little bit more about that, in this last six to eight weeks, one thing that you thought about was cutting yourself. What other ways did you think of killing yourself? [gentle assumption]

PATIENT:   Really none. I mean, there are so many options. Sometimes I drive down the road and think it would be so easy just to run into a telephone pole, but then you don't have the guarantee that you are going to die, for one thing, and it just makes more hardship on your family.

CLINICIAN:   Yea. Now did you ever specifically get into a car with the intention of driving off the road? [behavioral incident]

PATIENT:   No. I get in the car with the intention of not knowing what I was going to do but not necessarily that in mind.

CLINICIAN:   What other ways have you thought of killing yourself? [gentle assumption]

PATIENT:   Really that's all. I would never hang myself. I saw a lady that had been hung and that was disgusting.

CLINICIAN:   You said you would never do it. Did you think about it and rule it out or . . . ? [behavioral incident]

PATIENT:   Well, it was there but it was just [pause] I wouldn't do it. It was an option.

CLINICIAN:   Did you ever get a rope out?

PATIENT:   No.

CLINICIAN:   What other ways? [gentle assumption]

PATIENT:   I don't think there were any other ways.

Notice that Barbara made a blanket denial in response to the last gentle assumption. This denial signals the moment to utilize the next validity technique, denial of the specific, in an effort to see whether other methods may be still hidden. Any new method will be explored using behavioral incidents as before. After the most common methods have been reviewed, there will be a graceful movement into a determination of the frequency and intensity of the suicidal ideation over the past two months. Note the use of the validity technique of symptom amplification as it is employed to help with this clarification:

CLINICIAN:   Did you ever think about [pause] you mentioned shooting yourself. What about carbon monoxide poisoning or anything like that? [denial of the specific]

PATIENT:   No. We don't have a garage. So there's no place to do that.

CLINICIAN:   Did you ever think about jumping off a building? [behavioral incident]

PATIENT:   No, that would hurt. I'm not a great one for pain. [she smiles]

CLINICIAN:   How about driving your car into traffic?

PATIENT:   Nope.

CLINICIAN:   Okay. Good. You had mentioned cutting yourself. Have you ever thought of stabbing yourself or anything like that? [denial of the specific]

PATIENT:   No.

CLINICIAN:   Now, how much time do you think . . . if we look over the last couple, or say six, weeks, on a given day, how much time do you think you spent thinking about killing yourself? [behavioral incident]

PATIENT:   A lot. More than usual.

CLINICIAN:   Two minutes a day? Three hours a day? Ten hours a day? [symptom amplification]

PATIENT:   It just seems to be in my thoughts. I don't really know how much time I actually spent. The day that I wrote the letters and stuff, it was over the course of, like, a week I guess, and it was every day. It was every day I thought of it. I woke up in the morning thinking about whose letter I had to write but umm. . . .

CLINICIAN:   So it was very much on your mind and just wasn't an impulsive. . . .

PATIENT:   [patient cuts clinician off] Oh no, it's been there.

CLINICIAN:   What about in the past, have you ever attempted to kill yourself?

We have just begun to move into the region dealing with past events. But before making this transition, a few important closing points dealing with the exploration of recent events is in order, including a look at a second style of sequencing the questions in this region.

First, with regard to deciding whether Barbara would be best served in our outpatient group versus an inpatient unit. At this point in the interview, I was leaning toward admitting Barbara into the crisis group. Despite some significant risk factors and considerable suicidal planning, she had revealed a powerful motivator for not committing suicide—her children. In addition, there was consistent evidence that Barbara was motivated toward safety as shown by her keen attention to her weekend crisis plan, her removal of the gun, and her cooperative attitude during Paul's assessment and my own. In addition, she appears to be responding well during the interview itself.

Her affect is more natural, bits of humor have emerged, and she appears to be feeling more comfortable as I am proceeding with the CASE strategy. This "therapeutic" benefit of the CASE strategy is common. It appears to stem from the client's surprised relief at being able to talk about suicide, an intimate and taboo topic, with an interviewer who listens in a nonjudgmental and calm way. I have found that after they become comfortable with consistent use of the CASE Approach, clinicians become more matter-of-fact and reassuring during their elicitation of suicidal ideation. Clients quickly realize that the CASE clinician is at home in this territory and will neither underreact nor overreact.

I mentioned earlier that a beneficial but rather peculiar "side effect" of using behavioral incidents is the fact that they often trigger clients to spontaneously discuss the pros and cons of killing themselves. As Barbara poignantly illustrates, this listing can provide important clues to the way a client is leaning. Sometimes, at such moments, a new line of questioning can add even more information about the client's leanings by leading the client to openly discuss what he or she hopes to achieve by the act of suicide. In his wonderfully insightful and very practical book, *Suicide Risk,* John Maltsberger points out the diversity of clients' views about the impact of their own suicide:

1. Suicide is a gateway leading into a dreamless sleep (nothingness).
2. It will effect reunion with someone or something which has been lost.
3. It will be a way of escaping from a persecutory enemy, interior or exterior.
4. It will destroy an enemy who seems to have taken up a place in the patient's body or some other part of himself.
5. It will provide a passage into another, better world.
6. One can get revenge on someone else by abandoning him or by destroying his favorite possession (the patient's body), and one can then watch him suffer from beyond the grave.[10]

The patient's reactions to these views can provide insight into his or her motivating drives toward death and perhaps into the imminent risk of a suicide attempt. These motivators for suicide can be surprisingly powerful and sometimes odd, especially in people who see no other way of resolving their current pain or who find existence, as we know it, to be a bleak proposition. This possibility was recently highlighted in the mass suicide of thirty-nine members of the Heaven's Gate cult in a wealthy suburb of San Diego. The idea that suicide could provide a means of passage to a better world was the driving force behind their deaths. The cult members anticipated passage to a better world aboard an alien spacecraft that just happened to be tagging a ride inside the tail of the Hale-Bopp Comet.

I mentioned earlier that there is a second style of sequencing the questions in this region. In this also popular style, the clinician first generates the entire list of suicide methods contemplated by the client and then goes back to explore the extent of action taken with each one using behavioral incidents.

In this approach, after the clinician is done exploring the presenting method, gentle assumption is used to identify the second method, if indeed one has been considered. In the first approach, the clinician would have proceeded to use behavioral incidents to delineate the extent of action taken on this new method. Not so in this approach. As soon as the second method is uncovered, the clinician asks another gentle assumption, such as, "What other ways have you thought of killing yourself?" This use of gentle assumptions is continued until the patient answers that there are no other ways. The clinician does not stop there. The interviewer proceeds to use denials of the specific repeatedly until the list is done. Figure 6.4 illustrates the differences between this approach and the one previously described.

At this point, the clinician then returns to each method in turn and uses a string of behavioral incidents to find out how far the patient has gone in taking actions toward self-harm. For instance, the clinician might say, "Earlier, you mentioned that you had thought of shooting yourself. Is there a gun in the house, or is one available to you?" A series of clarifying behavioral incidents would follow concerning the actions taken with the gun. After completing his or her determination of the extent of action taken by the patient on this second suicide method, the interviewer will use the same tack with the third method, and so on down the line.

As with the first strategy, after all methods are explored with behavioral incidents, the clinician checks on the frequency, duration, and intensity of the recent ideation with a question such as: "Looking at all

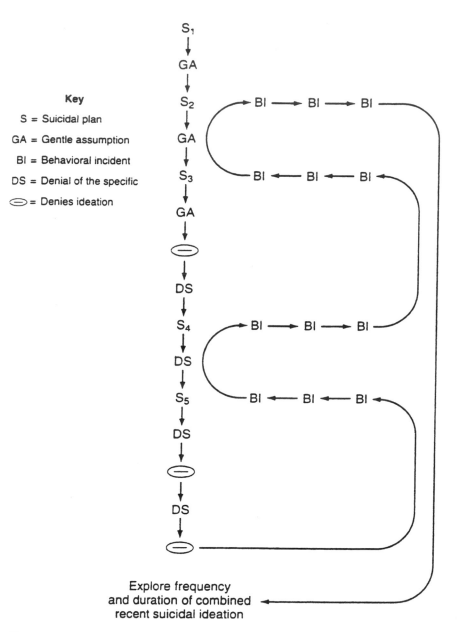

**Figure 6.4**   Alternative exploration of recent suicidal ideation. Adapted from S.C. Shea. *Psychiatric Interviewing: The Art of Understanding,* 2nd Edition, W.B. Saunders Company, Philadelphia, 1998.

these methods combined, over the past six to eight weeks, how much of any given day are you spending on thoughts of suicide?"

Both approaches are easy to remember. In the first one, as each method is uncovered, the clinician uses behavioral incidents to follow the extent of action taken. In the second one, a list of all the methods is uncovered first before any of them is explored in detail with behavioral incidents. Readers can try both methods and decide on a preference, or perhaps develop entirely new methods. There is no "right" method. But the important point for becoming a more skilled clinician is to consciously develop strategies as opposed to relying solely on intuition or habit. In Region 3, we will explore the interviewing methods utilized to elicit evidence of suicide attempts in the client's past history. In some respects, this is the simplest region to explore.

## REGION 3: EXPLORATION OF PAST SUICIDAL EVENTS

Curiously, during an initial assessment, clinicians sometimes spend too much time in this region. Patients with extensive histories of suicidal attempts and gestures (for example, some people suffering from a borderline structure) may have extensive past histories of suicidal material. One could spend the appointment hour just reviewing this material, but it would be an hour poorly spent.

Under the time constraints of a busy practice and managed care, initial assessments usually must be completed in an hour. When time is at such a premium, the question becomes: What past suicidal history is important to gather? My answer is: Gather only information that could potentially change the decision on the safe disposition of a patient. Using this principle, the clinician should explore the following key points:

1. What was the most serious past suicide attempt? (Is the current ideation focused on the same method? Practice can be deadly in this arena. Does the patient feel boxed in by current stressors in the same way as when the serious suicide attempt was made?)
2. What is the approximate number of past gestures and attempts? (Large numbers here can alert the clinician to issues of manipulation, and consequently less concern, or they may alert the clinician

that the patient has truly exhausted all hope—a cause for more concern. In either case, it is important to know the number.)

3. Going back beyond the previous two months, when was the most recent attempt and how serious was it?

Responses to the above questions may ferret out information that could alter the decision about safety. For instance, a discovery that Barbara had taken a life-threatening overdose about a year ago and was admitted to an intensive care unit would prompt serious concerns about her current safety. The overdose history would raise a red flag for it would indicate that her current suicide method had been practiced once to near-fatal perfection. Moreover, Barbara would have already demonstrated that she possessed both the motivation and the ingenuity to bring a suicide attempt to fruition. Of even more concern would be the fact that she had not spontaneously mentioned such a serious attempt earlier in the interview. Her tone toward suicide had somehow implied that suicide was quite foreign to her. This discrepancy would be disturbing for it would suggest that the interviewer did not have a good handle on the validity of Barbara's story. In a similar vein, if Barbara admitted to a string of attempts or gestures in the past, one would have to question the reliability of her current assurances of safety.

Here is what Barbara's past history holds:

CLINICIAN: What about in the past, have you ever attempted to kill yourself? [behavioral incident]

PATIENT: No. I've thought about it. I've talked to the doctor about it.

CLINICIAN: Okay.

PATIENT: But I haven't done it.

CLINICIAN: Have you ever, when you were younger, say teens, junior high, done a slight gesture, a couple of extra pills, thinking maybe it "would kill me or hurt me," anything like that? [behavioral incident]

PATIENT: No. I was a happy-go-lucky kid, Miss Congenial USA. When I look back at then, death was far from my thoughts.

CLINICIAN: Was there ever a period of time where you did have some suicidal thoughts other than the last three years? [behavioral incident]

PATIENT:   No. None that I remember.

CLINICIAN:   Now in the last three years, have there been other attempts at all? [behavioral incident]

PATIENT:   There have been other thoughts. I don't think there has been anything drastic. [pauses] I remember asking my husband if he would cry if I died. And there have been times where I have just prayed to God that, so that I wouldn't have to commit suicide, if he would give me cancer or something.

CLINICIAN:   Okay.

PATIENT:   Because my family could handle that better than. . . .

CLINICIAN:   The suicide?

PATIENT:   [patient nods head in agreement] Thinking I gave up.

CLINICIAN:   Do you feel, now getting back to the present time, do you feel like giving up? Where are you at?

Not much here, which is good news. No material has surfaced that would suggest Barbara is acutely dangerous. There are no past attempts or gestures. Barbara even implies that there has been little previous suicidal thought. Notice my persistence in probing despite her initial denial of past attempts as shown with my question, "Now in the last three years, have there been other attempts at all?" As mentioned earlier, with regard to suicide, it is a good rule of thumb to always ask at least twice. My inquiry did not uncover much suicidal ideation, but it dug up a curious comment. What are we to make of this statement? "There have been thoughts. I don't think there has been anything drastic. [pauses] I remember asking my husband if he would cry if I died." Puzzling. It is hard to picture Barbara's question *not* appearing surprising and disconcerting to her spouse, for it implies, almost aggressively, that her spouse may not care very much. At the very least such a question would strike many spouses as surprising and, at the worst, it would be off putting. It's the type of comment that a clinician would file in the back of his or her head under the general category of, "Is there some characterological dysfunction here, perhaps of a passive–aggressive nature?" With Barbara, that would prove to be a valid question. Much later in the interview, I discovered that the answer was "Yes." The discovery demonstrated one more advantage of the CASE Approach as a comprehensive strategy for eliciting suicidal ideation. Because suicide is taboo and is a "hot" topic, its discussion can bring to the surface characterological defenses that might otherwise be hidden for much of the interview.

Having finished an exploration of the region of past events, the clinician will now turn to what is arguably the single most important time frame with regard to predicting imminent dangerousness, the present.

## Region 4: Exploration of Immediate Events

This region focuses on the question, "What is this client's current suicidal intent as we speak?" Besides exploring any suicidal ideation that the patient may be experiencing during the interview itself, the clinician inquires whether the patient anticipates thoughts of suicide after he or she leaves the office or the emergency room. The content of this region is most easily remembered as devoted to the time frames of Now/Next.

It cannot be emphasized enough, that if there are continuing concerns about the safety of the patient or the validity of the patient's self-report, corroborative sources are critical. In the case of Barbara our crisis intervention team and our LMS clinicians were in close contact with Barbara's husband. It is important to evaluate such existing support structures and, if need be, design specific interventions and plans for their use.

In this region of the CASE Approach, the task of "cementing" crisis plans is frequently facilitated by asking questions such as, "What would you do later tonight or tomorrow if you began to have suicidal thoughts again?" From the patient's answer, one can often surmise how serious the patient is about ensuring his or her own safety. The answer also provides a chance to brainstorm and finalize plans for just such an occurrence. The clinician asks the patient, point-blank, whether he or she is feeling suicidal at present with questions such as, "Right now, are you having any thoughts about wanting to kill yourself?"

This line of questioning leads the clinician into the mildly controversial realm of "safety contracting." Although some experts wedge themselves solidly in the camp of always using safety contracts ("It makes good forensic sense and may deter the client from acting on suicidal impulse") or solidly in the camp opposing safety contracts ("It's so silly; if a client wants to kill himself, he'll simply lie, so why insult his intelligence?"), I prefer a different tack. People are complicated. Their responses to safety contracting are quite variable. With some people, safety contracting may serve a valuable function. With other people, it may be useless or, even worse, serve as a stage for counterproductive manipulation and theatrical "stand-offs," especially in an emergency room. In the CASE Approach, the clinician is asked to use his or her clinical judgment to determine whether safety contracting is appropriate for a unique individual in a unique set of clinical circumstances. If it is appropriate, use it. If it isn't, don't. One won't always be right, but there will have been an attempt to suit the clinical intervention to the immediate needs of the client, as opposed to following the rigid dictates of a school of thought.

With this philosophy in mind, let's take a closer look at the issues surrounding safety contracting. I feel that it can be a very useful tool with some people, but probably not in the way most clinicians envision it. The single most important thing to remember about safety contracting is that it provides no guarantee of safety whatsoever. I once had a patient overdose two hours after making a safety contract in my office.

Can a safety contract act as a relative deterrent? To my knowledge, conclusive proof one way or the other does not exist. Probably, with certain individuals, safety contracts sometimes can function as deterrents. The more powerful the bond with the clinician and, probably, the more concrete the contract (e.g., a written document), the more powerful the deterrents. It is hard to kill oneself. Anything that makes it even harder may function as a deterrent. Given a sense of long-standing commitment and trust in the therapist, the patient may hesitate to break his or her word. In contrast, the deterrence power of a safety contract made with a first-time client is probably markedly less.

In the realm of litigation, the documenting of a safety contract in the initial assessment may provide some mild forensic support in a lawsuit but not a lot. It might help support that safety was probed in some detail, which might make it harder to prove negligence on the clinician's part. This protection would probably be enhanced by a careful wording of the written record of the use of the contract, using observations that would be of value in defending why the clinician felt the safety contract was a good one. For instance, the clinician might write: "The patient was able to make a sound safety contract with me, showing good eye contact, a genuine affect, a firm handshake, and a natural and unhesitant tone of voice."

If one is meeting the patient for the first time—perhaps in an emergency room—is a safety contract an effective deterrent? In such one-time situations, safety contracting is probably minimally, if at all, effective. Still, if the patient has bonded quickly, as Barbara did with her crisis worker on Friday night and as she was doing with me in my interview, safety contracting may have a very mild deterrent effect. No one knows for sure because no good empirical studies have provided answers to date.

But in my opinion, deterrence is not the main reason for using a safety contract, especially in the context of an initial meeting. The process of negotiating a safety contract is better utilized as an exquisitely sensitive assessment tool. At the time of presenting the safety contract, the interviewer scours the patient's face, body, and tone of voice for any signs of deceit or ambivalence. Here is the proverbial "moment of truth." This juncture of the interview is, potentially, the best window into the patient's true suicidal intent.

A clinician who is purposefully using the process of safety contracting as an assessment tool may completely change his or her mind about releasing a client, because of the client's responses: hesitancy to contract, avoidance of eye contact, or other signs of deceit or ambivalence. The interviewer, trained to notice such nonverbal clues of ambivalence, can simply ask, "It looks like this is sort of hard for you to agree to. What's going on in your mind?" The answer can be benign or concerning.

It is also important to realize that, with certain people, it is best to avoid the whole issue of safety contracting. Some patients with borderline or passive–aggressive characteristics may become embroiled in manipulation around safety contracting issues. Around 2:00 A.M., in a teeming emergency room, this challenge may be tossed back at the clinician: "I don't know what to tell you. I guess I'm safe. On the other hand, I can't see into the future. Do you know anybody who can? I ain't got a crystal ball, you know? So I'm not guaranteeing nothin'. You got a problem with that?"

A decision on whether to ask for a safety contract with a person suffering from severe character disorder is best addressed by directly talking with the client's ongoing treatment team or therapist. As we shall see in the next chapter, the CASE Approach is often markedly altered with such clients. The most effective method for eliciting suicidal ideation in a client with a borderline personality disorder may be strikingly different from the method most useful in a client with mature defenses who is presenting with a panic disorder. And both of these approaches may be different from the method that will prove most useful with an actively psychotic client. The CASE Approach must always be flexibly adapted to meet the unique needs of each client.

A final note on this region is worth mentioning. It is important to explore the client's current level of hopelessness and to know whether the client is making productive plans for the future or is amenable to brainstorming concrete plans for dealing with current problems and stresses. It is critical to see whether the patient is interested in follow-up mental health care and to what degree this interest is genuine.

With these ideas in mind, let's return to our interview with Barbara. At this point, I am feeling that admittance to our crisis group is her best chance for a rapid recovery. Nevertheless, the finalization of the outpatient option is entirely contingent on her responses to my exploration of the region of immediate ideation. Several questions into this new region, I will make a brief sojourn back into the region of the presenting event because I realized that I had not asked her about suicidal ideation over the weekend. Barbara proceeds to misinterpret my question—"Are you having any suicidal thoughts in the past couple of days?"—as a reference to the past week. This unexpected sidetrack turned up a bit of surprising information:

CLINICIAN:   Do you feel, now getting back to the present time, do you feel like giving up? Where are you at?

PATIENT:   I don't know.

CLINICIAN:   Do you feel hopeless at all?

PATIENT:   I feel worthless. [crying]

CLINICIAN:   Do you see any hope?

PATIENT:   I don't know. That's what we're trying this for. [reaches for tissue offered by clinician]

CLINICIAN:   Yea. That's why I'm asking, because, you know, I think if you can have some hope, we can help you to get yourself mobilized and try to deal with some of this stress, and also try to help you to control any suicidal thoughts you might have. Are you having any suicidal thoughts in the past couple of days? [behavioral incident]

PATIENT:   Yea.

CLINICIAN:   I know this is hard to talk about, but you're doing a good job. [said gently]

PATIENT:   Thursday I had a headache for like four days, four or five days. And it just wasn't getting any better, and I just couldn't stand it. And I just thought that if I swallowed up the pills that were in my pocketbook that maybe something, maybe I would die, maybe I would go to sleep and that would be the easy way out.

CLINICIAN:   What stopped you? [behavioral incident]

PATIENT:   I don't know what stopped me.

CLINICIAN:   What other thoughts did you have recently—in the last couple of days? [gentle assumption]

PATIENT:   Just to put the plan in motion and then this [pauses] all hell broke loose.

CLINICIAN:   [clarifying intonation] . . . when you told your friend you were thinking of killing yourself?

PATIENT:   Yea.

CLINICIAN:   You weren't hospitalized, were you? [behavioral incident]

PATIENT:   No. They wanted me to be hospitalized. Dr. Jeffries [primary care physician, called from E.R.] wanted to put me in the hospital on Friday. And then a psychologist from downstairs at the clinic came up and talked to me and then got me into this program, so that this was an alternative to going to 4-Grey [inpatient psychiatry unit].

CLINICIAN:   Good. We like to think this is a good alternative, and it keeps you out of the hospital. I think you will find the group to be very supportive. The therapists are gifted and can maybe help you to turn some of this around.

Barbara's response to my inquiry regarding hopelessness was revealing and, in a strange way, reassuring. She did not endorse "feeling hopeless." Instead, she reported feeling "worthless" and proceeded to cry. I was a bit surprised by the closeness of her pain to the surface, and she was, no doubt, still in a good deal of pain, but her distinction between "hopeless" and "worthless" was important. Granted, feeling worthless is an extremely painful experience, but feeling worthless does not automatically cast a black shadow over the future. Feeling hopeless often does. In the discussion of risk factors, in Chapter 3, the work of Aaron Beck suggests that, over time, hopelessness has a high correlation with attempted suicide.

With Barbara, the possibility for change, implicit in her lack of endorsement of a sense of hopelessness, was given validity by her next comment in reference to the crisis group: "That's why we're trying this for." This was a quiet, yet powerful statement reflecting her safety, for it indicated that Barbara was already making plans for the future. She had decided that she would be in the group—a subtle verification that she was not planning on imminent suicide.

At this point, I used a series of behavioral incidents to reexplore some of her recent suicidal ideation. It was a bit surprising to hear that, in the days immediately before her presentation to the emergency room, she had toyed with the idea of impulsively overdosing on the pills in her purse. The crisis team had not uncovered that information. But this impulsivity appeared to have subsided over the weekend. One clearly received the impression, from Barbara and from her husband, that the immediate suicidal crisis had passed.

At this point I am almost ready to complete the suicide assessment. Two other facts bode well for Barbara's safety. In Chapter 3, on risk factors, I emphasized that one of the keys in the assessment of acute dangerousness is a no-nonsense consideration of the quality of the support available in the local mental health system. In this immediate system, Paul and his talented LMS clinicians offered a reassuring alternative to hospitalization.

The other reassuring fact was that, earlier in my interview, it became apparent that several of the more disturbing risk factors for suicide were missing in Barbara's case. Drinking and substance abuse were not part of the current presentation, there was no history of suicide in the family, and Barbara had no psychotic features. This information confirmed that Barbara lacked the elements of the triad of lethality that would have suggested a need for immediate hospitalization. She was not presenting with a serious suicide attempt, and she did not have any psychotic process. Finally, the CASE Approach had indicated that she was not intending imminent suicide.

Although Barbara had some evidence of low-grade personality dysfunction, she did not give evidence, in the earlier parts of my interview, of having a full blown Axis II disorder such as a borderline personality disorder, nor did she appear to be dramatically manipulative. Consequently, I felt she was a good candidate for utilizing safety contracting as a means of assessment. I was ready to admit her to the LMS group as long as the process of safety contracting did not reveal any hidden hesitancies or ambivalences.

CLINICIAN:   Good. We like to think this is a good alternative, and it keeps you out of the hospital. I think you will find the group to be very supportive. The therapists are gifted and can maybe help you to turn some of this around.

PATIENT:   Good.

CLINICIAN:   Right now, are you having any intentions or thoughts of killing yourself?

PATIENT:   No.

CLINICIAN:   Do I need to be worried or you need to be worried or Paul [the group therapist] that you are going to walk out of here and kill yourself?

PATIENT:   No.

CLINICIAN:   Can you contract with me that you will absolutely promise to talk with us or the crisis team, 24 hours a day, before you would ever try to hurt yourself?

PATIENT:   Yup.

CLINICIAN:   Can you shake on that?

PATIENT:   Okay. [patient shakes]

CLINICIAN:   Okay, can you look me in the eye while we are shaking? [patient smiles and looks clinician in the eye] I take this seriously and that is your responsibility, and I trust you.

PATIENT:   I am. [looks relieved]

CLINICIAN:   You let us know. Our goal is to keep you out of the hospital. And, hopefully, in the group you can get some real help.

PATIENT:   Okay.

CLINICIAN:   I know this has been tough to talk about because suicide is a scary thing and sometimes people feel badly about having thoughts of it. But hopefully you are going to learn that people who can talk about it tend not to do it. It's when you don't talk about it that it becomes more dangerous. So always let us know. [client is showing very good eye contact throughout this area and seems genuinely motivated] There is a huge difference between—and you've already discovered this—between having suicidal thoughts, having them more frequently, planning them, more frequently, more frequently, getting everything together, getting to the point, trying it, before you actually would hurt yourself. We can intervene at any given one of those levels, and that is important to remember.

PATIENT: Okay.

CLINICIAN: Now with all of the intense pain that you have been having, have you begun to drink anymore to help with the pain?

PATIENT: No. I'm not much of a drinker anymore.

The elicitation of suicidal ideation is done. Barbara made a convincing safety contract and truly appeared to be relieved. The CASE Approach had functioned not only as a sound assessment tool but as a means of immediate therapeutic intervention. It was time to go on with the process of gathering further diagnostic and biopsychosocial information, as evidenced by my movement into a more detailed history of her past alcohol use.

With Barbara, we have seen how a clinician gathers the information regarding the client's suicidal ideation and interweaves it with his or her knowledge of the client's risk factors, which was gathered in earlier sections of the interview and from corroborative sources of information. These twin databases are then used as the basis for the actual clinical decision making.

During this assessment process, something else has also been accomplished—something very important. The interviewer has helped the patient to share painful information, which, in many instances, the patient has shouldered alone for too long a time. At a different level, perhaps the thoughtfulness and thoroughness of the questioning as illustrated with the CASE Approach have conveyed the message that a fellow human cares. To a client, such caring may represent the first realization of hope. Such was the case with Barbara.

The sensitive, yet matter-of-fact nature, of the CASE Approach often helps the client feel safe enough to invite the clinician into his or her secretive world of suicidal thought. This invitation does not go out lightly. It is restricted to those who know the language of suicide. And, as Anne Sexton so cogently stated at the beginning of the chapter, the language of suicide is the language of method: gun, knife, carbon monoxide. The CASE Approach is a conduit into this world and a way of becoming fluent with the language spoken there.

## NOTES

1. Sexton, A.: "Wanting to Die" in *The Norton Anthology of Modern Poetry*, edited by R. Ellman and R. O'Clair. New York, W.W. Norton & Company, 1973. p. 1202.

2. Othmer, E. and Othmer, S.C.: *The Clinical Interview Using DSM-IV. Vol. 1: Fundamentals.* Washington, DC, American Psychiatric Press, Inc., 1994.

3. Morrison, J.: *The First Interview: Revised for DSM-IV*, New York, Guilford Press, 1994.

4. Benjamin, A.D.: *The Helping Interview: With Case Illustrations*, Boston, Houghton Mifflin Co., 1990.

5. Sommers-Flanagan, R. and Sommers-Flanagan, J.: *Clinical Interviewing.* New York, John Wiley & Sons, Inc., 1999.

6. Shea, S.C.: *Psychiatric Interviewing: The Art of Understanding, 2nd Edition.* Philadelphia, W.B. Saunders Company, 1998.

7. Shea, S.C., 1998, pp. 98–131.

8. Shea, S.C. and Mezzich, J.E.: Contemporary psychiatric interviewing: New directions for training. *Psychiatry: Interpersonal and Biological Processes* 51: 385–397, 1988.

9. Shea, S.C., Mezzich, J.E., Bohon, S., and Zeiders, A.: A comprehensive and individualized psychiatric interviewing training program. *Academic Psychiatry* 13: 61–72, 1989.

10. Maltsberger, J.T.: *Suicide Risk: The Formulation of Clinical Judgment.* New York, New York University Press, 1986, p. 87.

PART THREE

# PRACTICAL ASSESSMENT OF RISK: FLEXIBLE STRATEGIES AND SOUND FORMULATIONS

CHAPTER 7

# Putting It All Together: Safe and Effective Decision Making

When a doctor tells me that he adheres strictly to this or that
method, I have my doubts about his therapeutic effect . . . I
treat every patient as individually as possible, because the
solution of the problem is always an individual one.

Carl Gustav Jung, M.D.[1]

## INTRODUCTION

NO SUICIDE assessment is identical to any other. Even if the same clinician and client are involved in back-to-back assessments, the second assessment will differ from the first because the act of performing an assessment will change the two people and their relationship. The sharing of intimate material—suicidal ideas, suicidal plans—is an act of trust. The client's willingness to share such ideation now and in the future will hinge directly on the sense of safety the client intuits from the words, gestures, and eyes of the clinician.

Numerous other factors determine the unique characteristics of a suicide assessment: the clinical setting (e.g., psychiatric inpatient unit

191

versus school counselor's office), the familiarity of the clinician with the client (e.g., initial assessment versus ongoing therapy), the possible psychopathology of the patient (e.g., no personality disorder versus borderline personality disorder), and the psychological set of each participant (e.g., the acutely intoxicated client or the exhausted clinician after many nights on call).

To "put it all together," the clinician must understand the interplay of the above factors with the three tasks of any suicide assessment: (1) uncovering risk factors, (2) eliciting suicidal ideation, and (3) arriving at a clinical formulation based on the first two databases. The interviewer's ability to make a sound decision as to whether an individual client can safely leave or must be hospitalized depends on the interviewer's ability to view each suicide assessment as a unique undertaking. The needs of the client and of the clinician, both of which are ultimately shaped by the demands of the clinical environment in which the interview unfolds, are the cocreators of any suicide assessment.

Of the three tasks of suicide assessment, risk factor elicitation is probably the most straightforward. Risk factors are generally of a historical and epidemiologic nature; to gather them, the interviewer is not nearly so dependent on the vicissitudes of the client. In contrast, the most effective style of eliciting suicidal ideation is as variable as the nature and needs of the two participants. Its success is equally dependent on the client's willingness to share and the clinician's skill at fostering this willingness. The type of "slant" used in making a clinical judgment can also vary greatly, depending on such factors as familiarity with the client and the client's characterological structure. Consequently, in this chapter, we will focus on the need to flexibly undertake the second and third tasks of suicide assessment—eliciting suicidal ideation, and arriving at a clinical decision—for they pose the most formidable challenges to the clinician.

We will first focus on the various ways in which an experienced clinician can, and should, flexibly adapt the CASE Approach. Next, a trio of clinical gremlins—inconsistent data, fluctuations in clients' clinical conditions, and erratic social supports—that can interfere with the risk assessment process are described, along with remedies for the errors of overprotectiveness (inappropriate hospitalization) and underprotectiveness (discharge of a client who subsequently attempts suicide) that may result from their presence. Finally, we put everything together by examining seven clinical vignettes that attempt to illustrate all the principles discussed in this book.

No better way exists for learning about the practical performance of difficult suicide assessments than looking at difficult suicide assessments as they play out in the real world of hectic clinics and chaotic emergency rooms. These clinical vignettes are designed to demonstrate the need for flexibility and creativity. Effective clinicians strive to shape their techniques and strategies to the needs of the individual patient. Such was the advice suggested in the opening epigram of this chapter, as wise today as it was nearly fifty years ago, when Jung first wrote it.

## THE ASSESSMENT SETTING: ITS ROLE IN FLEXIBLY ELICITING SUICIDAL IDEATION

*"Toto, I've a feeling we're not in Kansas anymore. . . . "*

Dorothy, in the movie *The Wizard of Oz*

Part of the art of performing sound suicide assessments is "knowing where you are," from a clinical standpoint, when you are doing them. The clinical setting has a distinctive phenomenology, as do the two participants in any suicide assessment. More specifically, sitting in a private office with a well-known patient who has mature defense mechanisms is a different world from sitting in an emergency room with an unknown patient who has a borderline personality disorder. The first situation is Kansas, the second is Oz.

The basic principles of the CASE Approach are equally applicable in all settings. However, depending on the specifics of the clinical situation at hand, there are distinct differences in how these basic principles are most effectively applied. We will begin by delineating a framework that allows us to discuss the unique needs of these varying assessment settings in a practical and concise fashion.

The framework is built on two axes (see Figure 7.1). The first axis, the axis of familiarity, extends from situations in which the clinician is performing an initial interview with an hitherto unknown patient to the opposite extreme, in which the therapist is engaged in ongoing therapy with a well-known client. The second axis, the axis of character pathology, extends from interviews with clients who have few if

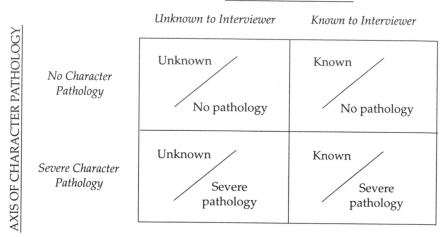

**Figure 7.1**    Matrix of assessment settings.

any severe characterological problems to interviews with clients who are struggling with severe characterological problems. These characterological disorders may include classic disorders such as borderline personality and narcissistic personality, as well as the "acquired personality disorders" often seen with severe substance abuse.

The flexible application of the CASE Approach pivots about the demands of these two axes. By conceptualizing them as forming a two-by-two matrix resulting in four distinct assessment settings, we can more clearly delineate the differences created by their interactions.

To some degree, the four assessment settings are artificial; clients do not always fit them neatly. But the matrix can provide a useful starting point for discussion. Let us begin with two brief examples. The most obvious decision facing a clinician before utilizing the CASE Approach is the extent to which the interviewer should fully explore the four chronological regions described in Chapter 6: (1) presenting events, (2) recent events, (3) past events, and (4) immediate events. For our first example, if one were performing a suicide assessment with a patient who is in ongoing therapy, it would not be necessary to explore past suicidal events, for they should be well known to the clinician by that time. Much of the region of recent events may also be known, thus eliminating the need for its exploration as well. The therapist would, however, explore the regions of presenting suicide events and immediate suicide events exactly as described in Chapter 6.

For our second example, representing a much more complex strategic decision, the clinician must decide how much time should be spent on the direct assessment of suicide events, as outlined in the classic application of the CASE Approach, in contrast to the use of crisis intervention/cognitive therapy techniques in an effort to defuse the suicidal crisis itself. For instance, in ongoing work with a patient with a borderline personality disorder, it is often rather remarkable how well a skilled therapist can help the client to transform the suicide crisis by utilizing cognitive-behavioral techniques. Indeed, much of the "suicide assessment" entails determining how well the patient has responded to these therapeutic maneuvers. In essence, the cognitive therapy has become an integral part of the suicide assessment.

With such patients, a detailed focus on their actual suicidal ideation, as dictated by a full application of the CASE Approach, could lead into a malproductive and manipulative escalation of "suicide talk." Thus, an experienced therapist, working with an ongoing borderline patient, will appropriately modify the CASE Approach. This is the ideal, but the ideal may not be practical. A crisis worker performing an initial assessment on a similar borderline patient who is unknown to the system may or may not be able to utilize the same therapeutic interventions as effectively. In this situation, a standard application of the CASE Approach may prove to be the most effective and reliable method of determining immediate suicide risk. The crisis clinician flexibly makes this decision on an individual basis with each borderline client.

The latter situation—a crisis clinician interviewing a borderline patient who is unknown to him or her—illustrates that a number of other axes can have an impact on the phenomenology of the suicide assessment. For instance, the axis of familiarity is concerned with whether the client is known to the interviewer, but there is also the question of whether the client is known to "the system." If known to the system—the client has a therapist or may frequently visit the emergency room—the crisis worker may be able to utilize the aforementioned cognitive techniques more effectively. This increased effectiveness may come from reviewing the case with the client's therapist or consulting a prospective treatment plan designed by the client and his or her longitudinal treatment team. Sometimes, the therapist may even prefer directly providing the therapeutic intervention by phone. Such pivotal advantages could not be gained with a patient unknown to the system.

Among the other axes that alert a clinician that it may be advantageous to modify use of the CASE Approach are:

1. Presence or absence of psychosis.
2. Indicators of agitation or imminent violence.
3. Ability of patient to provide coherent and valid information.

It is worthwhile to explore some of the strategic implications of these three axes before looking at the ramifications of the four assessment settings delineated by our matrix.

As described in Chapter 3, the presence of psychosis suggests the need for additional questioning. The reader will recall that three areas warrant the clinician's attention with actively psychotic patients: (1) command hallucinations, (2) thoughts or feelings of alien control, and (3) hyperreligious ideation dealing with self-harm, such as self-sacrifice in a Christ-like fashion, or self-mutilation. The next question is: Where should such questioning be placed within the four time frames of the CASE Approach?

Often, the clinician will be able to explore these areas in a naturally unfolding fashion early in the interview, while first exploring psychotic process. If not easily broached at such a point, these explorations can be woven into the CASE questioning itself. This is most effectively accomplished while exploring Region 1 (the presenting suicide events if a presenting suicidal event indeed exists) after imperceptibly guiding the conversation to suicide-related topics that may be affectively charged with psychotic process. Such explorations often dovetail into Region 2 of the CASE Approach—recent suicide events.

Earlier in the following interview, the patient had alluded to voices, perhaps of a command nature, but was cagey about discussing them in any detail at that time. Once within the exploration of the presenting events, the clinician is going to deftly readdress this psychotic process:

PATIENT:  I've thought of different ways of killing myself, including a gun and a knife. I don't know which is better.

CLINICIAN:   Jim, earlier you had mentioned the voices to me and how much they've been increasingly bothersome. Do they ever tell you which is better or suggest other ways?

PATIENT:   Sort of.

CLINICIAN:   What do they say?

PATIENT:   They sort of tell me that I'd better choose a way that works, that I can't afford to fail them.

CLINICIAN:   What do they mean by "fail them?"

PATIENT:   [sighs] I don't know exactly. They just think I let them down. They always call me a no-good fucking failure.

CLINICIAN:   Do they ever tell you to use the gun or the knife?

PATIENT:   [odd smile] They prefer the gun.

CLINICIAN:   What exactly have they told you to do with the gun?

PATIENT:   [patient leans forward and whispers] "Shoot yourself, Idiot. Shoot yourself." [sits back and smiles]

The clinician could just as easily have pivoted into the topic of alien control, instead of command hallucinations: "Jim, earlier you had mentioned that you felt pressured to do things by the demons inside you. I was wondering, do they ever tell you to shoot yourself or use the knife?" With a little creativity, the clinician could even have used the cue statement as a means of raising dangerous hyperreligious ideation: "Jim, you had been saying that you felt that God had plans for you, that you had a destiny of sorts. I'm wondering if you felt that God or Satan wanted you to kill yourself with the gun or the knife?" In all of these instances, one can see how the exploration of suicide-specific psychotic process can be gracefully woven into the exploration of the presenting or recent suicidal ideation.

As the interview proceeds, another problem sometimes facing an interviewer is the growing concern that the client is not capable of providing coherent or valid information. The question then becomes: "How much of the CASE Approach should I do?" With the tight time constraints typical of current clinical practice, one does not want to be wasting time gathering invalid information.

Such conundrums tend to arise with patients suffering from dementias and/or deliriums. But similar problems can also arise with intoxicated patients or with psychotic patients who have a severe problem with loosening of associations or other marked evidence of a formal thought disorder. One important concept to remember is that such patients may be at a higher risk of impulsive or inattentional suicide. Even if they are not making a lot of sense, their nonsensical suicidal babble may provide unexpected evidence of significant risk, especially with delirious patients. For instance, I remember a hospitalized delirial patient on a medical unit who hinted that suicide was imminent. It turned out that he was developing a delusion that hospital staff members were going to torture him during the night. He decided he needed to kill himself in order to prevent the experience of torture, " 'Cause they're gonna kill me anyway, when they're done."

Consequently, with such patients, I tend to carefully explore the presenting events (if present), the recent events, and the immediate events exactly as I would with any other client. One alteration that I make, which may shorten the CASE Approach with these patients, is with the exploration of past events. If I feel that a patient's dementia precludes an accurate rendering of past suicide events, I may enter this region only briefly with the patient and subsequently seek out a more reliable corroborative source, such as a spouse or other family member, for past suicidal history. In clients with severe dementias, there may be a minimal (or essentially no) role for eliciting suicidal ideation, because no meaningful data may be forthcoming.

Another factor that may impinge on the clinician's ability to implement the CASE Approach, especially in emergency room settings, is the possible escalation of the patient toward violence. One should attempt to elicit suicidal ideation with all patients, but if a patient is responding with an escalation of agitated or threatening behaviors, it's time to back off and get safety support. The questions asked should focus on the elicitation of presenting suicidal ideation and immediate suicidal intent. If the patient is to be admitted, the full CASE Approach can be utilized after the patient has arrived on the unit and has had time to calm down. In the emergency room, the team dealing with such an agitated patient will make a concerted effort to carefully interview corroborative sources who may be able to provide pivotal information regarding the patient's immediate suicide potential.

Now that we have looked at some of the generic factors that affect our method of implementing the CASE Approach, let us explore in detail, cell by cell, the strategic implications of the four assessment settings delineated by our matrix.

Assessment Setting 1: Eliciting Suicidal Ideation from a Client Who Is Exhibiting Mature Defenses and Who Is Unknown to the Interviewer

This clinical setting represents one of the most common types of suicide assessment. It appears in a myriad of contexts, including private practices, outpatient clinics, offices of high school and college counselors, emergency rooms, substance abuse clinics, drug rehabilitation centers, and hospital units. Other than the adjustments required by the presence of psychosis, cognitive impairment, or agitation, the CASE Approach can be used without any significant alterations other than those warranted by some idiosyncratic need of the client.

Assessment Setting 2: Eliciting Suicidal Ideation from a Client Who Has a Severe Personality Disorder and Who Is Unknown to the Interviewer

By severe personality disorder we are referring to the following diagnoses: borderline personality, paranoid personality, schizotypal personality disorder, poorly compensated histrionic personality disorder, poorly compensated narcissistic personality disorder, and some variants of antisocial personality disorder. Clients with significant substance abuse may also present with "pseudo-personality disorders," as evidenced by the ongoing presence of severe interpersonal dysfunction similar to the above disorders but acquired as defensive armor secondary to their addictions. A sizable group of people with substance abuse also have comorbid full-blown personality disorders as well. Substance abuse patients who also have these disorders, especially those with borderline, narcissistic, or histrionic personality disorders, often present in crisis. Consequently, these interviews are quite common in emergency rooms, hospital units, and substance abuse centers, but they can occur in any clinical setting, including a school counselor's office.

In some respects, initial assessment of these patients is one of the most challenging tasks a clinician can face. Their presentations are frequently highlighted by a fury of emotion, demanding attitudes, manipulative intentions, and a train of disgruntled friends and support persons, who may have many demands of their own. In short, this presentation is a crisis clinician's bread and butter.

The CASE Approach can bring a level of calmness to this clinical storm. When implemented by a clinician familiar with its nuances, it can provide a sound and reliable framework from which to operate. Clinicians who use the CASE Approach consistently with many patients over a period of years begin to develop a reliable sense of when manipulation is present as opposed to lethal intent.

But, as mentioned earlier, the application of the CASE Approach with these clients comes with a built-in dilemma. Such clients often "up the ante" when questioned directly about suicidal thoughts and plans, as is characteristically done with the CASE Approach. In my opinion, this manipulative process of the client is best looked at as an acquired skill that has probably proven to be a reliable solution for gaining interpersonal and professional support during periods of crisis. It is not so much an act of malice as it is an act of habit. With such patients, we do not want to reinforce this pattern. The clinician is in a bit of a bind, for he or she does not know the patient, but must, at some level, learn about the patient's suicidal planning without fostering suicidal manipulation.

Let's look at this commonly encountered dilemma in more detail. The clinician does not want to positively reinforce manipulative suicide banter by focusing on suicidal ideation, as would be done during a full implementation of the CASE Approach. On the other hand, no clinician can reliably recognize manipulation in a first encounter with an unknown patient, nor be sure that the unknown patient may not impulsively act out if denied his or her wishes. Consequently, the clinician must attempt to gather the best possible database on lethality, a task ready-made for the CASE Approach.

In the worst possible scenario—the client is unknown to the interviewer and to the mental health system, and no corroborative sources are available—the CASE Approach should, in my opinion, be fully utilized. Timely use of the CASE Approach may help to cut through the presenting distortions while providing a framework for determining whether hospitalization is necessary. If aware of the potential for secondary gain, the clinician can frequently minimize it by attempting to de-escalate the client's intense affect via sound crisis intervention before eliciting suicidal ideation. The ability to develop an early alliance, while simultaneously attempting to tone down the immediate crisis via concrete problem solving and solution-focused intervention, can often decrease manipulation and exaggeration during the subsequent CASE Approach interviewing.

In the worst case scenario described above, the clinician has limited options. The client's suicidal ideation will, in the last analysis, have to be taken at face value, for the client is totally unknown to the system. In such a manipulative situation—the unknown client knows exactly what "hot" words to utter to ensure hospitalization—we may have to admit to the hospital despite our gut feeling that admission is not necessary. When such unknown patients are admitted to a hospital unit, the extent of their manipulation around suicidal ideation often becomes quickly apparent on the unit. However, it is sometimes found that the client was truly in a suicidal crisis.

Thus far, in our exploration of this second assessment setting, we have been emphasizing clients who have severe personality dysfunction and are unknown to the interviewer and the mental health system. In an alternate scenario, it is common to find, especially in emergency rooms, that such a client is unknown to the interviewer but well known to the mental health system. A determination of the client's familiarity with the mental health system should be one of the first priorities of a clinician in these assessment situations.

This process can play itself out in the emergency room setting, where it is most often encountered. Three resources are immediately available to the clinician: (1) other emergency room personnel who may know the client, (2) the client's ongoing therapist or case manager, and (3) old records on file. All three resources should be tapped, in my opinion, no matter how late the hour.

Emergency room nurses and staff can provide invaluable insight into the history of a client's presentation. Staff members may be able to volunteer specific information regarding the client's propensity for manipulation, and helpful suggestions for how to transform the ongoing manipulation. They may know of specific social supports who may be able to help stabilize the client or to provide support in an effort to prevent hospitalization. Experienced staff may be able, intuitively, to tell the clinician whether a client who presents with a severe character disorder has the same "feel" as when manipulation was attempted in the past, or whether the presentation feels different this time, suggesting the possibility of imminent danger. Sometimes, a staff person may be particularly adept at helping a specific client transform suicidal crises. It may then be wise to let this person handle the first interaction with the client.

These suggestions reaffirm that emergency room staff are often invaluable and can help to prevent many unnecessary hospitalizations. The initial interviewer should keep one caveat in mind, however: Sometimes, emergency room staff "have had enough" of a particular patient. Secondary to burnout and/or difficult countertransferential feelings, some staff may have a biased attitude toward a specific patient. This attitude, which may emerge in a single staff member or in the majority of the staff, is usually displayed with angry or sarcastic comments about the client. Such anger may lead staff members to unconsciously provide suspect advice. A borderline patient who frequently presents in crisis to the emergency room may then be discharged inappropriately and found later to have completed a suicide, because, "Oh, she always presents like this." Each clinical presentation should be viewed as unique and weighed on its inherent characteristics. Clinical decisions are made easier by knowledge of a patient's past presentations, but they should not be bound by this knowledge.

For an interviewer who is unfamiliar with a borderline client, perhaps the single best resource in the emergency room is the client's therapist and/or case manager. One of the most common mistakes I have seen in an emergency room setting is the hesitancy of the clinician to contact the therapist of a borderline patient because "It's late at night" or "We ought to be able to handle this without bothering the therapist at home." Bother them. Any therapist who works with clients who have severe character disorders should be willing to consult with emergency room staff at any time of the day or night. It goes with the territory.

The power of ongoing therapists to help transform suicidal crises before suicidal action is taken and to prevent unnecessary hospitalizations is formidable. Some therapists, especially those working with the Dialectical Behavior Therapy (DBT) model, prefer talking directly with the client. Many non-DBT therapists prefer to not talk directly with the patient but can provide the crisis clinician with invaluable tips for how to use cognitive/behavioral therapeutic interventions that proved to be effective with the client in the past. As the client recognizes familiar techniques, recalls past successes at transforming crises, and feels the continuity of care provided by the clinician's contact with the therapist, new solutions may appear. The suicidal crisis may abate.

The ongoing therapist can also provide an up-to-date assessment of recent risk factors and stressors, and should be consulted as to his or her opinion on disposition and crisis support planning. It is often very reassuring to a client to know that an appointment can be arranged with the therapist the next day. Such stabilizing information may be the necessary ingredient to prevent hospitalization. As noted earlier, one of the decisions facing a clinician using the CASE Approach is whether to employ safety contracting while exploring the region of immediate ideation. The therapist can provide specific suggestions along with useful input as to whether safety contracting will trigger manipulative "suicide talk" with this particular patient. The goal is to weave the emergency room interventions into the continuity of the ongoing outpatient care. From a forensic standpoint, the clinician's consultation with the therapist adds the bonus of making it difficult to prove negligence on the clinician's part if something should go wrong following disposition.

When consulting with therapists, the clinician should keep in mind some of the same caveats associated with emergency room staff, especially therapist burnout or countertransferential issues. Once again, DBT-trained therapists tend to be ahead of the game; their use of an ongoing weekly consultation group often helps them to minimize such countertransferential problems. But any therapist, on any particular night, can be prone to give a biased opinion, and the interviewer must always keep this possibility in mind.

A therapist and a clinician may disagree on disposition issues, but I have seldom seen this situation in an emergency room setting. Just keep in mind, that the final decision in the emergency room must be made by the clinician doing the emergency room assessment and/or by his or her supervisor. This clinician, alone, is in the best position to intuit dangerousness from the nonverbal indicators that can be assessed only through direct face-to-face interaction with the client. A therapist contacted at home does not have this most important of all databases and, unlike the clinician, is not legally responsible for the final emergency room disposition.

A third resource for a clinician interviewing an unknown client with severe character pathology is the information that can be provided by hospital charts and clinical records. Such records may not be available, especially at night, but if they are available, they are worth a survey. Previous emergency room notes, the last entry written by the therapist, and any initial assessments or discharge summaries are particularly important.

Past manipulative interactions as well as a careful recording of the triggers and the seriousness of previous suicide attempts may be documented. The knowledge gleaned from clinical notes can directly impact the use of the CASE Approach by shortening the need to explore the region of past suicide events, thus giving less material for manipulative suicide banter. The charts are a resource for valid history, which, if contradicted or omitted by the client in the interview, may arouse the clinician's suspicion that the client may not be providing valid information during the current episode.

All of these resources—emergency room staff, the client's therapist or case manager, and previous clinical records—can be utilized to augment the data from the CASE Approach and may point to effective methods of adapting a strategy to cope with difficult patients. The clinical challenges shift yet again as we enter our third assessment setting, which is created by the axes of familiarity and character pathology.

ASSESSMENT SETTING 3: ELICITING SUICIDAL IDEATION
FROM A CLIENT WITH MATURE DEFENSES, DURING THE
COURSE OF ONGOING THERAPY

This clinical setting is one of the more common situations for mental health professionals, substance abuse counselors, and school counselors. We will assume that, in the initial assessment, the clinician performed a well-rounded CASE exploration of all four chronological regions. The dyad has now moved on in the counseling process, and suicidal ideation is appearing or continuing as a problem. How exactly is the CASE Approach to be used in these psychotherapy and counseling sessions?

As mentioned earlier, there is no need to repeat Region 3 (past suicide events) unless, for some reason, the clinician has new doubts about the validity of the information initially obtained. Otherwise, the CASE Approach unfolds in its natural sequencing. If the client has begun to develop suicidal ideation since the last visit, which may have been anywhere from one to four or more weeks ago, explore the presenting ideation exactly as described in Chapter 6. After exploring this information, which will probably cover the past week, the clinician can proceed to explore Region 2 (recent suicide events) back to the last meeting time. (If there are doubts about the validity of material related to the entire previous two months, this time frame should also be fully explored.) Following the completion of Region 2, Region 3 (past events) is skipped, and the clinician proceeds to explore Region 4 (immediate suicide events).

In my opinion, the single most important point to remember in ongoing psychotherapy is to continue to ask about suicide at every session until the therapist feels comfortable that the client is no longer experiencing suicidal ideation. When this point is reached, it is no longer necessary to ask on a weekly basis, but I check back about once a month just to make sure suicidal ideation has not returned. With a consistent use of this approach, clients with mature defenses quickly learn that it is okay to talk about suicide and that the therapist is comfortable with the topic and, indeed, expects to be kept alerted to its presence. This unfolding reciprocity—the therapist's interest in hearing about suicidal ideation, and the client's willingness to share it—provides a wonderful safety net for clients with mature defenses.

One of the hidden traps in doing longitudinal therapy is the fact that a client can become suicidal and still look fine in the sessions. Indeed, some clients, even those with mature defenses, may choose to present a misleading "good face" to the therapist, for they want to come across well to this respected figure whom they trust and would like to please. In a more ominous scenario, some clients may have decided to move toward suicide and do not want to share their plans or give any hint that there is a problem, for fear the therapist will try to intervene. Such secrecy is much harder to "pull off" if the client is directly and routinely asked about suicidal ideation, but it is easy to maintain if the client is never asked about it. The results of not asking are the so-called "unexpected" suicides in ongoing therapy which are often mislabeled as being impulsive when, in reality, they were often simply not detected.

Several other clinical pitfalls are inherent in suicide assessment with patients in ongoing therapy or counseling. The CASE Approach is a wonderful safeguard against each of them. It is easy with a client who seems to be improving to be lulled into the use of opinion-oriented inquiries, as opposed to behavioral incidents, about suicide. These validity-suspect questions may lead to spurious answers. Some opinion-oriented questions arise from an unconscious need on the part of the clinician to find that the suicidal thought is diminishing. A decrease in suicidal thoughts is good for the client and less stressful for the therapist. It is important to make sure that the style of questioning does not bias the client toward responses that are less likely to cause the therapist stress. Opinion-oriented questions may sound like this:

1. "Your suicidal thoughts aren't much of a problem anymore, are they?"
2. "You're still in good control of your suicidal thoughts, right?"
3. "Have your suicidal thoughts gotten better since we last met?"

The first two questions are leading in nature and, in my opinion, counterindicated. They subtly suggest that the clinician is looking for an answer of "Yes," and an overly compliant patient will be only too glad to oblige.

The third question can certainly be asked, but it should be followed with behavioral incidents that pin down the exact amount of suicidal thought as opposed to the client's impressions of frequency or relevance. Effectively worded behavioral incidents could include questions such as: "In the past week, how many days did you have thoughts of suicide, even if fleeting in nature?" and "On your worst day this week, how many times did you think of killing yourself—ten times, twenty times?" This last example shows a symptom amplification tied onto the behavioral incident. In the CASE Approach, the actual nature of the specific suicide methods should be addressed with behavioral incidents ("What ways came to your mind this week?") or a series of denials of the specific ("Did that thought of overdosing come back again?") The use of the CASE Approach ensures that a potentially dangerous mistake—reliance on client opinion as opposed to behavioral inquiry—is avoided.

Another common problem is that therapists in ongoing therapy forget to reaffirm safety contracting. Although there remains debate as to the efficacy of safety contracting, if it is to work, it makes sense that it will work best when it is routinely reinforced. In ongoing work, some clinicians actually like to use written contracts, although I have not found them to be necessary. In my opinion, it is in this assessment setting of our matrix—clients with relatively mature defenses in ongoing therapy—that safety contracting may prove to be most effective as a deterrent to suicide. Moreover, in the CASE Approach it will be recalled that safety contracting is utilized more as an assessment tool than a deterrent. In this population, I am convinced it can be helpful in uncovering dangerous ambivalence, and even movement toward imminent suicide, with a minimum risk of instigating gamesmanship on the client's part. As usual, the safety contracting is done during the exploration of Region 4 (immediate suicide events), where it falls quite naturally.

Perhaps the trickiest problem in this cell of the matrix, most commonly arising in outpatient settings where clinicians tend to see clients "on the hour" and the clients tend not to be in crisis mode, is the tendency to not telephone corroborative sources. This problem often occurs in school counseling offices, mental health clinics, and substance abuse outpatient departments. But it is most troublesome in private practices, where the isolation of the therapist is often most extreme.

In these settings, when a client unexpectedly presents with a crisis with the rapid onset of suicidal ideation and another client is waiting for his or her appointment to start promptly, I find it very easy to forget that it might be best for me to contact a relative or other corroborative source, especially if I sense that my client may be minimizing his or her suicidal intent. Such calls take considerable time but can be invaluable. The outside source may know of much more ominous expressions of suicide than the client has admitted, or may even provide information suggesting the need for commitment. These sources may also be pivotal in providing help with appropriate social support that could help to prevent an unnecessary hospitalization. We will talk much more about contacting corroborative sources, and the complex issues surrounding patient confidentiality, later in the chapter. The bottom line is: If it even crosses your mind that a call to a corroborative source may be of help in determining risk, you should probably make that call.

We can now explore our final assessment setting, where we will find the most extensive changes in the CASE Approach.


## ASSESSMENT SETTING 4: ELICITING SUICIDAL IDEATION DURING ONGOING THERAPY WITH CLIENTS WHO HAVE SEVERE PERSONALITY DISORDERS

For the sake of simplicity, we will use, as our prototype for this discussion, longitudinal psychotherapy with patients coping with a borderline personality disorder. People with borderline process have often found suicidal threats and/or parasuicidal activities, such as self-cutting and self-burning, to be surprisingly effective solutions for reducing intense emotional pain. The secondary gains received via such actions—sympathy and attention from friends, time off from work, excuses for not attending to responsibilities, becoming the focus of acute attention in the emergency room and prolonged attention during hospitalizations—can contribute toward a vicious cycle of suicidal storms. Patients who feel that other people do not care about them can attempt to prove otherwise by presenting in dramatic and affectively charged fashions that may demand responses from significant others. Although maladaptive in the long run, such dramatic presentations provide a useful and effective service in the short run. Many of these patients, especially early in treatment, will have a propensity to "up the ante" when presenting with suicidal ideation.

In ongoing therapy, the clinician helps to transform this vicious cycle by rewarding independent thinking, applied problem-solving skills, and evidence of the patient's efforts to avoid dependency-producing solutions such as hospitalization. As we noted earlier, the potential problem with a full implementation of the CASE Approach during ongoing therapy is that it can exacerbate counterproductive "suicide talk." But when the client is well known to the therapist, there exist tremendous advantages and opportunities for the therapist that would not be available to an interviewer new to the patient. Indeed, helping clients to transform these suicidal crises is one of the major learning laboratories for such clients in ongoing therapy.

There are many ways of approaching these crises. In this section, I will delineate some of the core principles at work during the assessment of the client's dangerousness. The art lies in de-emphasizing the actual assessment of the presenting suicidal ideation and plans, until an attempt has been made to first transform the crisis with cognitive/behavioral techniques that have been well established with the patient beforehand. If the crisis is resolved, there is no need to continue with most of the CASE assessment, and the risk of reinforcing suicidal talk vanishes. If the crisis is not relieved, the clinician can then finish the CASE assessment in an effort to determine the degree of acute dangerousness.

My goal here is to demonstrate how the CASE Approach is modified—indeed, greatly minimized—with such patients. I am not attempting to teach or demonstrate how to perform the cognitive therapy that helps to resolve these crises. Such therapy is tricky; it should not be attempted without extensive training. To learn more about such effective treatment interventions, the interested reader can consult no better source, in my opinion, than the innovative writings of Marsha Linehan.[2]

What basic principles are at work when assessing such patients in ongoing therapy? If the patient presents with newly erupting suicidal ideation, an approach I find to be frequently useful is as follows:

1. Acknowledge the pain (avoid any debates about how serious the suicidal ideation is).
2. Acknowledge that suicidal ideation has appeared.
3. Briefly explore the region of presenting events using the CASE Approach. (This is a rough sketching out of the extent of planning, to note the severity of the suicidal planning and to see whether grounds for commitment are available. This information is needed in case the patient escalates during the attempt at cognitive therapy and tries to leave abruptly, perhaps to impulsively act out the suicidal ideation. Such abrupt disengagement is not common in the hands of skilled therapists, but, even with them, it can happen, especially if the patient has been drinking heavily and consequently cannot respond appropriately to the cognitive work.)

4. The exploration of presenting suicidal ideation is done using behavioral incidents and in a very matter-of-fact manner, making sure not to provide secondary gain via the intensity of the clinician's concern about dangerousness.

5. Remind the patient of his or her method of resolving intense affect and/or suicidal ideation that they have agreed to use when such emotions/thoughts arise. It is often useful to stroke the patient for such successful transformations in the past. There should be no surprises here. The patient is asked to use techniques that he or she has been practicing and that he or she has agreed to use.

6. Have the patient review the steps of the strategy in concrete terms so as to avoid any confusion. This also offers opportunities for providing positive reinforcement for remembering the steps or carrying the slip of paper on which the steps are written.

7. Help the patient to employ the cognitive/behavioral techniques.

8. If the crisis is resolved move on to prospective homework and contingency planning.

9. Enter the region of immediate suicide events, but, in contrast to the classic CASE Approach, enter not so much asking about suicidal ideation/intent but reinforcing that it has already been transformed and that the patient has done an excellent job of handling the crisis.

10. If the patient responds to safety contracting, now is the time to employ it. If they don't, simply reinforce the commitment to the co-designed homework/intervention plan. Do not use safety contracting in patients who escalate or manipulate around its use.

11. If the patient does not respond to the cognitive therapy and continues to escalate, then the clinician can return to the more classic CASE format in an effort to ferret out the degree of dangerousness. Since the patient is well known there will be no need to explore the region of past events.

Using the above principles, let us see how the CASE Approach effectively interfaces with cognitive therapy for transforming suicidal ideation. We will look at a reconstructed intervention by a skilled therapist. The following dialogue is *not* meant to teach or model cognitive therapy, although readers will see such therapy effectively employed in this demonstration of the effective modification of the CASE Approach while performing longitudinal therapy with borderline patients.

The time is 2:30 A.M. on Saturday morning. It is a godforsaken time to be receiving a telephone call from an emergency room. But Meredith, an experienced clinician, is used to it, for she specializes in helping people with borderline personality disorders. The caller, a charge nurse who has built up a great relationship with Meredith over the years, opens the conversation with a quick plea, "Meredith, hi. It's Janet down at the E.R. Sorry to bother you at such an hour, but Mary is down here and she's beating down the doors to get in. You gotta help us. I really don't think it's in her best interest to be admitted. Can you work your magic with her? [pause] Pretty please. I'll owe you big time."

Meredith has been working with Mary for several years, with very good progress. Mary has markedly decreased both the number of her hospitalizations and the number of days during each hospitalization. She has not had a serious suicide attempt in fourteen months. Her self-cutting is minimal. Meredith has helped her to develop a sound cognitive/behavioral approach to handling suicidal ideation, and Mary has successfully utilized it on many occasions. At times, Mary still is prone to suicidal crises, usually precipitated by anger at her on-again/off-again boyfriend. Tonight is one such crisis:

CLINICIAN:   Hi, Mary. It's Meredith. What's up?

MARY:   You got to tell them to let me in here. I can't take it anymore and I'm not kidding around. I'll kill myself if I don't get in tonight. I just can't take it. [starts crying]

CLINICIAN:   Sounds like you're in a huge amount of pain.

MARY:   I am. I'm gonna kill myself.

CLINICIAN:   Sure sounds like you're thinking about it.

MARY:   No. I'm going to do it, if I don't get help. [said testily] I'm not just thinking about it. [upping the ante]

CLINICIAN:   I believe you. [pause] What way have you been thinking about killing yourself? [entrance into the presenting region of the CASE Approach]

MARY:   Same old way.

CLINICIAN:   Overdose?

MARY:   Yea.

CLINICIAN:   Have you been drinking tonight?

MARY:   No.

CLINICIAN:   Great.

MARY:   Yea. I don't need that shit to kill myself. I'm not an alcoholic. I just want to be safe tonight. I'm not gonna start drinking again. That's past history, you know that. [said testily]

CLINICIAN:   Sounds like that's the part of you talking that wants to take care of yourself. That's impressive that you're still feeling that, even though you are in such pain and thinking of killing yourself.

MARY:   Yea. I guess so. [sounds unconvinced]

CLINICIAN:   Did you get any pills out to overdose on? [continuing to matter-of-factly explore the presenting region with behavioral incidents in order to get a quick read on the degree of dangerousness]

MARY:   Sort of. [crying again]

CLINICIAN:   What do you mean when you say "sort of?"

MARY:   I bought a bottle of benadryl and have some old aspirins too. I'm gonna do it. I know I am. [starts crying louder]

CLINICIAN:   Have you taken any of the pills?

MARY:   No. Not yet.

CLINICIAN:   Okay. Sounds like we have our work cut out for us. First off, is there anything I can do to help you stop crying so that we can talk about possible admission? You know, anything I can do to help you get a little bit better control so we can talk better? In fact, why don't you take the three deep breaths like you do in the therapy hours when you want to regain control? [Note how markedly shorter the exploration of the presenting suicide region is in this use of the CASE Approach. Normally, the clinician would begin to walk the patient through the suicidal ideation in detail, creating a verbal videotape. Other methods of suicide would also be explored. But the clinician already has what she wants in this situation: a reading on the severity of the planning. There would even be grounds for commitment, if necessary. Now it's time to see whether Mary can turn the situation around. If she can't transform it, Meredith will return to the topic of suicide later and use a more classic CASE Approach to clarify dangerousness. But the hope is that such an exploration will not be necessary.]

MARY:   [patient takes three deep breaths] I'm all right. I can get it under control. I'm just in so much pain, Meredith. [crying lessens]

CLINICIAN:   Well, you sound in better control. Nice job. You know, over the past six months, I've noticed that you've really been able to control your crying much better. Even when you're in tremendous pain, like tonight. I find that really impressive.

MARY:   Thanks.

CLINICIAN:   Let's get right to work. If we got to hospitalize you, we got to hospitalize you. [The therapist is wisely not pitching a battle over hospitalization even though she doubts it is necessary and is going to try to avoid it.] Let's see where you are at. [pause] Obviously, I don't have my notes in front of me, so help me out here. What's the first step in your plan for transforming suicidal thoughts?

MARY:   Can't you just tell them to let me in here?

CLINICIAN:   I don't recall that being the first step. [said with humor]

MARY:   Very funny, Meredith. [said with a gentler tone—her intensity is decreasing]

CLINICIAN:   Hey, I'm not backtracking on our agreement. And I respect you too much, and the hard work you've done the past two years, to not follow through. We made an agreement that you would always use your therapy techniques before we ever consider hospitalization. And I'm going to hold you to that because I trust you. You know that. [Notice that the contract that is being emphasized here is not a safety contract but the client's contract, made much earlier in therapy, that she will agree to work toward solutions and improved management of her affective storms.]

MARY:   Yada, yada, yada. [pause] Okay, but I still want in. [tone of voice is definitely calmer. Meredith is on the right track and can feel the crisis shifting.]

CLINICIAN:   What's the first step again? Do you have your urge control list?

MARY:   Yea. I got it in my purse. I'll get it. [returns] I know this by heart anyway, almost.

CLINICIAN:   Great.

MARY:   [sighs] If I get the urge to hurt myself or kill myself, I'm always supposed to ask myself who or what am I mad at?

CLINICIAN:   And what's the answer to that question tonight?

MARY:   Oh. Jerkhead.

CLINICIAN:   You mean, Don?

MARY:   Who else.

CLINICIAN:   What did he do tonight?

MARY:   He stood me up. Can you believe it?

CLINICIAN:   Well, actually I can. Hasn't he done that before on several occasions?

MARY:   Yea.

CLINICIAN:   In fact, if I'm recalling right, about a year ago he did that and it really hurt a lot. I think you were feeling suicidal that night. Do you remember it? It was back in the summer.

MARY:   Oh yea. I remember it all right.

CLINICIAN:   You did a nice job of transforming your anger away from yourself that night. How did you do that? Had you developed your urge control list by then?

MARY:   Yea. That was one of the times we first used it.

CLINICIAN:   Well, you've done a nice job creating that list. It's one of the best that I've seen. [pause] Let's put it to work again. What's the second step?

MARY:   I'm supposed to remind myself that: "I'm a good person. I can't always stop people from being mean. But I'm not going to let their behavior make me hurt myself. I'm not the problem here."

CLINICIAN:   Good. Help me to understand what that means to you, because I know it's important to you.

MARY:   I don't know. [pause] I guess it means, "Don't let the assholes get to you."

CLINICIAN:   You got a way with words, Mary. [they both chuckle] Do you believe that?

MARY:   Yea. Yes I do.

CLINICIAN:   Did you stand Don up tonight?

MARY:   No!

CLINICIAN:   When you think it through using your list, does it make sense to you that you should hurt yourself because Don did something stupid again?

MARY:   Not really. But I'm really sick of his shit.

CLINICIAN:   You know, I'm glad to hear you say that. That statement is something important you have come upon. Because in the past it was hard for you to admit that. I think we should talk about what you can do about his behavior in our next session and to what degree you want to tolerate it. It would be very valuable. We're learning something here tonight. You're starting to look out more for yourself. That's good. I'm not sure, but I think you're starting to transform your pain, just exactly the way we designed your plan. Now what's the third step again?

MARY: Well, I'm supposed to remind myself that I've developed some better ways of releasing my anger than turning it on myself.

CLINICIAN: Yea, I remember that step. Aren't the next steps some specific ways?

MARY: Yea.

CLINICIAN: What's the next one?

MARY: I'm supposed to listen to my favorite piece of music.

CLINICIAN: Which is . . . ?

MARY: It's a Bach CD.

CLINICIAN: Have you gotten a chance to try that yet?

MARY: No, not really.

CLINICIAN: Good. There's one thing you haven't tried yet that often helps. What's next?

MARY: Oh, this one I really like. [sounding more positive and involved] I'm supposed to take a warm shower for ten or twenty minutes.

CLINICIAN: Have you tried that?

MARY: No.

CLINICIAN: Good. You got something else to try. Sounds like a nice one. Do you think you'll need ten minutes or twenty minutes? [conveying control to the client via choice]

MARY: Oh. I'd need the twenty tonight, that I can tell you.

CLINICIAN: Good choice. You know, Mary, I know that going to the E.R. is always an ultimate option for you when you are transforming your suicidal thoughts, but I remember it being the last solution on the list. I know from working with you that sometimes the anger comes on so quickly and intensely that it's understandable to drop down to the last step before trying all of the other steps first. But, you know, it's a good list. Let's see if it can help get rid of the pain tonight. Because that's what we want. If we can get rid of the pain without the hospital, then so much the better. You've made excellent progress with that these past two years.

MARY:    Are you going to try to convince me that I don't need to be admitted?

CLINICIAN:    No. [pause] I'm asking you to find out if you need to be admitted by trying the urge control techniques you've worked so hard to create over the past two years. If you find after trying them, you still need to come in, then we need to bring you in. [pause] Here's what I'd like to do. When we get off the phone, I want you to start with your list and really give it a good effort. It's actually a fun list. Listening to Bach. Hot showers. Sounds pretty good to me. Give it your best shot. I can squeeze you in for an appointment at 10:00 A.M. tomorrow, and we'll review the progress. If you still need to come into the hospital, we'll bring you in. [pause] Deal?

MARY:    Yea. I think I can do that. You'll bring me in if I need it? No hassles?

CLINICIAN:    No hassles. [pause] It would have to be a short stay, of course.

MARY:    Oh yea. I know that. I don't like staying in the hospital a long time anymore.

CLINICIAN:    Maybe we'll need to bring you in, maybe you need that. [gentle paradox]

MARY:    Well. I might not. We'll just have to see.

CLINICIAN:    Oh yea, I just remembered something. You remember our agreement about what to do if you buy any pills with the thought of hurting yourself, so you need to flush those out tonight as soon as you get off the phone. [This foray represents a brief entrance into the region of immediate suicide events, the region in which contingency planning is traditionally done in the CASE Approach.]

MARY:    Oh yea. Right. That's not a problem.

CLINICIAN:    You know, you should be proud of what you're doing tonight. You're really turning this around.

MARY:    Yea. I feel a little better, but I still might need to come in.

CLINICIAN:    We learned some important stuff tonight. Tomorrow we'll brainstorm on how to get that urge control list out before your anger takes off too fast. I bet we come up with some good ideas.

MARY:    Yea, okay.

CLINICIAN:    So just review for me the plan for tonight, to make sure I was clear.

MARY:   I'm gonna get off the phone and get rid of the pills. Then I'm going to work on the list. And tomorrow we'll see how it went. If I still feel a need tomorrow to come into the hospital, we'll do a brief stay.

CLINICIAN:   Are you comfortable with that agreement?

MARY:   Yea. I'm comfortable with it.

CLINICIAN:   You know what? I'm quietly hopeful it's going to work for you, because I already see some lessening of the pain. You're using the techniques well already. If you need to give me a call later tonight about making one of the techniques more effective, feel free to do so. But I don't think that will be necessary. [pause] Any last questions?

MARY:   No. I think I'm set. [pause] Janet is sure gonna be surprised.

CLINICIAN:   How do you mean?

MARY:   Oh, she thought I was out of control. She thought I was going to try to force my way in. [sort of chuckles]

CLINICIAN:   Well, that didn't prove to be true. It's always fun to give Janet a pleasant surprise. [they both chuckle] See you in the morning. Could you please put Janet back on?

MARY:   Yep. Thanks. See ya.


Meredith has earned her pay tonight. We have seen a therapist deftly help a client to transform a suicidal crisis while potentially avoiding hospitalization. In such instances, the CASE Approach is flexibly altered to minimize escalation or secondary gain for "suicide talk." The clinician is well aware of when she is doing assessment work with the CASE Approach and when she is doing intervention with cognitive therapy. What is interesting is the fashion in which the cognitive therapy has become an integral part of the overall assessment. In essence, the interviewer is assessing the impact of the therapy as the key component as to whether the client is imminently dangerous.

Meredith has learned from experience that, with this particular patient, it would have been a mistake to try a safety contract. In the past, such safety contracting has sometimes undercut the hard-earned transformation of the suicidal crisis that had already been achieved with the cognitive therapy. In such instances, Mary has rapidly focused on her inability to predict the future with the result that the crisis was rekindled and unnecessary hospitalizations have resulted. In contrast, Meredith chose to focus on an agreement to "do the therapy" and to meet with Mary the next day. Mary's agreement to do this work and "be around" to discuss it tomorrow is, in reality, an indication of her safety without needing to resort to a safety contract per se: an area ripe for prompting a patient to over-focus on "suicide talk."

Sometimes, an emergency room clinician or crisis clinician can also use similar techniques with a client they've seen before in crisis, especially if a well-written prospective treatment plan has been co-designed and agreed on by the client, the therapist, and the emergency room staff. Such prospective treatment planning is often pivotal in helping such clients to avoid unnecessary hospitalizations. If Mary had continued to escalate, then Meredith would have used whatever aspects of the CASE Approach she felt were of use in clarifying Mary's immediate risk.

We have now seen methods of modifying the CASE Approach with clients presenting in all four of the assessment settings created by the axes of familiarity and character pathology. As suggested by Carl Gustav Jung in the epigram of this chapter, flexibility is the key to success. Thus far in this discussion, we have focused on the need to modify the actual method of eliciting suicidal ideation in each cell, and the potential impact of these modifications on the subsequent risk formulation. We will now take a look at three factors that can greatly complicate the actual process of the risk formulation itself.

## CLINICAL GREMLINS THAT COMPLICATE RISK ASSESSMENT

### GREMLIN 1: INCONSISTENT DATA—TREACHEROUS WATERS

We have already seen that a client could have many of the risk factors for suicide but not be imminently dangerous. But if a client has a large number of risk factors yet denies any thoughts about suicide, such an inconsistency between risk factors and reported ideation may signal that the client is hiding information.

This situation is more likely if the client tersely or angrily denies current suicidal thought or curtly insists that suicide has never even crossed his or her mind. A total lack of suicidal ideation in clients riddled with risk factors is not the norm. Most of these clients will have had at least fleeting thoughts of suicide. In contrast to such terse denials voiced by clients purposely withholding suicidal ideations, clients who are merely hesitant to share their suicidal ideation will often nondefensively admit to such fleeting thoughts but will add something like, "Oh, I would never do it." Moreover, a patient who is actively contemplating suicide and hiding it may be cagey about discussing suicidal ideation and/or angry if probed. The discrepancy between numerous risk factors and a blanket denial of any suicidal thought may suggest the need to contact corroborative sources.

There are many other traps waiting for the unwary clinician that are betrayed by the presence of inconsistent data, especially during emergency room assessments. Always review past records if they are available. Be on the lookout for discrepancies between the client's reporting of past suicidal history and the written records of past suicidal activity. Inconsistencies here may be a red flag that the client is not providing valid data. Benign memory lapses or a desire not to "get into that stuff again" may be the cause. At other moments, the response may suggest deceit. For instance, a patient who is seeking inappropriate hospitalization or drugs may emphasize current suicidal thought but will not want to bring up previous E.R. visits during which his or her ulterior motives may have been exposed. A telephone call, with the client's permission, to other emergency rooms where the client has presented may be enlightening regarding evidence of malingering in the client's case history.

To clarify the nature of such discrepancies, I have often found it useful to ask questions such as, "You know, Jim, I was just reviewing your chart, and it looks like you were seen in the E.R. for suicidal ideation about two years ago. When we were talking about past suicidal thoughts, you didn't mention that. Do you remember what was going on that night?"

This tack does not provoke confrontation, but it puts the patient on notice that the clinician is resourceful enough to check old records for consistency and wily enough to note discrepancies. As the patient then describes the incident in question, it is often easy to spot deception or to note that the patient responds emotionally as if caught in the act of lying, which suggests that fabrication was indeed attempted. If at all possible, review the chart before interviewing the client.

Another common problem, especially in emergency rooms, is the client's story changing over time. This is particularly apt to occur with someone who was not the first interviewer or was not present when the client was first brought into the emergency room. A changed story is common when the clinician is the "Doc On Call" and the client has already been seen by a nurse or crisis clinician. As the client begins to realize that he or she could be hospitalized, perhaps even involuntarily, a cure suddenly occurs and no suicidal ideation was ever present: "Oh, I never said that" or "I don't feel that way anymore." Talk at length and in detail with anyone who brought the client into the emergency room or performed a previous assessment that night. If, because of a shift change in a backed-up emergency room, the initial evaluator went home, I recommend calling the clinician at home. Do not rely solely on the clinical note left in the patient's file.

If a patient has been transferred from another emergency room or you are part of an admitting team for a patient transferred to your facility for hospitalization, it is best to call and speak directly to the referring clinician. Transfer notes are often incomplete or sketchy. A client who was sharing valid suicidal ideation suggestive of real risk at the referring emergency room may suddenly decide to look better. He or she may have decided that hospitalization is not to his or her liking or that hospitalization will prevent a well planned attempt at suicide. I have actually had patients with presenting suicide gestures at a different emergency room deny them upon presentation for admission to our facility.

If a patient is delivered by police, someone at the receiving center should carefully interview the escorting officers. It is not at all uncommon for a patient, especially one who is acutely intoxicated, to completely change his or her story after arriving at the emergency room. In his or her home, the patient, perhaps with pill bottles in hand, may have clearly told the police that he or she was going to commit suicide. Within the emergency room, such actions are sometimes angrily denied. The only way to get the whole picture is to speak with the police. Always get a telephone number where the police officer can be reached if things get messy in the next couple of hours, and ask whether the officer is willing to petition for involuntary commitment if necessary to protect the patient.

A client's show of inconsistencies during the assessment should spark consideration of contacting corroborative sources such as family members or friends. One must ask the patient's permission for such contacts, but, as mentioned earlier, if there is genuine concern about dangerousness, corroborative sources should be contacted against the patient's will, for the patient's safety has a higher priority than confidentiality. If one needs to forgo confidentiality, it is often best to have consulted a supervisor first and then carefully record in the chart why both you and the consultant have deemed it necessary to break confidentiality. Such documentation may look like the following:

> Mr. Jackson, in his acutely intoxicated state, is denying any suicidal statements to the police. This is in direct contradiction to Officer Timothy Flint, who reported that the patient adamantly said he was going to shoot himself and he knew where to get a gun. The officer reports that the patient has a live-in girlfriend who may know more about any recent suicidal ideation. The patient has refused permission for us to contact his girlfriend. I have discussed this situation with Mary Fowler, the charge nurse, and with Dr. Jason, the on-call physician. We are all in agreement that, in order to get the needed facts to avoid unnecessary hospitalization or to determine that hospitalization is so critical for safety that involuntary commitment is indicated, we must override confidentiality and attempt to contact the patient's girlfriend. We have major concerns that he may be acutely suicidal.

Once this decision is made, I will generally tell the patient that we are going to override his or her refusal, and why. Frequently, at this point, the patient says something like, "Oh, go ahead and call her. You might as well get her involved, she's the problem anyway." If the patient is acutely agitated and I fear that a serious violent acting-out is likely if told about the override of confidentiality, I may opt to contact the corroborative source without telling the patient immediately and will carefully note on the chart why this is being done, after once again consulting with my supervisor.

When the corroborative source is called, be on the lookout for any inconsistencies between the client's report and the report of the corroborative source. Take the time needed to carefully engage the family member or friend before inquiring about the client's suicidal ideation, for such engagement can markedly increase the likelihood of receiving valid data from the corroborative source. Once the corroborative source is engaged the clinician explores the four regions of the CASE Approach asking questions about the client's presenting, recent, and past suicidal ideation. Even the region of immediate ideation is explored with the corroborative source with questions like:

1. "The last time you saw Jim, did he say anything about suicide— even if just a hint?"

2. "Did he express any comments about feeling hopeless or having no way out?"
3. "I know this is just your opinion, but your opinion is very important: "How dangerous do you think Jim is right now?"

Answers to these questions can be pivotal in uncovering critical evidence of imminent suicide. The interview with the corroborative source should employ all of the validity techniques and principles described earlier for using the CASE Approach with a patient. For instance, instead of asking, "Has Jim mentioned any other ways of killing himself?" the clinician might employ gentle assumption: "What other ways of killing himself has Jim mentioned?"

GREMLIN 2: FLUCTUATIONS IN THE CLIENT'S CLINICAL CONDITION—
UNEXPECTED STORMS

Psychopathological processes may run a fluctuating clinical course that is often related to the biochemical vicissitudes of the brain. Some psychotic processes, such as those seen in major depression, bipolar disorder, schizoaffective disorder, and schizophrenia, wax and wane. Delirial states are notorious for such fluctuations. At other times, it is the vicissitudes of the patient's self-control that can also precipitate unexpected clinical changes, as with acute intoxication secondary to alcohol or street drugs. In all of these cases, if suicidal ideation is caused by the underlying actions of these conditions, it too may fluctuate over time. Errors in clinical judgment ensue when the clinician is trapped by the immediate presentation of the client and assumes that "what you see is what you get."

Stated differently, the clinician must remember that the patient's imminent dangerousness is, in part, related to whether these state-dependent processes may reappear in the hours or days directly following the interview. As an example, a patient's command hallucinations may only manifest during peak periods of psychotic agitation or mania. During the interview, the patient may not be in such a peak period and may deny command hallucinations or report being in good control of them. Ten hours later, during an acute exacerbation of psychotic process or perhaps after several beers, the picture may be quite different. When weighing such a patient's dangerousness, one must make an educated guess as to what the future course will look like.

Because one of the best predictors may be the patient's history over the past two or so weeks, it is important to track the patient's recent history of the present illness. On several occasions, I have witnessed assessment clinicians being lulled into a false sense of a psychotic patient's safety because the patient did not appear psychotic in the interview. Some patients with psychotic process can "put it together" remarkably well, especially if faced with the prospect of referral for longitudinal outpatient care, potential voluntary hospitalization, or involuntary commitment.

Being aware of this trap is the first step in avoiding it. The second step is to carefully ask the patient to describe the most recent fluctuations in his or her symptom picture. The third, and often the most reliable, step is to speak with corroborative sources, such as family members.

It is not at all uncommon to hear a mother describe how a son with schizophrenia became agitated, talked to himself (hallucinating), screamed, or threatened suicide or violence late at night in the tormented confines of his or her bedroom, and to see the same son calm and cooperative during an interview at 1:00 P.M. It is critical to weigh the input of such corroborative sources very carefully often placing more weight on their report than on the client's self-report or appearance. Nothing is more frustrating to family members than having their concerns about the patient's safety or deterioration ignored because the clinician thinks the patient "looks fine now." In rare instances, a family member may be distorting the seriousness of the client's condition for malicious reasons, but I have seldom found this to be the case. Still, the clinician must keep such a possibility in mind.

Delirium is another complication for the assessment of suicide potential. By definition, deliriums fluctuate in intensity; often, they worsen markedly at night, a process known as "sundowning." Accompanying suicidal ideation may also fluctuate. When evaluating delirial patients on a medical ward during consultation, be sure to read the night nurse's notes carefully. Surprises may be waiting there. Also be sure to listen to nurses' concerns about erratic behavior suggestive of delirium, even though a patient looks fine to you now and may currently have a totally normal cognitive exam. This same patient may be delirial later at night. It is imperative to perform the appropriate lab tests and physical exam on such patients, to help determine the etiology of the delirial process so that appropriate treatment can be started.

I have seen clinicians delay an indicated delirial workup because, during morning rounds, "The patient looks great to me. There is absolutely no evidence of confusion that I can see, and I did a thorough cognitive exam." This trap is particularly easy for clinicians to fall into if the patient is intelligent and witty. During morning rounds, such patients may be engaging and enjoyable to chat with. At night, they may be frankly or subtly delirious, and the delirium may trigger dangerous suicidal ideation. The bottom line: Listen to the nurses. They know of what they speak.

We have been discussing situations in which the clinician mistakes a client as being safe when the client may be dangerous in the long run. The opposite can also be true, particularly with acutely intoxicated patients. During presentation to the emergency room, such patients may be voicing many suicidal concerns. At such times they should be listened to carefully, and hospitalization for observation may be in order, even though a "fried" emergency room staff may wish to turn away such patients to satisfy their own countertransference anger. As the alcohol wears off and impulsive urges recede, these patients may truly be safe again. This is a situation where the change in clinical condition has actually resulted in a situation in which the patient's immediate suicide potential may be suddenly much less now that he or she is in a nonintoxicated state.

With these patients, the presence of social supports and their own motivation to participate in appropriate substance abuse counseling can play major roles in determining their safety for discharge from the inpatient unit the next morning. Curiously, their social supports themselves may fluctuate over time—a situation well worth attention, for it can dramatically impact the decision as to whether a patient can safely be sent home.

## Gremlin 3: Social Supports—Safe versus Hostile Ports at Sea

As mentioned in Chapter 2, one of the cornerstones of performing a sound suicide assessment is an evaluation of the interpersonal matrix in which the patient is developing his or her suicidal ideation. Attention to the interpersonal milieu is of extreme importance not only in emergency room assessments but also in outpatient clinics and school counselors' offices. In outpatient settings, it is easy to overlook the importance of such evaluations because the clients often present alone without the presence of significant others.

In my opinion, all clients undergoing a suicide assessment should be asked about their interpersonal supports, attachments, and stresses. Particular attention should be given to romantic attachments and to anyone who is living with the client and to whom the client will be returning after the interview. If there are concerns about the safety of the client or the validity of the client's reporting on suicidal intent, a direct conversation with the client's significant other should be initiated by phone or in person, after receiving the client's consent. We have already mentioned the situations in which this contact would be made without the client's consent.

Here are some of the reasons for contacting corroborative sources such as family members and friends:

1. They may provide different, and potentially more valid, information on the patient's recent suicidal ideation and past psychiatric history.
2. They may know of extenuating circumstances, such as interpersonal stresses or substance abuse problems, that could directly impinge on the patient's safety. Out of shame or lack of insight, the patient may have omitted mention of these stressors.
3. They may be able to provide ongoing support that could allow the patient to avoid hospitalization.
4. They may be a resource for helping the patient to monitor and share his or her suicidal ideation.
5. They may have misinformation or prejudices about the patient's illness or suicidal ideation that can be transformed through psychoeducation from the clinician.
6. They may be extremely stressed by the disruptions associated with the patient's severe mental disorder (such as schizophrenia or bipolar disorder), and the clinician may be able to provide immediate support and avenues for future support, such as referral to the local chapter of the National Alliance for the Mentally Ill (NAMI). Keep in mind that sometimes family members also have severe reactive depressions having been worn down by the ravages of the illnesses in their spouses or children. They may

benefit from mental health referral. Occasionally we have uncovered suicidal ideation in family members, while doing our corroborative interviews, and have been able to provide prompt support and intervention.

7. They may be actively antagonistic toward the client, and their presence may represent a severely toxic interpersonal environment. Hospitalization or referral of the patient to a shelter may be indicated as an alternative to returning to the home environment.

Especially in emergency room settings, the final determination as to whether it is safe to send a patient home may rest on the clinician's assessment of the family milieu. In a meeting with the family, at which the client is present, the clinician can assess the degree of support the family can provide and the level of comfort, within the family, toward the idea of the patient's returning home that night.

Before meeting with the family, it is valuable to lay a sound and reassuring groundwork with the client. First, it is important to let the client know specifically why it may be of value to share some of his or her suicidal ideation with a significant other—for example, it increases the sense of trust shared with the significant other, eliminates the burden of bearing the thoughts alone, communicates to the significant other the degree of pain that is present, and encourages creation of a safe environment that is an alternative to hospitalization. Second, the client's answers to the following questions can be of help in determining what direction to take in the subsequent family meeting, while ensuring that the client is comfortable with the meeting's purpose and topics. It must be remembered that the discussion of suicidal ideation has been taboo in the families of most clients. For the sake of illustration, let us imagine that we are about to meet with a client's spouse. Before such a meeting the clinician might ask the client all or some of the following questions:

1. "Have you shared any of your suicidal ideation with your wife?"
2. "What made you hesitant to share those thoughts with your wife?"
3. "How do you think she will react if we decide to share your suicidal thoughts with her?"

[The answers to these three questions may suggest that it would be counterproductive to share the ideation with the spouse, necessitating a change in plans for such sharing.]

4. "Do you think she will be surprised?"
5. "How much of your suicidal thought do you feel comfortable sharing with her?"
6. "Would you be able to agree to have her ask about your suicidal thought over the weekend, before your appointment at our center on Monday?"
7. "If we decide that she can ask, how would you like her to ask so that you feel most comfortable?" (The clinician can simply wait for an answer after this open-ended inquiry, or, if the clinician feels a suggestion would make the client more comfortable, he or she might suggest: "For instance, would it be okay for her—once a day, say at night—to ask something like 'How did it go today, Jim? Did you have any of the suicidal thoughts we talked about last night?'")

If time permits, it is sometimes useful to meet with the family member or members alone first without the client present, to ensure engagement with them, to apprise them of the situation, and to prospectively de-escalate any responses from them that may be counterproductive with the client. During the client–family meeting, the clinician should facilitate open discussion and productive, matter-of-fact brainstorming. Concrete plans can be devised and discussed for helping the client navigate the time until his or her next appointment with a mental health professional. Keep in mind that you are asking this dyad or family unit to change a well-engrained taboo. A genuineness in the clinician and a well-timed sense of humor can often expedite this process. This reconstruction of dialogue may be of value as a model:

CLINICIAN: [addressing spouse] Jim trusts you immensely and wants to be able to share such thoughts if they arise, but he was afraid they'd be too upsetting.

SPOUSE: Oh, nonsense. [turning to her husband] I'm the person you *should* share this with. I adore you. [smiles, and Jim smiles] My gosh.

CLINICIAN:   [turning to Jim] Looks like a pretty open invitation to me, Jim. [smiles] She's not quite as fragile as you thought. [said with gentle humor in reference to Jim's earlier stated fears of what would happen if he shared his suicidal thoughts with his wife]

JIM:   [smiling] Yea. I guess not.

CLINICIAN:   In any case, [turning to wife] Jim wants you to ask him quite openly tomorrow whether he is having any suicidal thoughts, if you are at all concerned about how he looks. Do you think you can do that?

SPOUSE:   Absolutely. And [to Jim] I'll haul your butt down here if there's any problems. [both chuckle; Jim gives a sigh of relief]

CLINICIAN:   Jim, for your part, earlier you promised me that you would raise any suicidal thoughts (if they return tomorrow) with Mary. Can you still do that?

JIM:   Definitely. [pause] I don't think they're going to come back, but I'll share them if they do. I feel a lot better now.

CLINICIAN:   Great. Can you both make this agreement with each other? [both nod] Okay. Can you both shake on it? [both nod and then shake] Great. Why don't we wrap this up with a hug. You two look like you could use a good hug from each other. [they hug each other and begin to cry]

SPOUSE:   [to Jim] I love you so much. Everything will be all right.

JIM:   I love you too.

Throughout this process, the clinician is continuing his or her astute assessment, noting how well the two are communicating and relating. If friction had erupted, the clinician might have decided against the safety of returning Jim home. As the process unfolded with this couple, the clinician saw the opportunity to make further therapeutic interventions—for example, encouraging the couple to hug.

One final trap to avoid is the situation where interpersonal support might abruptly change. This can occur if the spouse or other support person has a drinking or substance abuse problem, is not responsible, is abusive, or is just putting on a front while the clinician is present. These possibilities can be explored with the client beforehand. A spin-off problem arises if there is someone else at home who may have a very different response to the client's return. Inquiries about *all* the people living at home should be a standard part of the assessment and will alert the clinician to the possibilities of this trap.

Thus far in this chapter we have reviewed the numerous complexities arising from the four assessment settings created by the axes of familiarity and character pathology, and the three common gremlins that can lead to faulty formulation by the clinician. Let us see how all of this fits together in actual clinical practice.

---

## SEVEN SUICIDE ASSESSMENT VIGNETTES

### CLINICAL VIGNETTE 1
### Student Presenting at a College Guidance Center

#### Primary Database

Jeremy Henderson presented for an initial session pretty much like most college freshmen who are feeling distressed. He complained of grade problems, indecision about his major, fears of letting his parents down, and social isolation. He had been a big fish in a little pond in high school, and he was now attending a major private university near where he lived. Although quite small for his age, he had rakish good looks, a winning smile, and a boyish charm. Because he was valedictorian of his high school class, it was assumed he was ready for the big leagues. He wasn't.

On his first two English Comp 101 papers, he received Ds. And Jeremy quickly discovered that calculus was not a pushover when everybody in the room had been a straight-A student in high school and university grading was done on a curve. When his father asked how things were going, Jeremy commented, with feigned assurance, "Just great, Dad. Everything is just great." He was painfully missing home, but did not dare return there for the weekends, for fear of being "found out." Instead, Jeremy was spending the weekends with his older sister, who lived nearby.

Upon interview, he acknowledged many persistent neurovegetative symptoms of depression. In fact, he met the criteria for a major depression, a fact that concerned the counselor. The CASE elicitation revealed that some suicidal plans had been contemplated, including overdosing and shooting, but Jeremy said that no actions had been taken. He denied any history of past suicidal ideation, and he knew of no fellow students who had attempted suicide. At one point, Jeremy broke down into tears and said: "I can't believe I'm a failure. I just can't believe it. What is everybody going to say?" During the exploration of immediate suicide ideation, he admitted to intense hopelessness. He made a hesitant safety contract. The hesitancy toward the safety contract bothered the school counselor, as did the fact that Jeremy refused referral to the consulting psychiatrist.

### Secondary Database, Formulation, and Disposition

Although the time allotted for the session was nearing an end, the counselor felt ill at ease with the original disposition plans. Jeremy's situational stresses and his interpretation of himself as a failure were striking, as was his sense of hopelessness. Coupled with the presence of serious symptoms consistent with a major depression, nonverbal clues during the process of safety contracting that were suggestive of deep ambivalence, and his refusal to follow up with psychiatric referral, the counselor felt that hospitalization might be in order. Unfortunately, she also felt that Jeremy would refuse to see a crisis clinician. More data were needed. She asked Jeremy if she could call his sister. At first he refused, but then he reluctantly acquiesced.

The sister's opening comment was, "Thank God, he's getting help. I'm so worried about him." She went on to share that she had seen him sitting forlornly in the guest bedroom and later found a bottle of aspirin hidden under the pillow. The counselor, armed with information from the sister that could be used as leverage for involuntary assessment, subsequently insisted on crisis assessment. Jeremy agreed to be seen by a crisis clinician at the local mental health center. During this assessment, he became quite tearful and revealed that he had been intending to commit suicide later that week, having stockpiled five bottles of pills. He was admitted for a brief hospital stay and did well.

While eliciting Jeremy's suicidal ideation with the CASE Approach, the counselor intuitively sensed that all was not as it seemed. The intensity of Jeremy's hopelessness, coupled with his numerous risk factors—adolescent age, male sex, presence of psychiatric disorder, and concrete suicidal plans—and an understanding, from a psychological perspective, that he was undergoing a massive assault to his sense of identity, all pointed toward high risk. The outstanding work by the counselor is highlighted by two actions:

1. Although not expected to be an expert diagnostician, she was well aware of the importance of screening for psychiatric disorders both

for medication assessment and because their presence can suggest high suicide potential.

2. She contacted a corroborative source. The information from Jeremy's sister proved to be alarming. His life may have been saved because the clinician was wise enough to make that contact despite tight time constraints and Jeremy's initial hesitancies.

The intensity and number of the risk factors served to alert the college counselor that perhaps "the full picture" was not being provided by Jeremy during the initial CASE inquiry. This prompted her to check with a corroborative source, which directly resulted in the assessment by the crisis clinician. In this second interview, the crisis clinician, using the CASE Approach, uncovered the extent of Jeremy's hopelessness and the determination of his suicidal intent. The uncovering of this intent and concrete planning, the third element of the triad of lethality, suggested the need for prompt hospitalization.

## CLINICAL VIGNETTE 2
### Return of Suicidal Ideation in Ongoing Therapy

*Primary Database*

Ken Rice is a 45-year-old African American store manager who has had difficulties with recurrent major depressions for years. He has benefited greatly from the recent use of maintenance antidepressant medication, and has not had a severe depression, requiring hospitalization, in over two years. He has been involved in a particularly ugly divorce and child custody battle. He has been working with a therapist for three months to overcome these issues and some secondary depressive symptoms. He has no history of alcohol or drug abuse, of severe medical problems, or of psychotic process. Two of his paternal uncles, one with bipolar disorder and the other with alcoholism and depression, shot themselves. Ken was named after the second uncle. He had two serious overdoses, three years ago and ten years ago. In their initial assessment several years earlier, careful diagnostic interviewing by the therapist revealed no evidence of a severe personality disorder. Two weeks ago, his wife won the child custody battle. On the good side, he has liberal visiting privileges with his children. On the bad side, he is devastated by the loss.

During the session, Ken became tearful. He commented, "There's no justice in this system. I don't even know why I try." He has had a return of some depressive symptoms, such as sleep disturbance and low energy, but they are intermittent in nature. He still is enjoying his visits with his three kids, and he smiles as he mentions them. During the CASE exploration of presenting and recent suicide events, he admits to a return of suicidal thought. Following the clinician's use of gentle assumption, denial of the specific, and behavioral incidents, Ken admitted to three methods: (1) gun, (2) overdose, and (3) hanging.

The use of behavioral incidents revealed that all of these thoughts were fleeting in nature. He had taken no action on any of the methods. When asked about hopelessness, he looked surprised and said, "I'm not hopeless at all. We're going to get through all this. I got the three best kids in the world." When the clinician used safety contracting in the region of immediate ideation, Ken smiled and commented, "You don't have to worry about me offing myself. I have absolutely no intention of doing that. I have to be there for my kids, now more than ever."

### Secondary Database, Formulation, and Disposition

Throughout their intermittent work together, over the years, the therapist had been periodically using modifications of the CASE Approach to keep the window open on suicidal ideation, for Ken had nearly killed himself twice. The two had grown to trust each other and felt quite open about exploring suicidal ideation. Consequently, the therapist had a good read on what Ken's ideation "looked like" and "felt like" when it was dangerous. (She had also worked with Ken shortly after his most recent serious suicide attempt.) Compared to her previous experiential database, Ken's current ideation was relatively benign. He did not appear to be developing a full-blown major depression. He lacked any of the desperation and hopelessness that were hallmarks of his serious attempts. There was no concrete planning, and no actions had been taken.

Despite risk factors such as his sex, two previous attempts, and a serious family history of suicide (including a family association of Ken with one of the dead uncles), an exploration of Ken's inner world via the CASE Approach indicated that he was handling the return of his suicidal ideation well. All three elements of the triad of lethality were absent—presentation with an immediately preceding serious suicide attempt, dangerous psychotic process, and evidence from the interview that the client is seriously intending imminent suicide.

The powerful alliance between Ken and his therapist represents a situation in which a safety contract may prove to be somewhat of a deterrent as well as an excellent ongoing assessment tool. In the latter regard, because the therapist had experience in watching the nonverbal behaviors of Ken while safety contracting—both when he was at risk and not at risk—the therapist had acquired an excellent feel for when Ken was contracting without ambivalence. This was the case today. There was no need to contact corroborative sources. She did make a note to alert Ken's psychiatrist about the current situation and suicidal ideation, so that they could brainstorm on any prospective treatment planning, for the next couple of months were sure to be tough ones for Ken.

## CLINICAL VIGNETTE 3
### Client with a Borderline Personality Disorder, Unknown to the Primary Clinician, Presenting in the Emergency Room

### *Primary Database*

Mary Beth Jarvis is a 27-year-old white single female who frequently visits the emergency room. In the past two years, her visits have decreased markedly, thanks to her hard work in ongoing therapy. No hospitalizations have been needed for one year. Mary Beth presents tonight with a chief complaint of, "That no-good son-of-a-bitch has finally done it to me now. If it will make her happy, I'll go ahead and kill myself." The "no-good son-of-a-bitch" in question is her on-again/off-again roommate, who apparently tonight threatened to kick Mary Beth out of the apartment at the end of the month.

Mary Beth has no history of psychosis, no concurrent major depression or panic disorder, and, despite a startling list of suicide attempts and self-cuttings, she has no history of a life-threatening act. She was sexually abused as a child; there is no history of suicide attempts in her family. During her stormy periods, Mary Beth has created more than her fair share of angry scenes in the emergency room. It is safe to say she is not a favorite of some of the E.R. personnel.

The interviewer is a first-year psychiatric resident new to the system. He has never met Mary Beth. When the charge nurse hands off the assignment, she tersely comments, "Whatever you do, don't admit her. She does badly in the hospital, and holy hell results. Let's just get her out of here quick." The clinician naïvely comments, "First, let me just see what's going on tonight." The resulting glare from the charge nurse suggested that his response was not exactly the one she was looking for, nor did her glare bode well for a fun night on call. As the charge nurse strode away, one could hear her commenting, "Oh great, everybody! Just what we need tonight: Albert Schweitzer is here."

An experienced nurse clinician who had been listening told the resident, "Don't worry, things have been pretty hectic here tonight. She's not always like that." As it turned out the nurse clinician knew Mary Beth well and had been impressed with her recent progress. The nurse clinician had good communication with Mary Beth's therapist and had helped to transform Mary Beth's suicidal crises several times during the past year, using cognitive therapy interventions developed by the therapist. The resident asked the nurse clinician if they could go in together; perhaps the nurse clinician could help again tonight. She agreed.

After engaging around the presenting crisis, the nurse clinician did a quick review of the region of presenting suicidal ideation. Mary Beth had bought various pills earlier that night, following her enraging conversation with her roommate. The nurse clinician began to try to help Mary Beth use her cognitive skills to transform her anger and, hopefully, dissipate her urge to kill herself. It did not work. Mary Beth became more agitated. With a slight slurring in her speech, Mary Beth snarled, "That shit is not gonna help me tonight."

Because the attempt at transforming the suicidal crisis had failed, the resident felt that a more careful examination of concrete suicidal planning was indicated. During the resident's subsequent survey using the CASE Approach, several other suicide plans emerged, including hanging, a plan that the nurse clinician had never heard from Mary Beth before. He also uncovered that the suicidal ideation had been brewing for a couple of weeks and was not solely in response to the argument tonight. As the nurse clinician and the resident returned to the nursing station, the charge nurse snarled, "I called the eighth floor, and they don't want another borderline up there tonight."

### Secondary Database, Formulation, and Disposition

At the suggestion of the nurse clinician, the resident called Mary Beth's therapist. There was no answer. The nurse clinician and the resident carefully reviewed the situation and the risk factors. The nurse clinician commented, "It just doesn't feel right. That's not the way it has been going with her recently, as we try her interventions. There is something else going on. [pause] I think I know what it is. She's been drinking. I have never seen her intoxicated before. Ever. And I've seen her about ten times before." The resident reviewed the chart. Drinking was atypical for Mary Beth.

It was apparent to the resident that the charge nurse's input should be carefully weighed because of her experience. As the charge nurse stated, Mary Beth probably does do poorly in the hospital. In fact, great progress had been made in keeping her out. On the other hand, the charge nurse was clearly angry with the patient, so her immediate insight was suspect. The resident decided that the nurse clinician was a far better source of input on Mary Beth tonight, and the nurse clinician seemed concerned. He subsequently decided to run the case by the psychiatrist on call, who also happened to know Mary Beth. The psychiatrist on call, the psychiatric resident, and the nurse clinician jointly decided that, although Mary Beth often regressed in hospitals, something was decidedly different about this presentation. Her acute intoxication was a wild card. The fact that her therapist's input was not available was also complicating their decision. Most importantly, using the CASE principle of evaluating the efficacy of the cognitive crisis intervention as one of the cornerstones of assessing such a patient's suicide potential, it was clear that the attempted intervention had failed. Usually, it doesn't. Tonight it did. The patient was admitted. A good decision was made.

Once again, the third element of our triad of lethality tipped the decision toward hospitalization. Despite a sound use of cognitive interventions that usually worked with Mary Beth, she continued to express the intent to kill herself. The fact that such ideation had been brewing for several weeks and was not just reactive in nature, coupled with the presence of a new plan, suggested that there might be something more lethal about this presentation. The intensity of her intent was considered to be even more disturbing because of the poor impulse control associated with acute intoxication, especially in an occasional drinker like Mary Beth.

The psychiatric resident showed excellent judgment at three different junctions: (1) he was not overwhelmed by the charge nurse's countertransference issues; (2) he recognized the opportunity to capitalize on the nurse clinician's superior skills and her experience in working with Mary Beth; and (3) he called his back up psychiatrist for consultation. Hospitalization would probably have been avoided if Mary Beth had responded to the nurse clinician's crisis interventions. And perhaps, if the patient's experienced therapist could have been reached, hospitalization might have been prevented through her input or even direct intervention. But as it stands, it was wise to bring Mary Beth in for a brief hospitalization until the alcohol cleared, her therapist could become involved, and resources for managing the new crisis could be tapped.

## CLINICAL VIGNETTE 4
### Mary Beth Presents with
### Self-Mutilation to Her Therapist

### Primary Database

Although Mary Beth's therapist was making a concerted effort to de-crease hospitalizations, she was in total agreement with the emergency room decision to admit Mary Beth on the night described above. She ap-preciated the E.R. team's attempt to reach her for input, and she was pleased that the team had tried to transform the suicidal crisis by using the techniques described in Mary Beth's prospective treatment plan. The E.R. staff had been correct in noting that this was not "just another one of Mary Beth's attempts to get in the hospital." Indeed, drinking be-havior had been one of the key factors in one of Mary Beth's more dan-gerous suicide attempts. The resulting hospitalization was quite brief. Mary Beth stabilized rapidly. But the destabilization of her relationship with her roommate, the precipitant for her most recent rages and sui-cidal storms, continued.

Five weeks later, Mary Beth presented for psychotherapy wearing a long-sleeved white blouse. The therapist would have needed to be blind to not notice the blotches of red seeping through the white fabric. Mary Beth apparently needed to make a point. Such a dramatic display was a return to an old behavior for Mary Beth, probably necessitated because she was not getting the needed relief from pain using her newly ac-quired and more mature coping skills. She simply didn't know how to handle the situation with her roommate, and so she resorted to what had worked in the past—self-mutilation.

Mary Beth's presentation provides an excellent avenue for discussing nonpsychotic self-mutilation, a phenomenon decidedly different from the desire to kill oneself. Typical methods of self-mutilation include: cutting, burning, fist pounding, and head banging. This phenomena is sometimes seen, as a transient and relatively isolated process, in people without borderline personality disorders who have been abused psychologically, physically, and/or sexually. More commonly, they are persistent methods of coping with stress among people with borderline personality disorders who have frequently been severely abused as well.

Acts of self-mutilation are often preceded by cognitions of abandon-ment, rejection, or being wronged, which are rapidly translated into in-tense feelings of anger and rage. Somehow, the turning of this rage onto one's own body seems to provide relief. During the actual moments of self-mutilation, the patient often is so depersonalized as to be oblivious to the pain, almost in a self-hypnotic state of sorts. Usually, the patient reaches a point where he or she suddenly feels an intense sense of relief, and the self-mutilation ceases. It has served its purpose well. It has provided a viable solution for ending the intense emotional pain. Often, this primary effectiveness is bolstered by the secondary gain that results as other people become aware of the mutilation: increased attention, concern, or even behavioral "goodies" like a trip to the E.R. or hospitalization.

Effective strategies for helping to end this vicious cycle are more appropriately explored in books on the ongoing treatment of people with borderline personality disorder. Once again, I refer the reader to the work of Linehan[3] and of Chiles and Strosahl.[4] I make no pretense to be able to address this complex treatment problem in this text focused upon assessment. On the other hand, I felt I should mention self-mutilation (sometimes referred to in the literature as "parasuicidal behaviors"), for no clinician can be performing suicide assessments for long without being asked to assess such a patient.

These patients are not trying to kill themselves. They are often quite good at making this distinction, if asked. Parasuicidal ideation is a learned method for relieving pain, not for ending life. Consequently, very often these behaviors do not require hospitalization. Repeated hospitalizations tend to feed this destructive process by providing secondary gain for maladaptive behaviors.

If the patient is known to the system, it is wise to contact the therapist or case manager for consultation on how to proceed with transforming the immediate crisis, as would be done with suicidal thought. A prospective treatment plan devised jointly by the client, therapist, case manager, inpatient unit, and E.R. staff can be invaluable in preventing unnecessary hospitalizations or, if necessary, making such stays brief. Hospitalization may be necessary if the crisis cannot be resolved or the threat of significant disfigurement is real. On occasion, these patients are simultaneously considering suicide, so hospitalization may be required for safety purposes.

The general approach to assessment of these patients is essentially the same as for assessing suicide potential in a patient with a severe personality disorder. The CASE Approach is greatly modified. The clinician makes a quick survey of the presenting self-mutilatory ideation and acting out, being careful to minimize any secondary gain. A concerted effort is made to transform the crisis by using the cognitive skills being learned by the client in therapy. If the transformation fails or the patient is new to the system to begin with, then a more standard implementation of the CASE Approach can be used to determine the extent of parasuicidal ideation and intent.

### Secondary Database, Formulation, and Disposition

In Mary Beth's situation, the therapist calmly noted that Mary Beth wanted to make a point. In a warm tone, and without condescension, she reminded Mary Beth that such a visual display of pain was not necessary and that she was always eager to listen to Mary Beth's concerns. Because she had a powerful bond with Mary Beth, she was able to add, with gentle humor, "That's rough on shirts, too." Mary Beth smiled.

Mary Beth began to intimate that maybe hospitalization was a good idea. But the therapist was able to skillfully guide Mary Beth into a productive use of her newfound cognitive skills. The parasuicidal crisis was transformed. No hospitalization was necessary. The cuts were superficial and did not require stitches. This is a nice example of a patient who presented with an actual act of self-mutilation but did not require hospitalization. Her superficial self-cutting did not fulfill the first criterion of the triad of lethality—presentation with a serious suicide attempt. This was not a suicide attempt, and the damage was far from serious. There was also no evidence of psychotic process and no expression of intent to actually kill herself or to self-mutilate in a disfiguring fashion.

### CLINICAL VIGNETTE 5
### Unknown Patient Brought to
### Emergency Room by Police

### Primary Database

Farrel Kraft, a 32-year-old white male, was brought into the emergency room at 8:00 P.M. on a Friday night, in curious circumstances. The police were called downtown to Mickey's All Night Grocery because the owner was suspicious that somebody was stealing from one of his stands. The supposed culprit was Farrel Kraft, who adamantly denied stealing anything. No stolen merchandise was found on his person. Lean and unshaven, with a look of vagrancy in his eyes, Farrel exuded the cheap scent of an alcohol-breath freshener. He was not acutely intoxicated, just moving in that general direction. The police didn't know exactly what to do with him. A passerby had told the store manager, who subsequently told the police, that Farrel had been loudly proclaiming that he was going to shoot himself. For want of a better disposition, the police decided to bring him into the E.R. to be "checked out." After hearing Farrel's story, the clinician was suspicious that he might be psychotic.

Upon interview, Farrel appeared subdued and depressed. His answers were vague but appropriate. Despite his initial hunch, the clinician found no loosening of associations, tangential thought, illogical thought, or any other signs suggestive of psychosis. Farrel denied hallucinations or delusions. He was well oriented and cognitively intact. When discussing the recent breakup of his first marriage and the loss of his two children, he began to weep. He reported being down on his luck—unemployed, debt-ridden, and friendless. He was currently living at the home of his aunt and was paying a nominal rent. He denied any psychiatric history or any suicides in his family. He seemed to meet the criteria for major depression and probable alcohol abuse, although he was cagey when providing history on his drinking, caustically adding, "My drinking had nothing to do with the breakup of my marriage. She's just a bitch."

Elicitation of suicidal ideation using the CASE Approach resulted in vague answers and comments that he had thought about overdosing or shooting himself, but he said, with an irritated tone, "I'll never do it." He angrily denied making any comments about shooting himself earlier in the evening. When questioned, the police officer said that Farrel didn't say anything about suicide to him directly, so the officer could not petition for commitment, and the officer had no idea who told the shop owner that Farrel was threatening to shoot himself. While exploring the region of immediate suicidal ideation with the CASE Approach, the clinician asked about hopelessness. Farrel paused and then said with a bitter tone, "Yes. Yes, I am hopeless. [pause] Is that a crime? Now let me out of here. I can do with my life what I want. It's a free country the last time I checked."

## Secondary Database, Formulation, and Disposition

The clinician was bothered by the inconsistency between the reported history that a passerby had heard Farrel loudly threatening suicide and Farrel's adamant denial that such a statement had been made. It didn't make sense to the clinician that a passerby would just make it up, and it was bothersome that, after denying that he had made such a comment, Farrel admitted that he had indeed been thinking about shooting himself. His affect was both depressed and erratic, not a good combination. There seemed to be a drinking problem, and the clinician felt that Farrel was a poor source of information on the extent of the problem. In addition, Farrel seemed profoundly hopeless. The clinician decided to ask Farrel if he could call his aunt. Farrel refused.

Everyone involved in the assessment—the police officer, the charge nurse, and the clinician—felt ill at ease. The clinician made a smart decision and called the psychiatrist on call. After much discussion, it was decided to override Farrel's objection and to call his aunt. When told of the decision, Farrel acquiesced, saying, "The old bag ain't gonna tell you nothing." He was wrong.

Mrs. Emily Jackson was both intelligent and concerned. Apparently, Farrel had a history of psychiatric hospitalizations for depression, alcoholism, and suicide attempts. He had been getting his life together—he was sober for five years—but, unfortunately, he did not handle the divorce well. Mrs. Jackson was quite agitated as she spoke. She related that she had unexpectedly happened by her nephew's bedroom door the night before, and saw him with a gun. She wasn't sure, but he might have been pulling it away from his mouth. She didn't know what to do and didn't think there was anything she could do. She wanted to know if he would be staying at the hospital.

Farrel was displeased by his aunt's information and demanded to leave. He required physical restraint. Despite numerous offers for voluntary admission, he repeatedly refused and was ultimately committed. Later, he would admit he had had a gun in his mouth and was seriously intending to kill himself, after "I got boozed up enough."

Farrel did not admit to suicidal intent at the time of the interview, nor was he actively psychotic. Thus, he did not seem to meet the last two criteria of the triad of lethality. In contrast, placing a gun into his mouth the day before presentation met the first criterion—an immediately recent and serious suicidal action. Upon further reflection, despite denying suicidal intent himself, he met the third criteria of the triad of lethality because his aunt's corroborative information about the gun suggested serious intent. Farrel is a beautiful example of clinicians carefully paying attention to inconsistencies between the patient's story over time and from the history gathered from corroborative sources. The interviewer made several excellent decisions including: calling the psychiatric consultant, thinking about the potential usefulness of calling Farrel's aunt, and deciding that the patient's safety concerns overrode the patient's confidentiality.

### CLINICAL VIGNETTE 6
### Unexpected Suicidal Ideation During Ongoing Psychotherapy and Medication Management

*Primary Database*

Julia Hartford was a hard-working no-nonsense 27-year-old charge nurse on a medical floor at a local hospital. She was prone to spontaneously arising major depressive episodes of a fairly severe nature but not severe enough to require hospitalization. Her family history was teeming with people afflicted with severe depressions. Two maternal aunts and her maternal grandmother had committed suicide. Julia did not particularly identify in a personal sense with any of the relatives who had killed themselves. She did not drink, and she had strong religious beliefs that suicide was wrong. She had often stated in therapy, "I'd never kill myself. My kids need me."

Julia was open-minded and psychologically savvy, and she quickly sought help when she was depressed. During her previous four episodes, she had responded well to a combination of psychotherapy and treatment with a selective serotonin reuptake inhibitor (SSRI). Her most recent depression, which occurred after she had stopped her medicine for about seven months, was not triggered by any particular stressors or psychological conflicts. The etiology of her depressive episodes seemed to be primarily biologic in nature. As she commented, "It just came out of nowhere. I had been feeling fine and things were going great in my life, which is why I stopped the med in the first place." This episode, more severe than most, was highlighted by numerous severe vegetative symptoms of depression and some significant suicidal ideation. She was promptly restarted on her antidepressant. To her great relief, shortly after restarting the antidepressant, her suicidal ideation completely disappeared. Both she and her psychiatrist felt that her suicidal ideation had arisen primarily as part of her biologically induced depression. Indeed, the ideation may have been an example of suicidal ideation directly triggered by pathophysiology.

Unfortunately, many of her other depressive symptoms proved to be more tenacious than in the past. The dosage was increased to a higher range and, eventually, a thyroid supplement was added as an adjunct agent. Both of these therapeutic maneuvers resulted in further improvement, but she continued to have too many symptoms to be satisfied with her degree of recovery. In particular, Julia felt overwhelmed at work and was reluctantly considering a medical leave of absence, an idea that stirred tremendous guilt in her.

She had a great therapeutic alliance with her psychiatrist, who was also providing her psychotherapy. Before switching to another medication, they decided to bump her antidepressant to its highest recommended dose, in the hope that it would finally "kick in" as it had before. This seemed logical because Julia was already obtaining significant, albeit partial, relief from this medication. Moreover, on three past occasions, this medication had led to total resolution of her depression. This last dosage increase was made directly before the psychiatrist left on a two-week vacation.

On the day of his return, there was an urgent-sounding message on his voice-mail from Julia's boss, "Can you fit Julia in today? She is really looking bad. I'm very concerned about her. I think something is very wrong." When Julia was seen that day, she did look bad. Usually fairly stoic, she burst into tears, saying, "I just don't know what's wrong. I just want this to all end." The psychiatrist was puzzled, for she had been doing progressively better and had not had suicidal ideation for many months. What was more puzzling, she said she was not much more depressed now. "That's not the problem, I'm just sick of it all. I'm just so wired up I can barely contain myself. Honest to god, I thought I was gonna strangle my husband today and he was just talking to me at the breakfast table. I'm screaming, literally screaming at my kids. [pause] I'm a horrible parent." [more intensely crying]

The psychiatrist was quite struck by the intensity of her agitation and anxiety, which seemed greatly out of step with the gradual improvement in her mood. Upon careful questioning, he uncovered that her increase in anxiety had been building up over the past two weeks. It was accompanied by marked disturbances in sleep, extreme irritability, very low stress tolerance, tearful episodes, and a new onset of what sounded like panic attacks.

Using the CASE Approach, some disturbing and peculiar suicidal ideation was uncovered, which she openly discussed because it had frightened her and she stressed repeatedly, "I don't want to die." She had noticed she had been becoming particularly wound up as the mornings progressed. This morning had been the worst to date. While in the bathroom, she suddenly had the urge to electrocute herself by putting the hair dryer in the bathtub. She had never had that idea before. She reported feeling compelled by it, although in her heart she didn't want to die. It scared her, and she threw the hair dryer into the bedroom. When asked whether the suicidal ideation felt the same as in the past, she quickly responded, "No. This was very different. It just came on so abruptly. It was very intense. And it felt different than anything I've ever felt before. It frightened me."

### Secondary Database, Formulation, and Disposition

On a surface level, it looked like Julia was having an agitated major depression and might need to be hospitalized, although she wanted to avoid hospitalization if at all possible. But a variety of circumstances did not resonate with this clinical impression. In the first place, if one reviewed her past psychiatric history, Julia did not typically develop agitation during her depressions. And in the second place, she had been showing progressive improvement, albeit incomplete, over the recent months. The degree of her anxiety was in sharp contrast to the relatively moderate intensity of her depressed mood.

The phenomenology of her suicidal ideation was very different from her presentations in the past. The clinician was quite familiar with them because he routinely checked them, using the CASE Approach. Normally, her suicidal ideation appeared slowly, almost insidiously. It lacked any impulsive tendency. The method was always overdosing, or driving her car off the road. The current ideation appeared abruptly, represented a completely new method (electrocution), and had an urgent and impulsive quality. The psychiatrist thought he knew what was going on.

Her antidepressant, which she took in the morning, was put on immediate hold. The psychiatrist suspected, and was subsequently proven to be correct, that Julia was experiencing a toxic behavioral state, secondary to the high dose of her antidepressant. An antianxiety agent was prescribed to immediately reduce her stress and agitation, because severe agitation has been noted as a risk factor for suicide attempts on inpatient units. Her husband was contacted and the situation was explained. Julia was tremendously relieved after hearing the probable cause of her otherwise unexplainable downturn in condition. She made a sound safety contract. Check-in calls were made that night, the next morning, and the next afternoon. Her husband agreed to stay at home the next day with Julia. Julia slept better that night. The next morning, she felt almost 50% calmer. By the next evening, she felt "almost back to normal." There was no return of any suicidal ideation. Within seven days, she was back to where she had been two weeks before.

Although her original medication had been very effective at rapidly eliminating the suicidal ideation related to her biologically triggered depression, it had not provided adequate relief from her other depressive symptoms over time. Pushed to higher doses, it created unacceptable side effects, possibly including some transient atypical suicidal thought. Julia was switched to a different antidepressant. Five weeks later, her depression was in complete remission.

A variety of factors allowed Julia to remain as an outpatient: her marked relief after hearing the physician's explanation, the genuineness of her safety contract, the absence of any suicidal ideation after the peculiar morning episode, the reliability and support of her husband, and the fact that the suspect agent had a short half-life suggesting its blood level would drop quickly allowing for a quick testing of the psychiatrist's theory. If any of these factors had not been true, the psychiatrist would probably have admitted Julia for observation as the med was stopped.

Such toxic behavioral states are relatively rare, but should always be kept in the back of the mind when using SSRIs, particularly at high doses. Her suicidal ideation was probably a secondary response to her medication-induced anxiety, but it may also have represented an example of suicidal ideation being directly triggered by the brain. There is no way to tell for sure. Clinicians should become suspicious of such toxic states whenever the characteristics seen with Julia's suicidal ideation appear: suicidal ideation is unexpected and inconsistent with past suicidal ideation; the patient reports the ideation as feeling very different from past ideation; the ideation has a peculiar feeling of intensity and impulsiveness that has never been present before; and the ideation appears to be erupting within a complex of other unexpected behavioral abnormalities not typical of the patient and suggestive of a toxic state.

## CLINICAL VIGNETTE 7
### Suicidal Ideation Uncovered During the Course of Substance Abuse Counseling

### Primary Database

Greg Baskins was a 27-year-old white male who spent much of his time going nowhere. Currently unemployed and living alone in a cheap apartment, he intermittently came in for outpatient substance abuse counseling. More often than not, he was a "no show." At times, he seemed to be tantalizingly close to being at "Step 1" and realizing his need for help, but he just couldn't maintain his commitment. At heart, Greg was a very good person. Alcohol often hid that fact.

He had been abused as a child. As an adult, he was abusive. He had overdosed on benadryl and two six-packs several years earlier, but denied recent suicidal ideation. One paternal uncle had alcoholism and had taken his own life. Greg's current social network consisted of a few frequently incoherent drinking buddies and the owner of the neighborhood deli, who had taken an interest in Greg. He denied current use of other street drugs, but had a history of cocaine and speed abuse.

Today, Greg entered the counselor's office with an unusually rapid step and plopped into the chair. His lean, handsome face had several days' growth of beard. There was no hint of alcohol on his breath, and he swore that he hadn't been drinking. He fidgeted with a dirty scarf hung about his neck, and he kept picking up odds and ends on the counselor's desk, such as paper clips and pencils. Normally, he was fairly calm when not drinking. The counselor sensed that Greg seemed unusually uptight.

To the counselor's surprise, Greg was more talkative than normal and more open about needing help, but his speech was rambling. For the first time in a long while, he talked about his sense of isolation and suddenly became tearful. He was experiencing a list of depressive symptoms and commented, "I just can't sleep, man. I gotta get some sleep. Do you know any docs who could get me some sleeping pills or something to calm me down?" Without any apparent trigger, Greg began to weep intensely. All of a sudden, he stood up abruptly. He looked about the room as if searching for something, and commented, "I've said enough for today. I think I'm going to leave now."

### Secondary Database, Formulation, and Disposition

Greg's presentation had become progressively odd. The counselor was concerned that Greg was showing soft signs of psychosis. The challenge was in figuring out a method of calming Greg and then proceeding to ferret out whether psychotic process was present and, if so, whether any of the dangerous types of psychotic processes were active—command hallucinations, alien control, or dangerous types of hyper-religious ideation. By getting Greg to talk more about his need for something to calm him down, he opened up about how wired he was. As the counselor had suspected, an old friend, speed, had reentered the picture as Greg's new drug of choice.

Sensing that Greg was preoccupied with his sense of isolation, the counselor moved him into a discussion around this area, hoping to uncover affectively charged psychotic process. Sure enough, it was waiting near the surface. For seven weeks, Greg had been speeding and crashing in his apartment. He denied any hyper-religious ideation or feelings of alien control to harm himself or others, but he had become paranoid. He had "heard sounds." Someone was pacing outside his doorway, and that same someone was drilling holes in his walls, ostensibly to watch him in his sleep, but "Lord knows what they could slip into my apartment through those holes. [pause] They're driving me nuts, and I can't take it anymore. I know I've been bad. And I know I've got a drinking problem. But, oh God, I don't deserve this." Greg began weeping again.

Careful use of behavioral incidents and gentle assumption revealed that Greg had decided earlier in the week to prevent "them" from getting at him and torturing him by slitting his own throat. Today he wasn't sure what was the right course of action. Using the CASE Approach to explore the region of presenting suicide events, the counselor found that Greg had placed a knife to his throat about a week ago. At this point, Greg mentioned for the first time that he thought he could hear voices outside his door whispering, "End it now. You're worthless. You'll be doing everybody a favor." Greg agreed to go to the emergency room for assessment and to see if they could help him with his sleep. He was subsequently admitted voluntarily with a provisional diagnosis of amphetamine-induced psychotic disorder.

The substance abuse counselor showed a great deal of clinical acumen in recognizing psychotic process in someone in whom he had never seen it before and who never had demonstrated it in his history. Furthermore, the substance abuse counselor remembered how to flexibly adapt the CASE Approach for exploration of the types of psychotic processes that could lead to self-harm or harming others. Part of the trick was to open the doorway of psychotic process by moving Greg into an affectively charged area. If Greg had refused evaluation at the emergency room, the counselor had adroitly uncovered good grounds for enforcing an involuntary assessment—Greg's holding a knife to his neck. The presence of the command hallucinations was also of great concern with regard to Greg's safety. Greg met two of the criteria of the triad of lethality. He presented with a recently dangerous act, and his command hallucinations represented one of the more dangerous types of psychotic process.

---

## CONCLUDING COMMENTS

In this chapter, we have tried to "put it all together" by looking at the delicate interplay of the principles discussed in the earlier chapters. We have seen in our closing clinical vignettes that, as we predicted, the extent of the patient's actual suicidal planning often offers the most valid window into his or her immediate dangerousness. Sometimes, the clinician is effective at eliciting the extent of the suicidal planning directly from the patient by utilizing strategies like the CASE Approach. At other times, when the patient is more determined to hide his or her plans, the extent of the planning must be carefully culled indirectly from corroborative sources such as family members, friends, therapists, and police. The ability to elicit this intimate information, coupled with our understanding of risk factors, etiologic factors, phenomenologic factors, and the complicating factors inherent in each unique assessment setting, can provide a window into the immediacy of suicide.

As clinicians, it is our mission to help uncover potentially reversible suicidal ideation in those who have been ravaged by the descent into their own suicidal maelstroms. We certainly do not pretend to offer all the means for ascending from this maelstrom. Life is difficult and not always fair. Despite our best efforts, some patients may decide to ultimately end their lives so as to end their pain.

But I am convinced that there are many other patients who, in the brief respite and time we offer them by preventing their immediate act of self-destruction, arrive at new answers and solutions. Through the help of medications, psychotherapies, the mobilization of supports, and the revitalization of their frameworks for meaning, many of these patients find hope. With this hope, they begin to ascend the walls of their maelstroms and life presents with a new freshness and sense of meaning. These once desperate patients will never forget the clinicians who listened with compassion and interviewed with skill, whether they met in the darkened halls of an emergency room or the afternoon shadows of a clinic office. To the deepening of this compassion and the development of these skills, we have dedicated ourselves in this book.

## NOTES

1. Jung, C.G.: *Memories, Dreams, and Reflections.* New York, Pantheon Books, 1961.

2. Linehan, M.: *Cognitive-Behavioral Treatment of Borderline Personality Disorder.* New York, Guilford Press, 1993.

3. Linehan, M., 1993.

4. Chiles, J.A. and Strosahl, K.D.: *The Suicidal Patient—Principles of Assessment, Treatment, and Case Management.* Washington, D.C., American Psychiatric Press, Inc., 1995.

# APPENDIX A

# How to Document a Suicide Assessment

For the average clinician, few events are as devastating as the death of a patient through suicide. That experience may be rendered even more distressing by one possible aftermath of such a death: a malpractice suit against the psychiatrist or other health care provider for failure to prevent that death. . . . Clinicians who are the target of such litigation describe the emotional reactions to being sued as resonating malignantly with the prompting of their own consciences and neurotic guilt, even in cases where the treater is objectively blameless and has rendered proper treatment.[1]

Thomas G. Gutheil, MD

There are only two kinds of clinical psychiatrists—those who have had patients commit suicide and those who will.[2]

Robert I. Simon, MD

## PART I   THE STUFF BEHIND LAWSUITS: THE ROLE OF SOUND DOCUMENTATION IN PREVENTING THEM

THERE ARE four pillars to preventing malpractice. The first three are obvious: good clinical care, consulting and referring when necessary, and the building of a good relationship with the client and the family of the client. The fourth pillar—sound documenta- tion—is less obvious, and it has slightly different characteristics from the other three predecessors.

If the clinician violates the first three pillars, it is possible that legitimate malpractice has occurred, in which case litigation may be both indicated and appropriate. The first three pillars share another common characteristic in the sense that much has been written about them. Indeed, the preceding pages of this book are dedicated to these topics, and, hopefully, provide a powerful base from which to practice effective clinical care.

However, what of the fourth pillar—sound documentation—how is it different? The first and most striking difference is that if the clinician violates this pillar then the clinician may be sued, and sometimes successfully sued, even if adequate or outstanding care was provided. As Thomas Gutheil so succinctly captures in the opening epigram to this chapter, it is hard to imagine a much more troubling and unfair double tragedy.

This appendix and the one following it are designed to help prevent such uncalled-for lawsuits. If you practice the principles outlined in this book, you will be providing good care, but you may still be at significant risk for a lawsuit, which brings us to the final distinction between the first three pillars and the last one.

Written information on how to create a sound forensic document is difficult to find in the literature, yet experts routinely emphasize the importance of making such documentation with comments such as the following by Comstock:[3]

> ...all mental health professionals participate in the responsibility for reasonable documentation of how each decision is reached and each treatment intervention is implemented.

But it is easy for experts on suicide prevention to give short shrift to the topic of how a clinician goes about creating reasonable documentation. I should know, because I unconsciously omitted a thorough exploration of this topic in the original edition of this book. Being genuinely concerned about conveying effective methods both for relieving the pain of our clients and for preventing unnecessary suicides, it is easy for a writer on suicide prevention to feel as if the job is done once this information has been adequately conveyed. The primary concern appears to be where it should be—on helping the client and practicing excellent clinical care, not on where it should not be—practicing defensive medicine.

However, there is a catch here. Unwarranted lawsuits do occur. Many of these inappropriate lawsuits may be the result of poor documentation. Thus, even competent clinicians, who are not well versed on effective methods for producing sound documentation, worry about lawsuits. Moreover, they should, for their lack of knowledge on sound documentation principles does put them at higher risk. The needless anxiety that results from a lack of knowledge on how to provide protection from malpractice through good documentation is decidedly unpleasant to experience. It can even get in the way of providing optimum care through the practice of defensive medicine and/or the development of clinician "burnout."

Fortunately, if well-trained clinicians are taught the fundamentals of sound documentation, the chances for being sued will be significantly reduced. If you provide good clinical care and you document this care well, the likelihood of actually losing a lawsuit is also lowered markedly. Ironically, giving enough attention to the protection against lawsuits provided by good documentation habits "up front" during graduate training, permits the clinician to stop worrying needlessly about litigation issues "down the road" during clinical practice.

This appendix, and the one that follows it, provides this much-needed information. As with the body of this book, an emphasis is placed on demonstration. As was the case with the interviewing strategies described in this book, it is important not only to tell "why" and "what" to do, it is equally important to show "how" to do it with an example of clinical dialogue. So it is with documentation. In addition to sharing my opinions on the "why" and "what" of creating a sound forensic document, I demonstrate the "how" of these principles by presenting examples of soundly written documentation.

There is a bright spot in this sometimes dark business of forensic liability. Good documentation not only decreases the likelihood of losing a lawsuit; it markedly decreases the likelihood of being in one in the first place. This bit of news is so important and can be so reassuring to clinicians, that it warrants a more careful look at how lawsuits unfold and how good documentation prevents them.

## WHY GOOD DOCUMENTATION
## KEEPS YOU OUT OF THE COURTROOM

We begin by addressing the pressing question as to "why" it is important to carefully document suicide assessments. The answers are many and not always as apparent as you might think. Lawsuits don't just manifest because a potential litigant wants to sue a clinician. Unless the litigant wants to act as his or her own attorney, the lawyer must accept the case. Before accepting a case, the lawyer must feel there is a very good chance to win the case, for he or she stands to make little or no money despite a huge investment of time if the case is lost.

Although we do not hear this voiced much among mental health professionals, most lawyers practice ethically. They are not out "to nail" good clinicians. Moreover, if they do not see malpractice, they do not attempt to create it. There are plenty of legitimate examples of very poor care out there; ethical lawyers have better things to do than pursue weak cases.

As with any field, there are also unethical lawyers out there. Paradoxically, their greed will work to our advantage as long as we document our quality work well. Here is why.

Whether ethical or unethical, greedy or on a legitimate mission to stop dangerous clinicians, the bottom line is that the attorney must predict the outcome of the case before the case begins or risk losing a lot of time and money. In this difficult decision process, the attorney's sources of information are limited: information from the plaintiff, information from other surviving family members, information in the public domain such as news media, and information from the clinical records. Let us look at the relative worth of each of these information sources to the prospective attorney.

Valuable information may come from the plaintiff and other survivors, but it may be tainted or biased because of personal interests and the complex dynamics and pains of a grieving survivor. The news media can be helpful but this information is notoriously unreliable. The attorney most desperately needs to talk directly with the clinician to find out exactly what was done. Only a deposition could achieve this end, and a deposition of the clinician is usually only possible after a lawsuit has already been filed. Moreover, the clinician's testimony would be biased as well.

The only source of information, on what the clinician did or did not do, that is readily available to help the lawyer decide whether to take on the case is the written record. You could argue that even though it was written by the clinician, often, not always, it is written before the clinician would have any reason to bias the information, so it might very well represent some of the most objective data that will ever appear in the entire course of litigation.

Lawyers, judges, plaintiffs, defendants, and jury members hold clinical records in high regard. There is also a certain mystique to the clinical record that perhaps gives it even more credibility than it deserves with the jury. However, the bottom line is simple: "If you don't write it down, it didn't happen." Whether just or unjust, if you did excellent clinical work but did not write it down, it is easy for a jury to think the worst. They may simply view your testimony as to your "good work" as an example of a clinician "just covering his you know what." Remember that there is going to be a skilled lawyer steering the jury exactly toward that conclusion.

So a prospective lawyer must decide whether a case is worth pursuing primarily from the clinical records. If the clinical records document clearly that malpractice did not occur, the greed of an unscrupulous lawyer would drive them away from the case, for fear of losing it or not being able to get a substantial monetary award from the jury. Excellent documentation of good care will also lead an ethical attorney to not accept the case, for he or she will not see evidence of malpractice.

Outside of good clinical care in the first place, what we write in the documentation of our suicide assessments is probably the single most protective factor in preventing an unfounded lawsuit. If you do good clinical work and document it well, a lawsuit is not likely. In short, the personal stakes of the lawyer will, paradoxically, protect the clinician.

Now what exactly does the lawyer do with the written records in an effort to determine whether to pursue a case? First, they read them extremely carefully, and often have their partners or legal aids also add opinions. In many cases, especially in the hands of a gifted and well-experienced malpractice lawyer, his or her years of experience will quickly reveal whether to accept a case upon first reading. Many cases are rejected, based primarily on what the lawyer reads from your notes, at this early stage. Second, if the lawyer thinks the case may be worth pursuing, then he or she will hand them to a clinical expert, who may or may not be a forensic psychiatrist. This clinical expert will generally, if the case proceeds, go on to be an "expert witness" for the plaintiff.

At this point in the process, an ethical expert witness is there to determine whether or not malpractice occurred and to relay that opinion to the attorney, who, you will remember, is trying to decide whether the case is worth taking. If there is no malpractice, the clinical expert will inform the attorney that the case is not worth pursuing and will also inform the attorney that, if the attorney does proceed with the suit, he or she will need to find a different expert witness, for an ethical expert witness will not testify against a clinician who did good work, that is, stayed within the standard of care.

A less ethical expert witness, the supposed "hired gun," and they do exist, on one level may want the case to proceed anyway. The reason for this desire is that the expert witness is paid by the hour and depositions, written opinions, and the long court hours that will follow if the attorney takes on the case, are quite lucrative. But, even hired guns don't savor going into a courtroom to be shredded by a gifted opposing attorney who is on a mission to protect a good clinician who did nothing wrong. Such shredding may also damage their reputations with professional colleagues who, appropriately, look down on such "hired gun" practices.

In addition, if an expert witness is shredded in one case, a shrewd defense lawyer in a future case, where this expert witness is once again testifying, can sometimes enter this previous court testimony to try to shake the credibility of the expert with the jury in the current case. In short, there are some significant reasons that a "hired gun" is not going to want to suggest pursuing a case that is unlikely to be won.

Again, the bottom line is simple: If good work was done, within the standard of care, and it is well documented, the expert witness generally will advise the lawyer not to proceed. It is relatively rare for a lawyer to proceed with litigation if a respected expert witness advises against it.

Another, more subtle but powerful force is at play here that will nudge the expert witness to tell the truth to the attorneys as to whether or not malpractice is present. From a business end, they do not want to be tagged as being "bad expert witnesses" among malpractice lawyers, a label that could markedly decrease requests for their future testimony. More specifically, expert witnesses often get "repeat business" from attorneys or friends of these attorneys, but this repeat business will not come if word gets out that this expert witness tends to steer attorneys headlong into losing cases. Once again, it is worth repeating that there are powerful, self-centered drives at work in the opposing camp to keep us out of court, but only if our documentation is sound and compelling.

There exists one final benefit to sound documentation that, at first glance, sounds a bit odd. Good documentation can help get you into court if you so desire. Keep in mind, that if an unjustified lawsuit has been filed against you, it risks damaging your reputation, affects privileges at hospitals, and may raise your insurance premiums. Unfortunately, you don't necessarily have the choice as to whether or not you get to prove your case, thus avoiding all of these negative results.

In most instances, malpractice insurance contracts have a "consent clause" in them. This clause states that the insurance company can settle "out of court" only after receiving your approval to do so. But if your insurance contract does not have such a clause, the insurance company decides whether or not to go to court. The insurance company, at the advice of its lawyer (a lawyer who only secondarily has allegiance to you, for his salary comes not from you but from the insurance company who retains his services) may choose to settle outside of court against your wishes. It is frustrating and painful to be forced to accept a lawsuit and pay damages when you did nothing wrong, and no one allows you the chance to vindicate your reputation.

A well-documented suicide assessment forms your best shield against such a painful situation. In a parallel fashion to what we saw with the potential plaintiff's attorney, as she was deciding whether to accept the case, the potential defending insurance company will poll its resources to decide whether to go to court or settle out of court. Their most relied upon source of information for making this decision will be the lawyer they have retained.

If this lawyer sees good clinical care and outstanding documentation of that care, she will most likely give the green light to a court battle in which the clinician has the possibility of vindicating himself. However, if this lawyer sees poor documentation, then despite good clinical work and over your protestations, this case will rapidly move toward settlement out of court. Good documentation is the critical key.

A well-written suicide assessment really can stop you from being sued, if there are no clinical grounds for the suit. It can also help to ensure that you will get your day in court, if you so desire. There are no guarantees here, but sound documentation provides the best insurance you can buy—and it's free!

On a more personal level, remember that sound documentation can prevent a good clinician from unfairly experiencing the intense agonies of an ungrounded lawsuit, which will undoubtedly draw out over several years, impacting dramatically on the clinician's daily happiness and practice. Remember that you will already be dealing with the exquisite pain of having lost a patient that you genuinely did your best to help. To have a lawsuit added to this grief is truly unsettling.

At this point, we should address the matter of time, for the insurance provided by good documentation is not entirely free, as I stated earlier. Granted it does not cost money directly, but good documentation increases your workload because it requires extra time. Such extra time could even indirectly translate into lost revenue. Let's take an objective look at how much time may be lost.

On a typical initial assessment, probably only a couple of minutes per client is added if you employ the principles outlined in these appendices. In a more complex suicide assessment, as seen in some emergency room (ER) assessments, thorough documentation will require at least an extra five minutes. On a very complex ER assessment, thorough documentation could require 10 or more minutes. At first such time increases may not seem overly problematic, but they tend to accumulate as the day proceeds. Having been the director of a busy psychiatric ER, I can tell you that those time parameters are costly. I can also tell you, that for me personally, they are worth every minute.

Adequate documentation of a suicide assessment is the standard of care as Simon implies in the *Concise Guide to Psychiatry and the Law for Clinicians*, "All suicide assessments should be recorded in the patient's chart at the time of evaluation. For the suicidal patient, an assessment of suicide risk should be made at each outpatient visit." [4] Exactly how thorough such documentation should be is somewhat debatable, but I am suggesting that it benefits both the clinician and the patient to be quite thorough, despite the increase in time such documentation requires.

With this in mind, it might help if I shared my own decision tree on the topic. I have found out that careful documentation of suicide assessment issues over the course of a busy day as an outpatient psychiatrist in a busy community mental health center used to cost me about 20 minutes a day, unless there were some unusually complex assessments. In short, I literally would leave the office around 20 minutes later (often less) each day. That's a sizable chunk of real time. It's a sizable cost.

On the other hand, here were the resulting benefits: I did not need to practice "defensive medicine" because I felt secure that as long as I was providing good clinical care and I was documenting it well there was little chance for a lawsuit. I seldom fretted about liability issues, this decrease in unnecessary fretting lowered any burnout feelings, and, clinically, my focus was where it needed to be—on providing good care for my clients.

Finally, and most importantly, an extra 20 minutes per day, dedicated to sound suicide assessment documentation, markedly protected me against the intense pains that accompany an unwarranted lawsuit. The torment associated with an unfounded lawsuit would affect me, my family, my career, and almost every minute of my daily practice for years to come. It cannot be overstated how much a lawsuit destroys the quality of life away from work, a time that may be plagued with second-guessing, replaying of the last words with the client, anger at the plaintiffs, worries about or anger toward your own defense team, and even concerns as to your own competence or how you will be seen by fellow colleagues. Good documentation of good clinical care can potentially spare one from all of this pain.

Because of these benefits, I gladly pay the extra 20 minutes per day. As you read the following appendices, you will have to decide for yourself. At the very least, these materials will provide you with the chance to make a wise choice for yourself.

One last comment: If a clinician routinely follows the documentation principles outlined next, you will become increasingly adept and efficient at good documentation. With each documentation, you will become faster, until it is remarkable how quickly a well-trained clinician can write up a complex suicide assessment, thus minimizing lost time. After years of clinical practice, the time commitments described above become less. I have seen this happen time and again with experienced clinicians when I was the director of an emergency room.

## WHY GOOD DOCUMENTATION HELPS TO PREVENT SUICIDES

We are almost done with our introduction to the "why" of performing sound documentation, but one could argue that the most important reason has not been addressed yet. The process of creating a sound written document can directly improve clinical care itself. This point is so important, and so seldom emphasized, it is worth a more detailed look.

The act of creating a good document can be of help clinically in two ways: (1) the actual content of the document can help a future clinician to make a better decision if our client is assessed in the future, and (2) the process of creating a sound document can push us to review the quality and comprehensiveness of our database, as well as lead us to reformulate the clinical assessment we have made based on that database. Let us explore both of these clinical benefits in more detail.

First, good documentation of how a client presented, what his or her risk factors were, and how we formulated a safety decision may be of extreme value to a future clinician, such as a crisis clinician in a busy emergency room where our client has suddenly appeared. The importance of the document is particularly striking if we are not available to the crisis clinician by telephone. Contrasting the client's current presentation to the baseline data to be found in our previously documented suicide assessment may prove to be invaluable, sometimes even life-saving.

We all know how daunting suicide assessments can be. Even the best of crisis clinicians, in the frenzy of emergency room work, can, if they are not careful, miss key information such as previous suicide attempts, problems with drugs and alcohol, or the presence of a significant other who may have critical information regarding dangerousness. A well-written assessment makes all of this pertinent information available to the crisis clinician. In addition, on any given night, the client may be displaying passive-aggressive characterological defenses that prevent the client from sharing the truth about key risk factors or suicidal planning. Again, our documentation may provide much needed information.

Second, and perhaps less obviously, good documentation provides an invaluable resource in the formulation of the client's immediate safety. Let me explain.

As the highly respected malpractice attorney, Skip Simpson, has noted, once a clinician has developed the habit of addressing key elements of suicide assessment in each and every suicide assessment note written, then the act of documentation, itself, essentially becomes a built-in checklist on good care.[5] This checklist function can prove to be a tool that helps us to spot important errors of omission that might otherwise be missed. Two examples will make the power of this internalized checklist more apparent.

Let us assume that the clinician learns to habitually ask himself or herself the following question during the writing of his or her suicide assessments: Did I contact any important collaborative sources such as a spouse, close friend, therapist, or person accompanying the client, such as a police officer during an involuntary commitment? This question may suddenly trigger a realization that a potentially critical source of information was missed, at which point this error can be addressed. Of all the errors I found while running our morning report for our night shift staff in our emergency room, failure to contact critical sources of information was the most common error. As noted earlier in the book, it is sometimes a fatal error. Good documentation practices—functioning as a trusted checklist—can help to eliminate this error.

Let us look at another example. In this instance, following the principles in this appendix, the clinician makes it a habit to always ask himself: If I consulted with another clinician on this case, did I record that I did and that the consulting clinician agreed with my formulation? Note by habitually asking yourself whether a consultation was recorded, it automatically makes you reformulate whether such a consultation may be indicated. If "yes" and not done, the adage "better late than never" is appropriate, and you can make the indicated consultation. Again, the clinician's use of a sound documentation protocol has effectively functioned as a checklist for good care. The development of a good documentation habit serves as the clinician's own best quality assurance measure—a guardian angel of sorts, as Skip Simpson calls it.

Our final point concerning how quality documentation directly enhances our provision of care is a simple one. If we take the time out to carefully write down our clinical formulation of risk, it pushes us to review the facts pointing toward safety and the facts pointing toward dangerousness. As we organize and review these facts, we may see them differently. In essence, we are being forced to review our clinical formulation. Sometimes the facts point away from our original decision.

In exploring the "Why" of doing good documentation of suicide assessments, we have covered a lot of ground. It is critical that clinicians have a clear-cut, no-nonsense understanding of why they are taking the time to carefully document their suicide assessments. Such understanding provides them with the motivation to document well, and the principles to guide the process effectively.

If you understand the implications of the following seven principles, you have taken a giant step toward staying out of a courtroom and toward ongoing improvement of care.

## SEVEN PROTECTIVE PRINCIPLES OF SUICIDE ASSESSMENT DOCUMENTATION

1. Good clinical documentation is the primary shield against malpractice litigation.
2. There can be no good clinical documentation, unless there has first been good clinical care.
3. Even if good clinical care has been provided, if there is poor documentation then the risk of malpractice litigation rises steeply.
4. There are two types of poor documentation:
   (a) The clinician didn't document the assessment.
   (b) The clinician did document the assessment, but documented it poorly.
5. The first legal purpose of a sound written document is to keep the clinician out of court.
6. The second legal purpose of a sound written document is to effectively defend the clinician if the case goes to court.
7. The most important reason to write a sound written document is to convey information to other professionals that may help the care of the client or may serve as a quality assurance checklist for the clinician which, if done effectively, will also result in a sound legal document.

With the understanding of the Protective Principles behind us, we are now ready to look into the nitty gritty of "what" do we document and "how" do we document it.

## PART II   STRATEGIES FOR CREATING SOUND SUICIDE ASSESSMENT DOCUMENTS

There exist a variety of clinical situations in which we perform a suicide assessment and subsequently need to document it. A sampling of these clinical situations includes: an initial assessment, an emergency room assessment, ongoing psychotherapy, ongoing medication checks, consultation and liaison assessments in a general hospital, assessments before a pass or a discharge from an inpatient unit or a substance abuse rehabilitation center, assessments in correctional facilities, nursing home assessments, and home visits/street assessments with outreach teams for people dealing with severe disorders such as schizophrenia or bipolar disorder.

All of these assessments have complex issues related to their documentation. Fortunately, the principles for sound documentation are quite similar in all of them. In this appendix, we look at some of these principles as they apply to one of the most complex clinical encounters—a comprehensive initial assessment of a client you might perform in an outpatient clinic or private practice. The principles delineated here will point toward useful strategies for all of the clinical situations mentioned earlier.

To create clinically useful and forensically sound written documents of suicide assessments, we need to understand the three "Hows" that form the matrix from which the written document emerges. These three "Hows" are:

1. How a written document is structured.
2. How the material in a written document can be used to help the client.
3. How attorneys use the written document to attack or defend in a malpractice suit.

Keep in mind that the entire written initial assessment—not just the documentation of the suicide assessment—is full of useful clinical information to help the client as well as information that may be used as "damning" evidence during litigation. For the interested reader, my previous book, *Psychiatric Interviewing: the Art of Understanding, 2nd Edition*[6] provides a practical and detailed look at the core principles of both documenting the entire initial assessment and performing the initial interview from which it arose. Indeed, much of the subsequent material on documenting suicide assessments was adapted from this text.

## How a Written Document Is Structured

The first "How" of the matrix—the structure of the written document—is seldom given the time it warrants in the training of young professionals. This lack of attention in graduate schools and psychiatric residencies is unfortunate, for an understanding of the structure of the written document forms the foundation that guides the clinician toward the creation of a document that is useful both clinically and forensically.

The different regions of the document fall into two broad categories: (1) database, recorded as objectively as possible, for there will always remain a subjective quality to some of this information; and (2) clinical judgment and formulation, both of which are truly subjective in nature.

With the above distinctions in mind, let us look at the documentation components of a standard initial assessment listed by either objective database or subjective formulation:

I. Database (objective areas):
   Identifying Information and Demographics
   Chief Complaint
   History of the Present Illness
   Past Psychiatric History and Treatment
   Social and Developmental History
   Family History
   Medical History
   Medical Review of Systems
   Mental Status
II. Clinical Formulation and Judgment (subjective areas):
   *DSM-IV-TR* Diagnostic Listing
   Clinical Summary and Formulation (includes suicide risk formulation)
   Triage and Treatment Plan (some clinicians incorporate this information into the Clinical Summary and Formulation)

This distinction between those parts of the document that are database and those that are formulation appears almost too obvious to be worth mentioning. But a misunderstanding of these distinctions often leads to weak written documents. In this regard, let us turn our attention to the second "How" that forms the matrix from which the written document emerges.

## How the Material in a Written Document Can Be Used to Help the Client

Earlier we saw "why" a well-written document can improve clinical care itself. Now we'll look at the challenging task of "how" to actually accomplish this task. Let's move from theory to practice. We will begin by exploring methods of documenting objective data and subjective formulation that directly impact on our own assessment of the client's risk.

Our first two examples amplify the use of the process of documenting the objective database itself as a form of quality assurance checklist. First, by developing a habit of carefully and methodically recording risk factors, the clinician may spot important errors of omission, such as a lack of data on the presence of comorbid psychiatric disorders, a family history of suicide, or the presence of agitation. Second, concerning the client's own unique history of suicidal ideation and behavior, we may spot that an entire region of the CASE Approach was missed such as "Past Suicidal Events" or that a specific region of the CASE Approach was poorly explored with subsequent gaps in vital information such as the extent of current suicidal planning and implementation.

Our third example moves to the act of recording subjective formulation, yet another rich arena for improving quality assurance via documentation. We will see how to make it work to our client's advantage. As you write down the specific sentence that documents your clinical judgment (e.g., "I do/do not feel that the patient is acutely suicidal because . . ."), the very act of reviewing which items to list to support your conclusion can serve as a test of the thoroughness of the database. The act of documentation is serving as its own means of monitoring the quality of the interview itself. In particular I find the following two questions to be of immediate usefulness:

1. "What specific information from my knowledge of the client's risk factors and the extent of his or her suicidal ideation supports the conclusion I am about to write?"
2. "Would these facts appear to support my conclusion to another good clinician?"

Occasionally I am surprised, and somewhat disconcerted, by what I don't discover when trying to answer these two questions. It is surprisingly easy to jump to a conclusion concerning suicide risk when pressured for time and dealing with a waiting room full of patients tired of sitting in an emergency room. Once again we see that careful documentation is not only a method of ensuring that important data is recorded, it is a method of making sure that the clinician has procured the important data that needs to be recorded.

We have seen how the process of making a sound document can actually help us to make better risk assessments. Let us now turn our attention to how the documentation of our suicide assessment can help future clinicians to make better risk assessments with the client we have just seen.

When documenting a suicide assessment, I always try to remember that I am part of a team of clinicians. It is a somewhat odd team, for the team members may not know who the other team members are or will be. It may ultimately be composed of a team of clinicians who don't even know each other. Indeed, at the time of my write-up, the clinicians on my future team may not even have completed their professional training yet. They may never know me directly. However, they will come to know me indirectly, and intimately, by the words that I am writing down—the words that they are now reading six months or two years after I have composed them.

I always write my suicide risk assessment with this future "shadow teammate" in mind. For at some distant time, he or she may be determining whether the client that I just interviewed is safe to leave an emergency room or is at imminent risk of self-harm. What he or she reads in my record may provide the pivotal information that helps to save a life.

The future crisis clinicians, emergency room staff, and "docs on call" are at a decided disadvantage in uncovering sensitive material when interviewing our client, especially if they have never seen our client before. Having run a psychiatric emergency room, I can assure you that these clinicians read our notes. Indeed, they count on them.

Perhaps the most basic, yet valuable, principle concerning the documentation of the objective database is also one of the most simple: Be complete. List in the HPI all the specific suicide methods, and the extent of planning and action taken on these methods, as relayed by the client. Our future teammate may be extremely busy, inexperienced, or simply having a bad day. In any case, he or she may have missed important types of suicide methods that the client has been contemplating. If our note mentions that such plans were contemplated in the past, it will signal the clinician to aggressively search for them in the present.

By the way, our "distant "shadow teammate may not be very distant in time at all. One of the most important areas where good documentation may prove to be life saving is when we are referring the client to another clinician for immediate assessment. For instance, after doing an interview in our outpatient clinic we may refer a client to an emergency room for possible admission secondary to our concerns of the client's dangerousness. Alternatively, a common situation arises when we have just seen a client in one emergency room and we are referring them to another hospital for admission either because our beds are full or the client is from another "catchment area."

As pointed out in Chapter 7, in these situations it is advisable to try to speak directly with the clinician who will be doing the assessment at the next destination in addition to passing on our write-up. However, this direct contact is not always possible. In such situations, it is imperative that we follow our basic rule—Be complete!—for clients are notorious for clamming up at the next emergency room or hospital. Sometimes clients, when being re-evaluated at the next facility, flatly deny suicidal ideation in an effort to avoid hospitalization. The only source of accurate information is the information that we documented. It is not an exaggeration to say that good documentation can be life saving in such instances.

Clearly, the actual content of the data in our note is of immediate utility to future clinicians. But the utility of our note goes beyond the content, because the database that we record may indirectly shed light on the actual clinical process that is unfolding in the future assessment. Let us see how.

One of the most important tasks facing our shadow teammate in the future, especially in an emergency room or during a crisis situation with an unfamiliar client, is the determination of the truthfulness of the client's responses. Is the whole picture concerning suicidal planning being described and, if so, is it being described in an accurate fashion? Is the data a valid reflection of reality or is it tainted by purposeful deceit or unintentional misinformation (as might be caused by unconscious defense mechanisms such as denial or rationalization)?

Here is where our careful documentation may play a role in helping our future teammate decide whether the client is providing valid data. For instance, after taking the history of past suicide events using the CASE Approach, the clinician can always compare their information with the same material, previously relayed to us by the client, from our recorded history. The data should be the same. If it is not the same, it raises the specter that the database being currently provided by the client may be suspect. This could trigger more interviewing or even alert our future clinician of the prudence of attempting to contact collaborative sources other than the client. It might even prompt the clinician to call us, an exchange that may result in powerful new information and a sharing of clinical perspectives.

In this section, we have seen a set of specific principles and techniques that show us the "How" of making the act of documentation directly useful to our clients. Now let's see how poor documentation helps the plaintiff's lawyer to hurt us and, conversely, how to write documents that help our own lawyers to protect us from unwarranted lawsuits.

## HOW ATTORNEYS USE THE WRITTEN DOCUMENT TO ATTACK OR DEFEND IN A MALPRACTICE SUIT

Lawyers have a nasty penchant for scrutinizing written documents with much more attention to detail than the clinician used while writing them. When doing so, these documents are scoured for errors of omission, inconsistent data, formulations that are not supported by the database, evidence that important information was not gathered, and frank errors in clinical formulation and judgment. It is worth mentioning again that, in an odd sort of way, it is not so much what we say in court, but rather, what we wrote in our offices, that determines the outcome of a lawsuit.

Although risking triteness, it really is true that a lawsuit is much like a chess game. Each attorney is attempting to build advantages while looking for weaknesses in the opponent's play. For every point made, the opposing attorney is looking for a counterpoint. For every strategy employed, the opposing attorney is looking for a counterattack. Make no mistake about it, the goal is to "take out" the opponent's king, and the play can become ruthless. It is particularly unsettling when we realize that we, personally, are the opponent's targeted king.

However, in at least one important aspect, a lawsuit is distinctly different from a game of chess. For the lawyers, the "game" begins after half of the moves have already been made. Thus, a malpractice attorney, considering whether or not to take on a case, finds himself or herself looking across a board in which half the game has already unfolded and the resulting positions of the chess pieces are on display. The attorney has the opportunity to see the play to date (whether good care occurred and good documentation was done). After surveying the board, the attorney will decide who is likely to win and whether it is worth joining in the fray.

As noted earlier, it is the clinician's documentation that best shows the play so far. This is why, as we stated in our Seven Protective Principles, a soundly written document is the single best shield against malpractice. Let us look at how attorneys read this chessboard, looking for advantages and disadvantages, so that we can determine how best to design our shields.

The initial point of attack for an attorney is the objective database. It is in the objective database that the telltale signs of negligence, as reflected by a sloppy or inadequate database will surface. There are two main regions of objective database in a suicide assessment: (1) risk factors and (2) the client's unique suicidal ideation, planning, and intent.

In this light, the first stop-off for the attorney is to see whether the common risk factors for suicide have been addressed in the written document. If not, an argument can be made that the standard of care was not met because the clinician did not address typical risk factors.

If you ask about a risk factor and the client answers no, be sure to write down this "pertinent negative." If you don't write it down, there is no proof that you asked about it. Documenting pertinent negatives—those things that you asked about, but the client denied—is one of the key protections to a legal attack of negligence, more specifically, of negligence reflected in an inadequate database. Thus, in the Family History section, if there is no suicide, you would write:

> The client reports bipolar disorder in his father, alcoholism in two paternal aunts. He denies bipolar disorder, schizophrenia, anxiety disorders, substance abuse, or any other psychiatric disorders. There is no history of suicide.

The second stop-off for the attorney is to see whether suicidal ideation, planning, and intent were adequately addressed. Bottom-line: If you gathered a good database using the CASE Approach, be sure to document it. If you don't document it, an effort will be made to prove that you didn't do it. Without the record of such information in the written document, your fate lies purely on who the jury now believes. Should they believe the plaintiff's attorney, who has had years of training in how to sway jury opinion, or you, who has absolutely no training whatsoever in swaying jury opinion and is, at the moment, absolutely terrified. It's best not to be in this boat. Document fully.

The third stop-off for the attorney as he or she is perusing the objective database is the opposite of the first two stops. This time instead of looking for missing data—suggesting a sloppy database— the attorney is looking for "damning data" whose presence suggests that this client was imminently dangerous and the clinician just missed the boat.

Here is where leakage of subjective data into the objective database can be quite troubling. In my opinion, the most common problem comes down to the ill-advised use of a single word—"suicidal." Use it with great caution. First, notice that the term "suicidal" is clearly a subjective opinion, and consequently does not belong in the objective database according to our principles on structuring. Second, notice that when it is used alone without qualifiers such as mildly, moderately, or severely, it is vague, and it is easy for a jury to assume its most ominous connotations. Third, notice, in a similar vein, that to a jury the word "suicidal" simply does not sound good. A juror could easily assume that if a clinician thinks a client is suicidal, then the client should, obviously, be in a hospital. They are unaware that this conclusion might not be the case if the client is only mildly or moderately suicidal and effective support plans have been put in place. All of these vagaries make the term "suicidal" a red flag if used in the objective database. It is intensified by the phenomena that if a subjective opinion is placed in the objective database of the written document, it seems to take on the mantle of being "a fact." As a fact, it can now appear more damning.

Before we see how all of these factors can combine to wreak havoc in our defense, I should mention two exceptions to our rule. There are two places in the objective database where the word "suicidal" can be used safely. First, if you are recording the exact words of the client and he or she used the word "suicidal" and, second, if it is being used solely as a descriptor of another word as with a phrase such as "suicidal ideation."

If you follow these easily employed principles, you will be safe. Don't follow them, and you will be sorry. The following example of an easily made mistake, if you do not understand these principles, will make the point of just "how sorry" more evident. The following written statement is part of the History of the Present Illness. You will recall that this is one of the objective areas of the written document:

> The patient presented to our emergency room. Apparently he has been very stressed over his recent divorce and has been suicidal off and on for about three weeks. Because he is concerned that the patient is suicidal, his outpatient therapist referred him to us for possible admission to the hospital.

Now let's see why there is a glow of excitement in the attorney for the plaintiff, while he or she is reviewing this chart, for here is the chess gambit that is being imagined for the courtroom:

ATTORNEY:    Dr. Jones, could you please read this sentence from your initial assessment to the jury. It is marked 2–6 on the first page.

DEFENDANT:    Yes. "Apparently he has been very stressed over his recent divorce and has been suicidal off and on for about three weeks. Because he is concerned that the patient is suicidal, his outpatient therapist referred him to us for possible admission to the hospital."

ATTORNEY:    So, at the time of your evaluation, you wrote that the patient, who is now dead from a suicide, was suicidal off and on for about three weeks.

DEFENDANT:    Well, you have to understand that what . . .

ATTORNEY:    Excuse me, I don't like interrupting you, but I'm not asking you to interpret what you wrote, I just want to know, did you write that this patient had been suicidal off and on for about three weeks.

DEFENDANT:    (frustrated sigh) Yes, but . . .

ATTORNEY:    You also wrote that another experienced clinician, on the very day of your exam felt the patient was "suicidal." Indeed, he referred you the patient because he was suicidal.

DEFENDANT:    Well, once again, you have to . . .

ATTORNEY:    Please, Dr. Jones, just answer with a "yes" or a "no." You will have a chance to describe your post-suicide reasoning later if your attorney wants to offer it. All I want to know is did you write it.

DEFENDANT:    Yes, obviously I wrote it. I just read it to you from my own record, which you are well aware of (said a bit tersely).

ATTORNEY:    Dr. Jones, I just want to clarify that we can assume that if you write something down, it is your opinion

DEFENDANT:    Yes, but I see what you are trying to do here.

ATTORNEY:    Dr. Jones, what I'm trying to do here is get at the truth, that's what I'm trying to do. Now, for some reason, by the time you were done seeing the patient, you changed your mind about him being suicidal. It is clear from your record that you thought he had been suicidal off and on for about three weeks. Obviously, by the end of the interview you had changed your mind.

Now what concerns me is why you changed your mind because you were right to begin with. The referring clinician, who also felt the patient was suicidal, by your own note, was also right to begin with. This patient was obviously suicidal. He is dead. You were obviously very wrong. That's what concerns me. That's what concerns the parents of the deceased. That's why we are here today. Thank-you, no further questions at this time.

Wow, what a mess! We had better have a good attorney on our side. Two good ones would be even better. Remember, in the courtroom, the jury will be weighing our sloppy record against the obvious pain of the grieving family members—a pain being effectively highlighted by the skills of an experienced trial lawyer. This one subjective word—"suicidal"—is a ticket to a nightmare if used inappropriately in the objective database. Let's see how all this could have been avoided by using the principles described earlier. Here is both a more accurate and, from a liability prevention standpoint, sound example of the written document from the same patient:

> The patient presented to our emergency room. Apparently, he has been very stressed over his recent divorce. He has had intermittent suicidal ideation off and on for about three weeks. Because of his fluctuating suicidal ideation, his outpatient therapist referred him to us to assess the severity of this ideation and to determine whether hospitalization may be necessary.

Gambit declined. No unnecessary advantage has been given to the opposing lawyer. Simply writing down the truth in unambiguous terms and keeping subjective opinion (the word "suicidal" unless used as a descriptor) out of the objective database has created a forensically sound document. We have forged ourselves a better shield.

The next question is how much did the shield cost to make. The answer is—next to nothing. Note that this simple safeguard created by keeping the objective database clean of subjective opinion, required almost no extra time whatsoever during the write-up, but look at the amount of potential misery it avoided for this clinician. When it comes to creating a sound written document—technique counts!

As we wrap up this section, we come to the second major attack point for a lawyer—the subjective formulation of risk. The attack plan is simple yet quite effective. The lawyer is looking for the following weaknesses in the clinician's development of his or her chess pieces:

1. The clinician has demonstrated incompetence or negligence in care.

a. Poor judgment—below the standard of care—when weighing the risk factors.

b. Poor judgment—below the standard of care—when weighing the extent of suicidal ideation, planning, and intent.

c. Did not tap critical collaborative sources of information such as spouses, partners, friends, family members, employers, client's therapist, or psychiatrist.

d. Did not educate nor rally the patient's available support systems in an effort to create a safer interpersonal milieu.

e. Did not obtain records or obtained the records but did not read them.

f. Did not consult when indicated.

g. Did not refer when indicated.

h. Did not set up appropriate follow-up care.

i. Did not provide the follow-up care that was offered.

j. Did not check to see if follow-up care was utilized, and, if not utilized, did not take appropriate steps to improve utilization.

k. Chose an inadequate or dangerous treatment intervention.

2. The clinician is competent, but acted maliciously:

a. Client is not admitted because the clinician/staff do not like the client.

b. Client is discharged prematurely because the clinician/staff did not like the client or the client's insurance "ran out."

c. Clinician could not make appropriate decisions secondary to vested interests in the client or has boundary violations with the client.

The previous outline forms a nice checklist of the dos and don'ts of suicide assessment, highlighting what a reasonable standard of care should be. If these have not been met, then a lawsuit may be both appropriate, and necessary, to prevent a weak clinician from doing further harm. In this chapter, we are assuming that the clinician has met these standards. Our question is how to create a written document that adequately shields a competent clinician from being inappropriately sued concerning his or her clinical formulation of risk.

The first tip is obvious, but in a hectic emergency room, I find it easy to forget to do—document that I did what I did. Such documentation is frequently done at the beginning of the formulation. Let us imagine that you were involved in a complicated suicide assessment that required contacting collaborative sources as well as consulting a colleague such as a psychiatrist on call. Here is an example of well-written documentation:

> After interviewing the patient and reviewing his charts, speaking with his mother and sister by phone, discussing the case with our charge nurse and reviewing the case with the psychiatrist on call (both of whom agree with my formulation), I feel that Mr. Jakins is not at immediate risk for suicide. Our reasons for this opinion are as follows: . . . .

Your defense lawyer will be smiling from ear to ear when he or she reads the above sentence in the chart. In addition, it doesn't take a long time to write it. By the way, as we have noted before, if the clinician develops the documentation habit of routinely reviewing whether such contacts occurred (and thus need to be documented) it may help the clinician to spot that an important source of information was missed. As we have seen so many times before, good documentation and good clinical care foster each other.

There is a useful caveat worth mentioning. As with the recording of the objective database, be sure to list "pertinent negatives" in the formulation. If you tried to reach a therapist and he or she is not at home, document it. If you can't procure a chart, document that you tried; if the client refuses to let you speak to someone and you do not think you have enough suspicion of lethality to override his wishes, document your reasoning; and, finally, if someone you contact cannot provide adequate information, state so (e.g., his wife was both hostile and acutely intoxicated when called, limiting the usefulness of her input). These pertinent negatives will serve you well in preventing a lawsuit, for they represent concrete evidence that it is unlikely that you were negligent. As such, they are critical alloys in our shield.

The next point may very well represent the heart of the matter regarding the construction of a good shield when documenting clinical formulation. Simply put, it is not only important to clearly document what your decision is concerning the client's suicide risk, it is equally important to describe how and why you arrived at this decision. Both subsequent clinicians and lawyers are interested in the how and why of your decision, not just the what.

For example, let us assume you have a patient who has chronic schizophrenia. He presents with some low grade command hallucinations to kill himself. After careful consideration of the many important variables in assessing his acute dangerousness secondary to these command hallucinations, you decide he is not at high risk now. Here is how *not* to record this decision:

> After reviewing the content of the patient's command hallucinations, I do not feel he is in danger of acting upon them at this time.

Notice that this documentation gives the "what" but not the "how" and "why" of the decision, thus opening the door for a talented lawyer to try to convince a jury that you used judgment that was below the standard of care. Since you have not written down how you made your judgment, your only defense are the words you speak in court, and the opposing lawyer will use every legal trick in the book to convince the jury that your words should not be given much weight.

We don't need to go there. With just a few written statements, the likelihood of such a scenario can be significantly reduced as illustrated next:

> Despite the fact that Mr. Everly is currently having some command hallucinations as described in the HPI and Mental Status, I do not feel he is likely to act upon them in the near future. In the past, on the few instances he acted upon them they were described as loud, hounding, and relentless. At such moments, he reported feeling out of control. The last time he acted upon them was over thirty years ago. Today the voices are reported as infrequent and soft. Mr. Everly does not appear to be bothered by them as reflected by his pleasant affect, indeed, he commented, "Doc, don't get bent out of shape about those voices, the devil has been talking to me for years and I haven't listened to him for years, and I'm not about to do so now." His wife is well educated on schizophrenia and knows both when and how to contact us if problems arise.

The importance of documenting the how and why of our clinical decisions is obvious from the above example. However, I must admit, when pressed for time, I frequently feel a pull to short-circuit this aspect of documenting my formulation. I try to avoid such short-cuts when documenting my formulation, if at all possible. But when short-cuts are made necessary by extreme time constraints, a knowledge of the above principles can help me to choose them wisely.

The cornerstone of many a wrongful death lawsuit is the idea that poor clinical judgment was used. And malpractice lawyers accept many cases, because they can almost taste the presence of poor clinical judgment as they read the chart. It is a well-documented written description of the "hows" and "whys" of a sound formulation that can quickly sour this taste in the mouth of a hungry attorney and push them toward a refusal to accept the case.

Before we proceed, let us review what we have learned about the general principles of writing a sound forensic document:

### Recording Objective Data:

1. Be sure to take the time to actually list the risk factors that you uncovered in the appropriate regions of the objective database

(HPI, Family History, Mental Status, etc.). This provides you with the data to support your formulation of risk in the subjective section and helps to show that you were not negligent in your duties of developing a database that meets the standard of care.

2. Be sure to document pertinent negatives regarding risk factors (e.g., "no history of past suicide attempts" in the Past Psychiatric History or "no history of suicide" in the Family History) so as to once again demonstrate that a thorough assessment was undertaken and that a search for the risk factors associated with a reasonable standard of care occurred.

3. Be sure to list both the positives and pertinent negatives discovered concerning the client's suicidal ideation, planning, and intent as uncovered using the CASE Approach or a similar method for uncovering such data.

4. Do not let subjective opinions leak into your documentation of objective data. This is particularly true of the word "suicidal" which should not appear in the subjective areas of the document unless it is used as a quote from the client or as a descriptor of another word as with the phrase "suicidal ideation."

**Recording Subjective Formulation:**

1. If not already documented in the previous sections on objective data, always list what resources were used in your formulation including, collaborative informants, other professionals involved in the client's care, hospital and clinic records, and consultants.

2. List the pertinent negatives in this regard such as anybody who you attempted to contact but could not reach or clinical records that simply were not available to you despite your attempts to procure them. Such documentation helps to demonstrate that you were not negligent in your attempt to gather information regarding the safety of the client.

3. Take the time to carefully document the "hows" and "whys" of your clinical reasoning that led to your conclusions on the client's immediate safety. Arguably such documentation is the single most important area of legal defense. If done well, you may significantly decrease the likelihood that an attorney will accept the case. It also makes your defense, if the case is taken to court, significantly easier.

At this point, we are ready to put it all together. We will take the three "Hows" of suicide assessment documentation and watch them in action as we employ them in concrete examples of sound clinical and forensic documentation of risk.

## THE BASICS PUT TO THE TEST:
## EXAMPLES OF SOUND DOCUMENTATION

### DOCUMENTING THE OBJECTIVE DATABASE

### *I. Documentation of Risk Factors*

The documentation of our first area of objective database—classic suicide risk factors—is the most straight forward. As mentioned earlier, the following points are worth remembering. Be complete for such completeness helps to demonstrate concretely that you were not negligent in hunting for risk factors. Be sure to document pertinent negatives concerning risk factors, such as "no history of past suicide attempts," for this action once again demonstrates thoroughness—an important aspect of meeting a reasonable standard of care.

Be aware that the various risk factors will be elicited in a variety of different sections of the clinical interview and will, in a parallel fashion, need to be documented in differing sections of the objective database. For example, risk factors will appear in the following sections of the objective database: Identifying Information and Demographics (risk factors such as sex and age), History of the Present Illness (risk factors such as current drug and alcohol use, current psychiatric symptoms, current psychotic symptoms, immediate stressors, and recent discharge from a hospital or recent visits to emergency rooms or contacts with crisis clinicians), Past Psychiatric History and Treatment (risk factors such as previous suicide attempts, responses to previous treatment interventions, presence of longstanding psychiatric disorders such as a borderline personality disorder or chronic bipolar disorder), Social and Developmental History (support systems, hostile interpersonal relationships, presence or absence of a life partner, details on current stressors and triggers), Family History (risk factors such as a history of suicide and suicide attempts in blood relatives, client's feelings, and/or identifications with family members who completed suicide), Medical History (risk factors such as the presence of chronic pain and/or the presence of a debilitating chronic or terminal illnesses).

For the sake of illustration, we will look at a well-documented Past Psychiatric History. Notice the clear documentation of past drug and alcohol abuse, a specific distant suicide attempt, and the pertinent negative of "no recent suicide attempts":

Past Psychiatric History: The patient reports a drinking history that included weekend drinking to the point of intoxication on many weekends from the ages of 17–23. She denies a history of blackouts, seizures, arrests for DWIs, or use of street drugs of any kind. No drinking for over ten years. She denies a history of schizophrenia, bipolar disorder, or other major psychiatric disorder. No past psychiatric care or hospitalization. At the age of 19, while under the influence of alcohol, she reports taking a handful of aspirin following a break-up with a boyfriend, but received no care at that point. Denies any other history of suicidal ideation or attempts.

## II. Documentation of Suicidal Ideation, Planning, and Intent

To "bring to life" the documentation of the second database needed in a suicide assessment—the client's suicidal ideation, it is valuable to show a prototypic documentation from an actual client discussed in this book. We will look at an example of how you might soundly document the suicidal ideation and planning of Barbara, who we met earlier in Chapter 6. If you will recall, we used a direct transcript of Barbara's clinical interview to illustrate the CASE Approach (pages 153–188). All examples in this section will be based on the information garnered from that interview, providing you with the rare opportunity to see the translation of actual clinical dialogue into a clinical document.

Before examining these examples, let's take a look at a few basic principles. As with the documentation of risk factors, in order to demonstrate appropriate thoroughness, you will want to be complete with your documentation of suicidal ideation and pertinent negatives reported by the client about suicidal ideation. The trick is to make sure such information is recorded in the appropriate regions of the objective database, and that no subjective data trickles in.

In the HPI, the clinician will describe all suicidal ideation and events that occurred in the current episode of the illness up until the time immediately before the assessment including the region of recent suicide events as they unfolded in the previous two months. In the Mental Status, the clinician will describe any recent suicidal ideation not already described in the HPI and any immediate suicidal ideation experienced during the interview itself (some clinicians include descriptions of safety contracting here and others include it in the HPI). In the Past Psychiatric History, all past suicidal information will be appropriately described as we have already demonstrated.

Notice how closely the different regions where we will record the client's suicidal ideation and behavior parallel the topical regions of the CASE Approach itself, which was utilized in gathering the information in the interview. If the clinician has utilized the CASE

Approach effectively, all of this data will be neatly waiting to "fall into place" in the written document.

It is often wise to include in the HPI or the Mental Status any direct and compelling quotes from the patient that may be used later to support the formulation that suicide risk is minimal. For instance, the clinician might document statements such as, "I would never kill myself. I just couldn't do that to my kids" or "As much pain as I'm in, I know I won't kill myself because it is a mortal sin. It's just not the right thing to do."

As we shall soon see, in our Summary and Formulation, we will refer to such statements as supportive objective evidence for our clinical decision. If ever taken to court, both you and your attorney will be greatly pleased by the presence of such concrete documentation. Such quotations also provide important clues to future clinicians, suggesting areas they can explore to see if such powerful deterrents to suicide are still active for the patient.

The documentation of "safety contracting" opens up an entirely new "can of worms." This particular documentation issue is complicated enough, and can play such a significant role in a lawsuit that it warrants a separate discussion that follows in Appendix B.

Let us now look at the documentation of Barbara's suicidal ideation and events as they might be recorded in the History of the Present Illness (HPI). We will refer to Barbara as Ms. Simmons. Somewhere in the body of the HPI, at a point that would chronologically make sense, the following would appear:

HPI . . . . (previous paragraphs) . . .

Over the past several months, Ms. Simmons has developed suicidal ideation. Her most recent plan was to stockpile various over-the-counter medications and, in the month of June, go to a remote cabin and overdose on these pills and shoot herself. She had gathered around twenty bottles of Tylenol-PM and Benadryl. There was already a gun in the house. She also wrote some suicide letters to important people in her life. On Friday night, a full month before she was intending to implement her plan, she spontaneously shared her thoughts on suicide with a friend agreeing to come to the emergency room for help.

Over the last several months, she also had some thoughts of driving her car off the road but denies ever getting into a car with this intention. She has had fleeting thoughts of hanging herself but has taken no action on such thoughts. She denies thoughts concerning jumping or carbon monoxide poisoning. Several months ago, she did have an incident of thinking of cutting herself on the arm. She had obtained a razor blade for this purpose but never did place the razor blade to her arm. She made a decision not to kill herself commenting, "I couldn't do that to my kids, I wouldn't want somebody else raising my kids." At the present time, she denies any suicidal thoughts or intentions.

This crisp and comprehensive summary provides a wealth of information for any future emergency room clinician who might be evaluating Barbara. The extent of the planning and the details recorded will emphasize to the clinician the seriousness of her thoughts while providing specific plans to inquire about to see if any further planning has occurred since we saw her. Notice how it will also provide a check on her validity as the clinician compares what she is now reporting about her past suicidal ideation and that the clinician now, thanks to our record, has an actual picture of what is the truth. It also provides a future clinician with possible grounds for commitment in some states, for the stockpiling of pills represents an action taken toward self-harm.

From a legal standpoint the thoroughness will make an attack of negligent interviewing hard to pull off. Clearly, the clinician was thorough as is further reflected by the judicious listing of pertinent negatives as with, "She denies thoughts concerning jumping or carbon monoxide poisoning." We have also wisely included concrete evidence that Barbara has a powerful reason to live by recording her own words as best we remembered them, "I couldn't do that to my kids, I wouldn't want somebody else raising my kids."

What we are not writing is almost as important as what we are writing. We are not making any subjective comments about this objective database—either suggesting that we feel Barbara is safe or not safe. Such impressions will be shared in our formulation of risk and do not belong here. On the other hand, we are carefully making sure that we are recording the raw data that is going to be used to support our ultimate formulation of safety.

This database does show that Barbara had a lot of suicidal ideation. Some clinicians might argue that the accurate recording of her ideation could look bad in court. So be it. It is the truth. Moreover, our goal is to record the clinical truth about Barbara's presentation so that future clinicians can make wise decisions. So far, we have only recorded part of the objective database. By the time we are done recording all of our raw data, it should make a sound case that she is safe. If it doesn't then we might be wise to rethink our decision. Maybe our risk formulation is wrong. This is why it is so important, while recording the objective database, to simply write down what we know—both factors suggestive of risk and factors suggestive of safety—and let the data point us toward the correct formulation of risk.

What is critical from a forensic standpoint is to make sure that we are not inadvertently leaving out the important raw data that actually supports our decision that the client was safe. Such errors of omission are easy to make when under tight time constraints, but they are critical not to make. If you practice the principles in this appendix, you will remember this need. With continued practice, you will become surprisingly proficient at recording important supportive data quickly.

At this early stage in the recording of suicide data in the HPI, Barbara looks fairly dangerous. In fact, an attorney contemplating taking the case on, although disappointed that negligence during the interview does not look like a promising line of attack, might be quite excited about the possibility that the clinician used poor clinical judgment, for, so far, Barbara sounds dangerous. In this regard, Barbara has extensive planning, she has the means to act on it, and there are even grounds for an involuntary commitment.

But watch what happens to this attorney's enthusiasm when we continue to simply lay out the facts accurately, making sure we document any facts that will support our ultimate formulation that Barbara is safe to go. If you will recall, Barbara was seen in the emergency room on a Friday night. This interview which we are now documenting, occurred on the subsequent Monday as part of an assessment to see if Barbara could become part of an outpatient crisis support group. Here is the next paragraph in our HPI:

> Barbara was both cooperative and thankful for the interventions in the emergency room on Friday Night. Her husband, who came to the Emergency Room, was responsible and concerned. All consulted on that night including the psychiatrist on call and the emergency room nurses and physician all felt Barbara was safe to go. She and her husband eagerly agreed to a plan whereby Barbara was to call the crisis team twice on Saturday and twice on Sunday for supportive counseling. Both the crisis team and Barbara report to us today that these sessions went very well, as is also corroborated by her husband. Barbara denies any suicidal ideation over this past weekend, a fact also corroborated by her husband who inquired of such ideation several times over the weekend. The gun was removed from the house as requested.

Any attorney, looking for a good lawsuit, is not finding one. In addition, notice the attorney hasn't even seen a single sentence from our formulation for risk. The hard data is protecting us. It is the simple act of accurately recording what we know that is forming our forensic shield. This objective data is pointing toward the fact that a decision that the client is safe seems appropriate from the information available at the time of the interview. In short, an adequate standard of care is being met.

One of the reasons Barbara provides such a good record for us to discuss is the fact that her presentation was a particularly complex one— much more high risk than many typical assessments. Thus, her case does two things: (1) it demonstrates that the application of a handful of basic principles can provide powerful forensic protection even in high risk cases, and (2) it reminds us that most assessments, and their subsequent documentations, are not nearly this complex or time consuming. Indeed, most suicide documentations can be done in several minutes. If you can apply these principles in a complicated case like Barbara's, you will find yourself easily, and with minimal time costs, employing such sound documentation practices in your everyday practice.

Let's now take a look at how we would record Barbara's suicidal ideation and events from her past. This will prove to be quite simple:

Past Psychiatric History:
   . . . (other past psychiatric history information) . . . Barbara has had some intermittent suicidal ideation from the age of 15 onwards, but has no history whatsoever of acting on these thoughts. She denies any previous suicide gestures or attempts.

Simple, quick, and accurate. Let's move to our documentation of her current suicidal ideation. This material will always appear in the Mental Status:

Suicidal Ideation: The client has had recent suicidal ideation (Please see HPI for details). At the present moment, and over the weekend, she denies suicidal ideation of any kind. She was able to make a safety contract with me, demonstrating both good eye contact and a firm handshake.

That's it! If you have documented the recent suicidal ideation clearly in the HPI, there is no need to duplicate it here. If you hadn't, then here is where it would be added. Generally speaking, if the client has had significant suicidal ideation it will have been already described in the HPI. Much more information on the documentation of safety contracting will be provided in Appendix B.

We are done with our discussion of documenting the objective database. All that is left is the documentation of our subjective formulation of her suicide risk. Again, by following the few principles we have already outlined, this will turn out not to be an overly difficult task at all.

*III. Documentation of the Clinical Formulation of Suicide Risk*

I would like to begin this section on the documentation of the subjective formulation of risk by noting two points. First, the clinical formulation is often the best place to document any consultation that you made with a colleague. As we mentioned earlier in the appendix, it is wise to list everybody with whom you discussed the case and state his or her agreement with your decision. Such a notation may look like this, "I spoke with the patient's therapist at home and also consulted with the on-call psychiatrist, both of whom are in full agreement with the plan." Consulting is probably the single best defense against the charge of negligence. However, it weakens markedly if not recorded.

From a clinical standpoint, consulting is often very beneficial, even for the most experienced clinician. I always use the following rule of thumb, if I'm wondering whether it would be a good idea to consult someone, it means it is a good time. And I do.

The second point concerns a common documentation practice to avoid. It has to deal with the design of the intake form or emergency room note itself. Specifically, some agencies create forms where it is expected that the clinician should "check off "or circle a "number" indicating the client's risk of suicide. The scales often range from one to five.

Right from the beginning, this notion should bother anyone familiar with the principle of keeping the subjective out of the objective database and vice versa. Here we have an example of trying to make something that is, and should be, inherently subjective in nature—our clinical formulation—into a quantifiable "fact" by giving it a number. Bad business! Assigning a number lends it a weight that can bite one in the face in court, as an attack attorney uses this inflated importance against the defendant. No matter whether you assigned a high or low number to the client's risk, if that client goes on to commit suicide, it is a lose/lose proposition in court. Let's see why.

Let us say we saw a client with many risk factors, and he was displaying marked suicidal ideation and planning. Consequently, we assigned the client a risk of five out of five. But we also had designed an outstanding support network with both the family and crisis clinicians to get the client through the weekend. As with Barbara, the goal was to get the client into a crisis group on Monday. Unfortunately, the husband who appeared to be quite responsible and reliable ends up going on a drinking binge and leaves the client alone. The client impulsively acts out and kills herself. Now look at the mess we are in because we assigned a high number to the client's risk, we have opened ourselves to an attorney's attack that might go like this:

ATTORNEY: Dr. Nathan, what was the highest number on your risk scale?

DEFENDANT: Five

ATTORNEY: Five?

DEFENDANT: Yes, five.

ATTORNEY: And could you please read to the jury what number you assigned the client's risk?

DEFENDANT: (sighing) A five.

ATTORNEY: Well, I'm a little baffled here (turns to the jury). You gave this client your highest level of risk. You literally can't get any higher risk of dangerousness on your scale. What exactly does it take to get someone in pain, who desperately needs the safety of hospitalization, into your hospital?

This line of questioning is not going well. It would not be going much better if you had given the client a rating of "four." The same argument could be used but now the words "the highest number" are replaced with "the next to highest number on your entire scale." That doesn't sound much better. And a gifted attorney will pound the message home to the jury.

It is almost as bad if you gave the client a low number, say a "two" and the client proceeded to commit suicide. Let us return to our courtroom:

ATTORNEY: Dr. Nathan, is it true that on your suicide risk scale a low number, such as one or two, indicates minimal risk and a high number, such as a four or a five means a much higher risk?

DEFENDANT: Yes.

ATTORNEY: Could you please read for the jury, what number of risk you assigned the client on the night of December 22?

DEFENDANT: A "two."

ATTORNEY: A "two"? That was your clinical estimate of this client's risk?

DEFENDANT: Yes.

ATTORNEY: Just for a point of clarification. Wasn't the client dead from committing suicide only eight hours after you gave them one of the lowest ratings of suicide risk possible on your scale? It's hard to be much more wrong in clinical judgment isn't it, Dr. Nathan?

Of course, your attorney is jumping up and down yelling, "Your Honor, I object." Well, your attorney can object all he wants. The bottom line is the jury heard the point, and it isn't going well for the home team. In my opinion, it is not wise to assign numbers to suicide risk. The formulation of clinical risk by nature is subjective. Keep it that way. Simply describe in detail how you arrived at your personal view of the client's suicide risk.

As stated earlier, take the time to demonstrate your clinical reasoning step by step. If you clearly documented that you took a careful history, contacted corroborative sources if indicated, consulted if necessary, and then used good clinical judgment, you can't have a much better shield against a lawsuit.

Let's see these principles at work with the documentation of our clinical formulation of risk with Barbara. Remember we don't have to write a thesis, we just have to clearly document the how and why of our reasoning so that it is clear to a future clinician or a jury member. If this clarification is hard to do, it suggests that perhaps our formulation may be wrong. Once again the act of carefully documenting our work serves as a built in quality assurance device for that work. Use it.

Clinical Formulation:
. . . (statements concerning other areas of clinical formulation such as differential diagnosis by *DSM-IV-TR*, psychological issues etc.) . . . Concerning suicide risk, Barbara presents a fairly complex picture. Several factors point toward significant risk including: a well thought out plan, the use of a gun as well as pills, the procurement of the pills, and ready access to the gun, an isolated place chosen for the suicide, and significant emotional pain. On the other hand, when looking at generic risk factors, there appear to be a great many factors pointing toward her immediate safety. Her age, sex, lack of current drug or alcohol use, lack of psychosis, lack of a family history of suicide, no previous history of suicide, and no debilitating medical conditions all lower her risk profile.

Even more powerful arguments for her safety appear when we look at specific safety factors for her. One month before she was to attempt suicide she leaked the information to a friend (strongly suggestive of a desire to get help), and she cooperated fully with the emergency room clinicians and appeared grateful for their interaction. And her commitment to her own safety was directly tested over the weekend. She responded with strong evidence of a desire to live as reflected by her contacting the crisis team, as she had promised, at the four specific times that the crisis team had scheduled for her. The crisis team reports she did good work during the telephone sessions. There was no suicidal ideation over the weekend. The gun was also immediately removed as requested by the crisis team. Her husband reports she had a much better weekend without any suicidal comments. During my own interview, she denied current suicidal ideation and voiced a strong commitment to stay alive for her children as reflected by her comment, "I couldn't do that to my kids, I wouldn't want somebody else raising my kids."

Although I believed there would be minimal deterrence value to a safety contract, for this was our first meeting, I used the act of safety contracting as a method for uncovering any evidence of ambivalence in Barbara concerning her commitment to her safety and found no evidence of ambivalence. She contracted with a genuine affect, good eye contact, and a firm handshake all done in a natural fashion suggesting she was comfortable with the commitment to work in our support group. All parties involved including Barbara, her husband, the Director of our crisis support group, and myself felt she was safe for outpatient care.

Keep in mind that Barbara was a high-risk candidate from a forensic point of view. She had well thought-out plans, had written suicide letters, had chosen an isolated area unlikely to result in detection, and even had presented with grounds for an involuntary commitment. If she had committed suicide two months after my assessment, she would have been a classic candidate for a lawsuit. But I think such a lawsuit would have been highly unlikely with the type of shield that we had produced by using a simple set of core documentation principles. Precious little room exists for forensic attack in this document. In contrast, it is a veritable bonanza of outstanding defense points. A lawyer looking to pick up a case, in which he or she has a high likelihood of both winning and landing a large settlement, will have to look elsewhere. This chess game has been played well.

In this appendix, I wanted to demonstrate the remarkable power of a well-written suicide assessment to prevent a lawsuit when a clinician has provided good clinical care. Now that we have seen these principles applied in a complicated case, where it behooves the clinician to take considerable time to carefully document, we can feel comfortable that in the vast majority of our assessments, the documentation process will be much shorter. Most suicide assessments can be documented in a fraction of the time it took with Barbara.

Extreme time constraints sometimes make employing these principles, to their fullest extent, difficult, and, in some instances, not practical. Hopefully, after reading about these principles, you, when placed in such situations, are now armed with the necessary knowledge to know in which cases documentation shortcuts can be taken and in which cases such shortcuts would be ill advised. You also now understand the possible costs of specific shortcuts and can make a wise decision on which documentation shortcuts you feel comfortable with making. At least now, you can make these decisions that may have major forensic ramifications, from a solid understanding of the possible consequences of these decisions. If we view written documentation as a form of insurance against malpractice, the goal of this appendix has been to make the clinician, whose increased time is the payment for this insurance, an informed consumer.

We end with two important caveats. First, having taught these techniques for many years, I want to emphasize that clinicians, with practice, become surprisingly rapid at documenting efficiently. In short, I do not believe that the time costs are very high in the long run. Second, we have seen repeatedly that the principles that help to make a written document more forensically sound, also significantly improve clinical care itself. And one can think of few places in our work where it is more important to provide the best possible care that we can, than in the assessment of suicide risk.

Once the principles of this appendix are understood, the clinician can feel a refreshing sigh of relief knowing the following: If we provide good clinical care and soundly document that care, using the principles of this Appendix, then we do not have to practice defensive medicine, for the likelihood of a lawsuit is remote. Thus, we can put our thoughts of lawyers where they belong—on a back burner. Instead, we can focus our attention where we have always wanted it to be—on caring about our patients and caring for our patients.

We began this chapter with the often-cited quotation by Robert I. Simon:

> There are only two kinds of clinical psychiatrists—those who have had patients commit suicide and those who will.

I would like to end with a corollary of that quotation:

> For those psychiatrists, who provided good clinical care, and through no fault of their own lost a patient to suicide, there are only two categories—those who are sued and those who are not sued.

The goal of this appendix is to make sure that all clinicians who provide good care, and, unfortunately lose one of their clients to suicide, are in the latter category.

## NOTES

1. Gutheil, T. G.: Liability issues and liability prevention in suicide. *The Harvard Medical School Guide to Suicide Assessment and Intervention,*

edited by D. G. Jacobs. San Francisco: Jossey-Bass, 1999, Chapter 31, 561–578.

2. Simon, R. I.: Taking the "sue" out of suicide: A forensic psychiatrist's perspective. *Psychiatric Annals 30:* 399–407, 2000.

3. Comstock, B. S.: Decision to hospitalize and alternatives to hospitalization. *Suicide Guidelines for Assessment, Management, and Treatment,* edited by Bruce Bongar. New York: Oxford University Press, 1992, Chapter 12, 216.

4. Simon, R. I.: *Concise Guide to Psychiatry and the Law for Clinicians, 2nd ed.,* Washington, DC: American Psychiatric Press, Inc., 1998, 143.

5. Skip Simpson, J. D.: Practice limited to psychiatric and psychological malpractice, (http://www.skipsimpson.com), personal communication, 2002.

6. Shea, S.C.: *Psychiatric Interviewing: The Art of Understanding, 2nd ed.,* Philadelphia: W.B. Saunders, 1998.

# APPENDIX B

# Safety Contracting Revisited: Pros, Cons, and Documentation

I T HAS been decades since the concept of the "suicide prevention contract" was first formally described in the literature by Drye, Goulding, and Goulding in 1973.[1] We don't know a lot more now about its proposed efficacy, with regards to deterrence, than we did then. In his excellent chapter on the topic, Miller cogently points out that some clinicians overvalue the effectiveness of safety contracts.[2] Moreover, Miller points out that even if a clinician is appropriately aware of both their potential advantages and limitations, there is very little formal training on when to use them, how to use them, and how to document their use. However, use them clinicians do.

Drew reported that 79 percent of the Ohio psychiatric inpatient programs that she surveyed reported using written no-suicide agreements.[3] In a survey of Harvard Medical School faculty, whereas virtually all the psychiatrists and psychologists polled had seen contracts used—indeed, approximately 75 percent worked in places where they were regularly used—60 percent to 70 percent stated that they had never received formal training on how to use them.[4] Such a conspicuous lack of training takes on a more ominous tone when it is realized that one of the more common issues in malpractice lawsuits, regarding wrongful death in suicide, is an undue reliance on suicide prevention contracts.[5]

*The Practical Art of Suicide Assessment: A Guide for Mental Health Professionals and Substance Abuse Counselors* provides a resource for the clinician that addresses this lack of formal training. In Chapters 6 and 7, I discussed some of the advantages and disadvantages of safety contracting, including areas where it may prove to be detrimental, for example, with some clients dealing with borderline process. I need not repeat this information here. However, in the hardback version of this book, I did not address the important issue of how to document the act of safety contracting. This appendix addresses this omission. Equally importantly, as with Appendix A, I will make an effort not only to show why and what should be documented, but to show exactly how safety contracting should be documented through the liberal use of prototypic illustrations.

Since the original publication of *The Practical Art of Suicide Assessment* in 1999, I continue to be impressed with the robust intensity of the debate surrounding safety contracting both among suicidologists and general clinicians. This ongoing, and always stimulating, debate as to the effectiveness of safety contracting warrants a second visit. Moreover, an understanding of how to use safety contracts will lead us naturally into a discussion of how to wisely document their use.

Regarding the topic of documenting safety contracting, we return yet again to one of our main guiding principles from Appendix A, "Good clinical care is good forensic protection, if well documented." If we use reasonable clinical judgment in deciding whether to use safety contracting—and how to interpret its relevance once utilized—and we then subsequently document this good judgment, the shield for a solid legal defense has already been forged.

Outstanding clinicians have weighed in on the safety contracting issue both strongly in support of its use and strongly opposed to its use. The question then arises: How can talented clinicians be at such categorically opposing ends of an opinion spectrum on a clinical tool that is employed by tens of thousands of clinicians everyday? Depending on which end of the continuum proves to be right, it would appear that a large number of very talented clinicians are obviously wrong. Or are they?

I don't think so; I believe that in a surprising and, paradoxical fashion, both camps are right. They are simply focusing on different angles to the debate and, depending on which angle one uses, the effectiveness of safety contracting appears to legitimately vary. Let us look at this supposed clinical paradox in more detail. The confounding problem seems to be that the debate has been oversimplified by two ground rules that have come to define the debate itself and, to some degree, in my opinion, may have led the debate off track. Let us see how this side-tracking has unfolded.

## A MISLEADING FIRST QUESTION: "IS SAFETY CONTRACTING A GOOD DETERRENT TO SUICIDE?"

The question usually at the forefront of the safety contracting debate seems to be, "Is safety contracting a good deterrent to suicide?" Unfortunately, this question, from both a research and a clinical perspective, is oversimplified. A more useful, albeit necessarily more complex, question is as follows:

> Does safety contracting ever serve as a deterrent (e.g., help to save a life) when considering its use with a unique client, who has unique psychodynamic defenses, unique characterological traits, a specific set of risk factors, and in the hands of a specific clinician, who has unique skills, a unique number of years of experience with suicidal clients, and has developed a unique therapeutic alliance with the client, while factoring in the critical situational caveat as to whether the safety contracting is being done in an initial interview versus ongoing therapy?

The answer, at this stage of research, is a categorical, "We don't know." Moreover, we might not ever know, for the number of research variables, for which there is a need for a control in such a project design, is formidable indeed.

Consequently, at present, the answer to the question whether safety contracting is an effective deterrent is, "Don't know for sure, but it probably depends on a variety of factors including who the client is, who the clinician is, and what the clinical situation is." At our current level of knowledge, it would appear that it might be premature to adamantly defend or attack safety contracting across all clients, as if the tool were meant to be used as a cookbook. Instead, we have a rich opportunity to re-open the debate as to whether with a specific client it might in some fashion help to save his or her life. Naturally, this ultimate decision must be made by each clinician and we are all entitled to our opinions.

My personal bias is that safety contracting is seldom a deterrence in initial assessments, although there can even be exceptions here. I also believe, as described in the text of this book, that safety contracting is sometimes counterindicated with certain clients, where it can foster the use of nonadaptive defenses and manipulative "suicide talk." In ongoing therapy, I doubt it is of much deterrence in many situations, for the forces that propel an individual toward suicide are massive indeed.

On the other hand, so are the forces of ambivalence that pose a powerful drive for life and for finding the solutions that help one to choose life. Consequently, in the hands of a well-trained and experienced clinician, who has developed a powerful alliance with a specific client, a safety contract may represent one factor that weighs the client toward life. In a patient with a strong super-ego and a lifelong belief in the importance of trust and "keeping one's word," it is easy to picture a safety contract as being one more, albeit small, reason to not act on suicidal thought. As we all know, in the complex weighing of the reasons to live against the reasons to die in the mind of an ambivalent client contemplating suicide, even a small reason can be a critical player if it tips the balance toward life. I have had clinicians describe such situations where they felt that safety contracting played a beneficial role in such a delicate weighing.

On the other hand, it remains important to carefully heed the problems that arise when safety contracting is misused:

1. Safety contracting should never be used instead of a careful and thorough suicide assessment as outlined in this book. (Some clinicians have been known to short-circuit a comprehensive suicide assessment once the client has made assurances of his or her safety.)
2. In some specific clinical situations, safety contracting may be an effective mild to moderate deterrent, but it should never be viewed as a guarantee of safety.
3. Safety contracting should never provide a false sense of security to the clinician, for such a false sense of security could result in inadequate follow-up with ongoing suicide assessments. As described in the text of this book, suicide assessment is not a static thing but an ongoing process.
4. Safety contracting may be counterproductive with certain patients, and must be judiciously employed.
5. If poorly done or poorly documented, safety contracting may hurt the clinician in court, not help (more about this later).

Where does all of this lead us with regard to the question of safety contracting as a deterrent. The answer is fairly simple. There is no good empirical evidence that supports safety contracting in a generic sense with all clients. (Thus, from this perspective, those who have argued against its use have correctly alerted us to the problems associated with a premature acceptance of its utility and with an unjustifiable over reliance on its effectiveness.) It is equally important to remember that there is not a shred of empirical evidence that safety contracting has not been a deterrent with specific clients in the hands of specific clinicians, for no such research, designed to include all of the variables listed in our previously suggested prototypic research, has ever been attempted. (Thus, from this perspective, those who have supported safety contracting have correctly alerted us to its potentially effective use with specific clients.)

In this regard it is interesting to note that a recent study showed that the majority of patients, from a sample of 135 inpatients admitted to a psychiatric unit with suicidal danger, rated written no-suicide contracts in a positive light. This study was not designed to determine deterrence, but it does show that these patients had some faith in the deterrent impact of no-suicide contracts, a fact worth noting in its own right.[6]

Thus, we find ourselves in an exciting crossroads in the study of suicidology. The debate can now move away from potentially premature arguments about the ultimate utility of safety contracting as a deterrent in an artificially generic pronouncement across all clients. Instead we can move toward the opening of doors to the design of sound research protocols, both quantitative and qualitative, that may provide fresh answers to the elusive, yet important, question of the efficacy of safety contracting with specific clinician/client dyads in specific clinical situations.

There is a second ground rule in this debate on safety contracting that has proven to be quite detrimental to an objective look at the pros and cons of safety contracting in actual clinical practice. However, this time the problematic ground rule is not a poorly defined question but a poorly supported myth.

## A MISLEADING MYTH: THE PRIMARY GOAL OF SAFETY CONTRACTING IS DETERRENCE

Somewhere along the line, this belief has become the foundation for the debate on the safety contracting issue. If this myth were true, then the value of safety contracting should, legitimately, be almost entirely based on whether it is effective in this regard. Deterrence may have been why safety contracting was first developed, but the art of safety contracting has evolved over the years.

Miller discusses several values—unrelated to deterrence—that may be provided by the act of safety contracting including an enhanced therapeutic alliance and enhanced responsibility in clinical outcome on the part of the client.[7] But Miller's factors focus on therapeutic advantages, whereas, I believe that the main role of safety contracting may have less to do with deterrence and therapeutic alliance and much more to do with the delicate art of data gathering.

Indeed, Drye, Goulding, and Goulding suggested that the act of safety contracting itself might provide valuable clinical data that could subsequently affect the decision as to the client's safety. They commented on the value of sharing "the evaluation task with the patient. Since he is the one who is making the decision to kill himself . . ., he has the best data—not only on how intense his urge is, but on how strong his controls are."[8]

One of the first to point out that safety contracting may play a major role in critical data gathering during a suicide assessment was Stanford and associates.[9] From the perspective of the emergency assessment of suicide potential, they felt the act of safety contracting could be used as an assessment tool to uncover the nature and severity of a patient's suicidal thought and intent, to identify specific troubling issues that may be triggering suicidal thought, and to evaluate the client's competency to make a safety contract in the first place.

Simon, in his pivotal article "Taking the 'Sue' Out of Suicide: A Forensic Psychiatrist's Perspective," hints at one clinical situation in which safety contracting provides some specific useful information when he comments, albeit without much enthusiasm, that "The contract against suicide is perhaps the most useful when the patient refuses to accept it. Then, at least, the clinician is not deceived by a disingenuous assent and a false sense of security."[10]

In the primary care arena, in a review of the role of safety contracting, Kelly and Knudson conclude that the "use of safety contracts may serve several useful purposes, including fostering a therapeutic alliance between the clinician and patient and assisting in suicide assessment."[11]

With the introduction of the CASE Approach to the literature,[12,13,14,15] it was suggested that not only is safety contracting useful as an assessment tool, assessing client ambivalence and commitment to safety may very well be the primary goal of safety contracting. "Deterrence" becomes a secondary goal. As the CASE Approach has gained in popularity over the years since its introduction, it is safe to say that many clinicians are now using "safety contracting" primarily as an assessment tool with potential deterrence as a hoped for, but not counted on, secondary goal. With this perspective gaining popularity, it is useful to look a little more deeply at how the act of safety contracting may provide useful information not otherwise available to the clinician.

The concept of using safety contracting as an assessment tool in the CASE Approach began in the mid-1980s as the CASE Approach was being developed at the Diagnostic and Evaluation Center at Western

Psychiatric Institute and Clinic in Pittsburgh, Pennsylvania. It was patterned on a common family therapy principle that if you want to see how a family works, it is often best to give the family a task to do. For instance, if you want to know who is "over controlling" in a family, the clinician could ask each member of the family who he or she thought was over controlling, useful data in its own right. However, the members of the family may be quite hesitant to share such information openly. On the other hand, if you want to find who, in actuality, is over controlling in the family, the clinician could give the family a task to do, during which, through simple observation, it would quickly become apparent "who the boss is here." The bottom line in this type of family therapy assessment is that the key to gaining valid data is to focus not so much on what the family tells the clinician and more on what the family shows the clinician.

And so it may be with the assessment of ambivalence in a potentially suicidal client. One of the best ways to obtain a valid look at the client's immediate degree of ambivalence is to give the client a task—contracting for safety—in which ambivalence may more easily show itself through, not only the content of the client's answer but also, the process with which the client conveys his or her answer—nonverbal leakage.

More specifically, while employing safety contracting consciously as an assessment tool, the clinician carefully looks for any nonverbal clues suggesting ambivalence, increased anxiety, or possible deception, suggesting that the client may, in actuality, not feel safe. Indeed, there may be actual nonverbal leakage that the client has intent for self-harm. A slight hesitancy, a turning away of the eyes, or the appearance of tears may signal to the astute clinician that the client has more intent toward self-harm than he or she had been willing or, perhaps because of denial or other psychodynamic defenses, been even capable of sharing earlier in the interview when directly asked about suicidal intent.

Personally, on at least two occasions in my emergency room work, the data I obtained by watching the nonverbals of my clients during safety contracting reversed my original clinical decision. In both instances, after doing a very thorough suicide assessment, as outlined in this book, I had decided that the clients would be safe to leave the emergency room. In both cases, when I asked the clients to make a safety contract, they hesitated, welled up with tears, and broke down. Both commented something to the effect of, "Dr. Shea, to tell you the truth, I just want to die." In both of these instances, this new data—only made available through the task of safety contracting—resulted in a decision to hospitalize, which both clients immediately seemed relieved to have made in retrospect.

In other instances, unexpected angry affect or impatience may first appear during safety contracting, alerting the clinician that "all may not be what it seems to be." Such anger can point toward impulsivity or characterological problems that may also suggest the wisdom of a re-thinking of the client's safety and/or the appropriateness of specific therapeutic interventions.

As with the family therapist assessment tool described earlier, I am convinced of the power of providing an individual client with a task to uncover the true feelings of the client. If, instead, I rely solely on the content of the client's answer when asked directly about safety, I may create a situation in which the client only tells me what he or she thinks I may want to hear. It is during the task of safety contracting that the client's true feelings of ambivalence may leak nonverbally. In this re-gard, over the past 20 years, I have found safety contracting to be a valu-able assessment tool for gathering information with many, but not all clients, in many, but not all, clinical situations. I refer the reader back to Chapters 6 and 7 for a review of those clients and clinical situations in which safety contracting may be problematic or even counterindicated.

## DOCUMENTING SAFETY
## CONTRACTING FROM A LEGAL STANDPOINT

Now that we have reviewed why safety contracting may be useful in suicide assessment and possibly useful as a deterrent with some clients, the next question is how do you document the act of safety con-tracting in a forensically sound fashion. If the clinician has used good reasoning as to why he used safety contracting and did not overly rely upon it as a deterrent, then he should be reasonably safe from forensic attack. Right? Wrong!

As highlighted in Appendix A, this protection is only true if the third Protective Principle of Suicide Assessment Documentation is observed—the sound decision making of the clinician was well docu-mented by the clinician. Keep in mind that, as we said in Appendix A, if you don't write it down, as far as lawyers and juries go, they are free to assume you did not do it. Concerning the topic of safety contracting, the potential lawyer for the claimant, in deciding whether to take the case, is looking specifically for evidence that the clinician naively placed too much emphasis on safety contracting as a deterrent.

Keep in mind that sound clinical documentation will never compensate for poor clinical care. If the clinician poorly used a safety contract by over relying on it in an initial assessment as a deterrent and subsequently cut short his or her suicide assessment, then the clinician may well have performed malpractice—a lawsuit may be legitimately in order.

On the other hand, if the clinician used safety contracting appropriately, as described in this book and elsewhere, then it is important that the clinician protect himself or herself from frivolous and/or opportunistic legal action. Naturally, there are never any guarantees against the placement of lawsuits, but if we adhere to the following principles, the risk of a lawsuit related to safety contracting is significantly diminished.

To demonstrate how, let us examine one of the highest risk situations for a wrongful death lawsuit—a client commits suicide several weeks after an emergency room assessment. If we can demonstrate documentation principles that can help provide protection in this high-risk situation, then these same principles may also help in lower risk situations as well.

We will look at the situation in which the clinician performed an excellent suicide assessment and instituted a well-thought-out suicide prevention plan agreed on both by the client and the significant others associated with the client. In short, there was no malpractice. As with many cases of suicide, our imagined suicide was not the result of poor clinical care nor lack of caring, but represents one of the tragedies that is an inherent part of the human condition and of clinical practice.

Furthermore, we shall picture a situation in which the safety contracting was used primarily as an assessment tool by the interviewer. The client readily made a safety contract and, at the time, appeared sincerely invested in living, despite a devastating divorce and custody battle. Since this was a first encounter with the client, the clinician put little weight on the safety contract as a deterrent. Our hypothetical client, at the time of her emergency room assessment, had no ambivalence and wanted to live, indeed, she was quite appreciative of the clinician's intervention.

Unfortunately, a completely unexpected severe loss (death of the client's only child in a car wreck) occurred several weeks after the assessment. The client, who had no prior history of drinking problems, drank heavily over a two-day period. The combination of a massive stressor and alcohol in an already struggling individual proved to be too much. The result was an impulsive and fatal overdose in an isolated hotel room.

Let us see first how *not* to document the safety contract. More specifically, let us see how a perfectly sound use of safety contracting, performed by an excellent clinician, could still land the clinician in court because of poor documentation.

The first documentation mistake occurs in the History of the Present Illness, where the actual record of the performance of the safety contracting was made. The clinician's documentation is short and sweet. As it would turn out, too short and too sweet: "The client made a no-suicide contract in the Emergency Room."

The second problem occurs later, when the clinician is documenting his clinical formulation as to why he felt the client was safe to leave. The clinician wrote, "Because of the client's ability to make a no-suicide contract coupled with relatively low risk factors, I feel the client is safe to go home with follow-up care as outlined below."

As we already found in Appendix A, the first problem here is that the description of the clinician's formulation is far too brief and generic to be effective—it really only documents "what he used" in his formulation not "how he used it." However, in this instance, the problem of brevity magnifies itself for the following reason. By placing safety contracting first and then only listing one other set of reasons for safety, it would legitimately appear to any well-versed reader that the clinician may have given marked, and possibly inappropriate, weight to the deterrence power of safety contracting. This is exactly what the plaintiff's lawyer is looking for. Yet, you and I know that the clinician did not do that. However, from the written record, no one else knows. Herein lies the problem. Unfortunately, we are watching an excellent clinician writing his own invitation to a lawsuit.

Such weak documentation has opened the door for an aggressive lawyer to pounce. In fact, an expert witness, reviewing the case in an effort to tell a lawyer whether malpractice occurred, might say, "I'm not sure from the records. He may have over-relied on safety contracting. I can't tell for sure. However, if he did, then there may have been malpractice. You'd have to depose him to find out. It's simply not clear to me what he did." And with that single statement, based on the only evidence provided by the clinician to the expert reviewer—the written record—a lawsuit is one step closer to being filed, despite the fact that malpractice did not occur.

Watch what happens when the clinician follows the basic principles we outlined in Appendix A for documenting objective database—record what happened, be complete, use direct quotes when highly supportive of your formulation—to the charting of the safety contracting itself. In the History of the Presenting Illness, the following statement appears:

> At the end of the interview, Mrs. Johnson made a safety contract with me, showing good eye contact, a firm handshake, and a genuine affect, adding, "Dr. Shea, although I feel very depressed, I could never kill myself. I need to be there for my son during this divorce. He needs me now more than ever."

Now watch how the clinician applies the key principle for documenting subjective material in the clinical formulation that we discussed in Appendix A—don't just record what your decision is, record the how and why of your decision-making process. In this instance, the clinician is showing how and why he feels the client is safe to go, as reflected by various factors, including how the client approached the safety contracting:

**Clinical Formulation**

After consulting with the charge nurse, we both agreed that the client seemed safe to go. Despite the fact that she is currently moderately depressed regarding her divorce and has had some suicidal ideation about shooting herself, as well as some potential difficult financial stresses, there are many factors suggesting her safety. There is no evidence of psychosis, no drinking or drug history, strong support from her parents and friends, no action taken on her suicidal plan, no gun in the house, no thoughts on how to procure a gun, and no other suicide plans. She is also currently healthy and young and has no history of suicide attempts. She responded well to my crisis intervention. During safety contracting, which was primarily used to more thoroughly assess any hidden ambivalence towards her own safety, she did not appear ambivalent. Both her verbal and nonverbal communications seemed genuine and spontaneous and were consistent with a genuine desire to live. I was particularly impressed with her powerful reason to live reflected by her statement concerning the need to be there for her eleven-year-old son. Our plans were shared with both the client and her parents who also agreed she seemed safe to go home. The client appeared thankful and agreed to the follow-up care outlined below.

Now let's see what our expert witness might be saying to the lawyer, who is considering whether to accept the case, "John, this looks like excellent care to me. There is no way this clinician could have foreseen the death of the child, and I honestly believe this woman would still be alive if there had been no accident. Looks like good care and excellent documentation. I would not be comfortable being a witness for you in this case. I see no malpractice."

This case is not heading for the courtroom. Moreover, it shouldn't, because the clinician provided good clinical care. But the reason it is not going to court is not only the fact that the clinician provided excellent care, it is the fact that he provided excellent documentation of his excellent care.

It is a good moment to see if we can uncover some of the principles that were applied to the above documentation that helped to create such an effective written assessment:

1. When documenting the actual act of doing the safety contracting in the History of the Present Illness (note some prefer to do this in the written section on the Mental Status, which is also appropriate), be sure to include any nonverbal descriptors that lend weight to the client's apparent commitment to safety. This data can be used to support the clinician's ultimate formulation that the client did not appear to be showing dangerously significant ambivalence at the time of the assessment and disposition. Such data observations can also be used to support the idea that with this particular client, the safety contract may have had some deterrent power if, indeed, the clinician believed this to be true.

2. Also be sure to document in the client's own words, with quotation marks, any comments by the client that support that the client has strong reasons to live. Such comments sometimes surface during the act of safety contracting, a phenomena that once again supports the idea that safety contracting can provide new and vital assessment information.

3. During the written documentation of your formulation, state plainly and in succinct terms why you are doing safety contracting (e.g., as an assessment tool, a deterrent, or both). Any time you are suggesting that it played a role as a deterrent tell why (remember there is no quantitative empirical data to support such a conclusion and you can bet that the claimant's lawyer is going to try to catch you and your expert witness on this point). Here is another example of effective documentation:

Although there is no empirical data proving or disproving the role of safety contracting as a deterrent, in this particular client, I feel it may play some role as an effective deterrent. Over the past three years in therapy, we have formed a strong therapeutic alliance based upon honesty and trust, two values that are very important to the client. She has a very strong superego and prides herself on honesty. At this point, I feel these factors coalesce to enhance the deterrent effect of "safety contracting" in this client. Thus, although not a strong deterrent, it may play a small but useful role in adding to the reasons that the client would not impulsively act on her suicidal thoughts and in this instance it appears to be a worthwhile clinical tool to utilize, in addition to its obvious use as an ongoing part of suicide assessment.

Sound documentation practices not only record that good clinical care happened, they prospectively help to ensure that good clinical care happens. Each of the above three principles for enhancing forensic protection actually also help to improve care. This is such an important and often underemphasized point that I feel I should demonstrate how.

In the first principle, we stated that a description of the nonverbals of the client during the act of safety contracting should be recorded. This documentation may help a future clinician in a powerful fashion. Let us assume that we are a psychotherapist at a Community Mental Health Center and have worked with a client for many months. On several occasions, suicidal ideation emerged. In each case, the client was not intending suicide and was comfortable with making a no-suicide contract. We note in our charts that "the client responded without hesitation, with good eye contact, a genuine affect, and a firm handshake." The client's suicidal ideation eventually vanished.

Three months later, the client unexpectedly appears at the Community Mental Health Center in crisis. The crisis clinician attempts to contact us but we are out of town. Despite good clinical interviewing and a reasonably cooperative client, the safety of the client is a little hard to tease out for the crisis clinician. The clinician has read our notes and decides to use safety contracting as an assessment tool. When approached with safety contracting, the client looks away and sighs, saying, "I guess I can say that."

The hesitancy of the client stands in marked contrast to the nonverbals documented in the previous notes on safety contracting, significantly increasing the crisis clinician's doubts as to safety. New data has been gained. Not only that, the new data is more useful for there is a comparison database provided by our documentation. The crisis clinician does not feel totally comfortable with the disposition and decides to ask the on-call psychiatrist to become directly involved.

Further interviewing uncovers that much more serious suicidal intent is present than first thought. All parties deem that hospitalization be utilized, including the client. Not only did the act of safety contracting by the crisis clinician play a pivotal—perhaps lifesaving role—but the documentation of previous safety contracting was crucial in helping the crisis clinician interpret the nonverbal message the client was sending.

In the second principle, we urged the clinician to keep an eye out for any specific statements that the client made suggesting strong reasons to live. In recent work, Jobes and Mann have elegantly pointed out that sometimes more emphasis needs to be placed not only on the critical reasons the client offers for dying but also on their reasons for living, for this internal debate may play a major role in their ultimate decision.[16] If the above principle is routinely applied to the documentation process, the clinician will develop the habit of looking for such information.

Sometimes the client spontaneously provides this information during safety contracting or earlier in the interview, but if it isn't provided, it is often useful to ask for it. Again, the habit of always documenting "reasons for living" tends to engender the search for such reasons in the interview in the first place. Indeed, if no such questions were asked, when the interviewer gets to the point of documenting the safety contracting, they will be reminded that this material was missed, perhaps prompting the need for further interviewing.

With the use of the third documentation principle from above—always document why you are using safety contracting—the clinician must clarify in his or her mind the task at hand, including the pros and cons of safety contracting with this particular client and also a clear vision of its limitations. Again, the habit of always addressing this critical issue in the documentation process helps to ensure that the clinician is doing it in his or her mind. Such careful thinking helps clinicians to avoid the misuse of safety contracting or an inappropriate reliance on its deterrent capabilities.

In all three of the above documentation principles, we see that documentation approaches, ostensibly designed to help protect against malpractice, are inherently effective in fostering better clinical care—a principle we saw repeatedly at work in Appendix A. Yet one more issue concerning documentation—both for forensic protection and clinical care warrants our attention—What do you write if you don't use a safety contract?

As we saw in the body of this book, there are certain clients and clinical situations where safety contracting may be problematic or even counterindicated in a relative sense. We will not review these situations here, but I find it useful when I do not use safety contracting to document why. I find this ensures that I am carefully weighing the pros and cons of safety contracting with each client, as well as providing forensic protection. Here is an example of what I might write with a client that I am seeing in ongoing therapy with whom I feel safety contracting is not appropriate:

> Because of Mr. Farings' individual defenses and dynamics, as reflected by his diagnosis of borderline personality disorder, I have decided that safety contracting may be problematic in his ongoing care. He has a long history of reverting into patterns of behavior viewed as manipulative (that actually only reflect his need for their use because of a lack of more effective skills) that sometimes result in unnecessary, and, in both my opinion and the opinion of the inpatient staff, counterproductive hospitalizations. More specifically, despite being safe, in some instances, he will hedge or refuse to agree to safety contracts, a process that has resulted in counterproductive inpatient admissions in the past. Instead, after always doing a thorough suicide assessment, I will rely on the client's eagerness and readiness to meet again and to work on jointly agreed upon goals as more valid reflections of safety as is in keeping with the therapeutic approach I am using with Mr. Farings (e.g., Dialectical Behavioral Therapy).

The above note, which merely goes back to the adage to describe why you are doing what you are doing, essentially shuts the door on a lawyer trying to "prove" that you did a shoddy assessment because you did not use safety contracting as an assessment tool. Your note provides the answer clearly and succinctly to the lawyer and the jury—safety contracting was carefully considered by you but ultimately viewed as a bad idea.

At this point, we have reached an end to our study of safety contracting and its documentation. We have seen that safety contracting is not a good idea for all clients. In those in which it is a useful idea, its ability to function as a deterrent probably depends on the specific client/clinician dyad and clinical situation. Despite significant limitation to its use as a deterrent, it seems to have excellent utility as a tool for helping to assess the client's degree of ambivalence and degree of immediate commitment to his or her own safety.

When using safety contracting as an assessment tool, a deterrent, or both, it is important to document its use carefully. Such careful documentation, paradoxically, not only protects from inappropriate malpractice suits but also helps to improve clinical care itself. Understanding the power of good clinical care coupled with good clinical documentation to markedly reduce malpractice liability allows the clinician to put concerns of liability on "the back burner" where they belong. Instead, by developing a habit of effectively documenting safety contracting, the clinician can focus attention on the art of providing sound suicide assessments without the nagging fear of litigation. Safety contracting can then takes its rightful place as one more tool that, if effectively utilized, might help us to save a life—a wonderful outcome for all involved.

## NOTES

1. Drye, R.C., Goulding, R.L., and Goulding, M.E.: No-suicide decisions: Patient monitoring of suicidal risk. *American Journal of Psychiatry* 135: 171–174, 1973.

2. Miller, M.C.: Suicide-prevention contracts: Advantages, disadvantages, and an alternative approach. In *The Harvard Medical School Guide to Suicide Assessment and Intervention,* edited by D.G. Douglas. San Francisco, CA, Jossey-Bass, 1999.

3. Drew, B.L.: No-suicide contracts to prevent suicidal behavior in inpatient psychiatric settings. *Journal of the American Psychiatric Nurses Association* 5: 23–28, 1999.

4. Miller, M.C., Jacobs, D.G., and Gutheil, T.G.: Talisman or taboo? The controversy of the suicide prevention contract. *Harvard Review of Psychiatry* 6: 78–87, 1998.

5. Simon, R.I.: Taking the "sue" out of suicide: A forensic psychiatrist's perspective. *Psychiatric Annals* 30: 399–407, 2000.

6. Davis, S.E., Williams, I.S., and Hays, L.W.: Psychiatric inpatient's perceptions of written no-suicide agreements: An exploratory study. *Suicide and Life-Threatening Behavior* 32 (1): 51–66, 2002.

7. Miller, M.C.: Suicide-prevention contracts: Advantages, disadvantages, and an alternative approach. In *The Harvard Medical School Guide to Suicide Assessment and Intervention,* edited by D.G. Douglas. San Francisco, CA, Jossey-Bass, 1999.

8. Drye, R.C., Goulding, R.L., and Goulding, M.E.: No-suicide decisions: Patient monitoring of suicidal risk. *American Journal of Psychiatry* 135: 171–174, 1973.

9. Stanford, E.J., Goetz, R.R., and Bloom, J.D.: The no-harm contract in the emergency assessment of suicidal risk. *Journal of Clinical Psychiatry* 55: 344–348, 1994.

10. Simon, R.I.: Taking the "sue" out of suicide: A forensic psychiatrist's perspective. *Psychiatric Annals* 30: 399–407, 2000.

11. Kelly, K.T., and Knudson, M.P.: Are no-suicide contracts effective in preventing suicide in suicidal patients seen by primary care physicians? *Archives of Family Medicine* 9 (10): November/December 2000.

12. Shea, S.C.: The chronological assessment of suicide events: A practical interviewing strategy for eliciting suicidal ideation. *Journal of Clinical Psychiatry* (supplement) 59: 58–72, 1998.

13. Shea, S.C.: *Psychiatric Interviewing: The Art of Understanding, 2nd ed.* Philadelphia, W.B. Saunders Company, 1998.

14. Shea, S.C.: *The Practical Art of Suicide Assessment: A Guide for Mental Health Professionals and Substance Abuse Counselors,* New York, John Wiley & Sons, Inc., 1999.

15. Shea, S.C.: Practical tips for eliciting suicidal ideation for the substance abuse counselor. *Counselor, the Magazine for Addiction Professionals* 2: 14–24, 2001.

16. Jobes, D.A., and Mann, R.E.: Reasons for living versus reasons for dying: Examining the internal debate of suicide. *Suicide and Life-Threatening Behavior* 29: 97–104, 1999.

# APPENDIX C

# A Quick Guide to Suicide Prevention Web Sites

## A GENERAL INVITATION

L ET ME BEGIN by inviting all of my readers to my home site at the Training Institute for Suicide Assessment and Clinical Interviewing (TISA). Our URL is easy to remember (www .suicideassessment.com).

The Web site is designed specifically for busy front-line clinicians, who are interested in learning more about suicide assessment techniques and specific tips on all aspects of clinical interviewing. It provides the "Interviewing Tip of the Month" and its Archive of Monthly Tips, as well as the complete journal article, *The Chronological Assessment of Suicide Events: A Practical Interviewing Strategy for Eliciting Suicidal Ideation.* If you like the CASE Approach and want to share it with colleagues, you can direct them to our Web site. This article provides a succinct and useful introduction to the strategy.

The TISA Web site was also designed specifically to be a resource for graduate students in their core courses on interviewing and counseling skills. The number of sites devoted to mental health on the Web is somewhat staggering. To help you sort through these many resources, on the TISA site, I have included a set of the 50 Web sites that I feel are some of the best sites available regarding mental health information, including suicide prevention. My goal is to create a user-friendly launch pad into the fascinating world of mental health Web sites for the interested reader. The TISA site is frequently updated to ensure inclusion of new sites.

For those readers who want to learn more about my scheduled workshops or how to arrange to have me brought to your center to provide workshops, you can locate that information on the site as well.

Please feel free to drop me an e-mail from the TISA site if you have any interviewing tips or questions about suicide assessment techniques. I am also always eager to receive feedback on how to improve *The Practical Art of Suicide Assessment: A Guide for Mental Health Professionals and Substance Abuse Counselors*. I hope that you enjoy the TISA site, and I'll see you on the Web!

## A FEW OUTSTANDING SUICIDE PREVENTION WEB SITES TO GET YOU STARTED

Here is an annotated listing of some key suicide prevention Web sites. I have tried to include at least one Web site that will be of immediate utility to all of the following groups: mental health professionals, advocates for suicide prevention, survivors of suicide, and people who are currently experiencing suicidal ideation. I believe these sites provide an outstanding gateway into the rich arena of information on suicide prevention.

### AMERICAN ASSOCIATION OF SUICIDOLOGY (AAS)
www.suicidology.org
A Web site packed with useful information including suicide facts, warning signs of suicide, support groups and crisis centers listed by state, a nice set of links, an active bulletin board for AAS members, and a bookstore dedicated to high quality books on suicide assessment, intervention, and postvention. This is a great organization to join and has a unique breadth of membership divisions including survivors of suicide, a clinical division, a crisis centers division, a prevention division, and a research division. AAS provides certification for crisis intervention centers. The site also provides information on the outstanding annual meetings of the AAS.

### AMERICAN FOUNDATION FOR SUICIDE PREVENTION (AFSP)
www.afsp.org
This Web site is also packed with useful information including suicide statistics, helpful information for survivors of suicide, and tips

on how to report suicide to the media. Another great organization to join, it has been very successful at raising money for research on preventing suicide. If you are a researcher looking for grant money, this organization provides grants and the Web site describes how to apply for them.

SUICIDE PREVENTION ADVOCACY NETWORK (SPAN)

www.spanusa.org

This Web site describes various ways, including advocacy letters, of enhancing awareness of the importance of suicide prevention from a local to a national level. The site has an excellent resource page for community organizers and provides updates on national events designed to decrease stigmatization and increase suicide prevention awareness. Another excellent group to join, SPAN has been a key supporter of "The National Strategy for Suicide Prevention."

INTERNATIONAL ASSOCIATION FOR SUICIDE PREVENTION (IASP)

www.med.uio.no/iasp

This excellent site provides an international arena for collaboration on suicide prevention. It publishes an interesting newsletter and updates on suicide prevention news from around the world. It also provides information on various awards for excellence in suicidology research. It is a nongovernmental organization that has an official relationship with the World Health Organization. The site will keep you informed about the annual meeting of the IASP Congress and provides information on its journal, *Crisis: The Journal of Crisis Intervention and Suicide Prevention.*

ENDINGSUICIDE.COM

www1.endingsuicide.com/mentalhealth/suicide_preven

One of the newest of the major suicide prevention Web sites, this site, which resulted from a contract with the National Institute for Mental Health, is dedicated to the task of functioning as a portal for all of the resources on suicide prevention available on the Web. It provides Web resources on the federal, national, state, and tribal level. It also provides interesting short articles on a wide range of topics from the "Neurobiology of Suicide" to an introduction to "The CASE Approach." There is also a bulletin board and an unusual interactive set of questions on general suicide prevention knowledge.

SA\VE—SUICIDE AWARENESS\VOICES OF EDUCATION

www.save.org

SA\VE provides education about suicide prevention and is a strong advocate for suicide survivors. This excellent Web site is a good starting point for anyone who is a survivor of suicide or has a family member or friend who is coping with suicidal thoughts. Informative readings cover a host of topics including questions on suicide, information on depression, what grief is like after a suicide, what to tell children after a suicide, and what to do if a loved one is suicidal. The site also has book lists, book reviews, and information on how to start a support group for survivors.

SUICIDE . . . READ THIS FIRST

www.metanoia.org/suicide

This remarkable site is a gift to all those who are having suicidal thoughts. In a sensitive and compassionate fashion, sound advice is provided that helps to destigmatize the process of having suicidal thoughts so that the reader can actively seek help. A collection of readings addresses topics of interest to people coping with suicidal ideation as well as people trying to help them, including titles such as "Why is it so hard for us to recover from being suicidal?" "Handling a call from a suicidal person," "Nine ways to help a suicidal person," and "Suicide warning signs." There are also links to Web sites, such as the Samaritans and online support groups that may help a person dealing with suicidal ideation. Outstanding links on depression and a list of self-help books for people coping with suicidal ideation are described with links to bookstores provided.

SURGEON GENERAL'S CALL TO ACTION

www.surgeongeneral.gov/library/calltoaction/default.htm

In 1999, a "Call to Action to Prevent Suicide" was released by the Office of Surgeon General David Satcher. This landmark document provided a huge increase in the momentum to improve awareness of the importance of suicide prevention in the United States. It opened the door to increases in research funds, public awareness, and the development of a national strategy for preventing suicide. It is a relatively short, well-written document that is both informative and historic. You can also find this document listed under the "Calls to Action" section of the Web site for the Surgeon General at www.surgeongeneral.gov.

## OTHER EXCELLENT SUICIDE PREVENTION SITES

In this section I have listed valuable Web sites on suicide prevention in alphabetical order. They can provide a rich array of new perspectives and sources of information to all those interested in preventing suicide.

Befrienders International (Parent organization of the Samaritans)
www.befrienders.org/suicide.htm

Canadian Association for Suicide Prevention (CASP)
www.suicideprevention.ca

Crisis Management in Schools Following a Suicide
www.ed.gov/databases/ERIC_Digests/ed315700.html

European Network for Suicidology
www.uke.uni-hamburg.de/ens

National Center for Suicide Prevention Training (NCSPT)
www.ncspt.org

National Organization of People of Color Against Suicide
www.nopcas.com

National Institute of Mental Health (NIMH) Research Consortium
www.nimh.nih.gov/research/suicide.cfm

National Strategy for Suicide Prevention (NSSP)
www.mentalhealth.org/suicideprevention

Preventing Suicide
www.cdc.gov/safeusa/suicide.htm

San Francisco Suicide Prevention
www.sfsuicide.org

State Planning for Suicide Prevention
www.wwu.edu/~hayden/spsp

Suicide Information & Education Center
www.siec.ca

Suicide Prevention Efforts in Norway
www.med.uio.no/ipsy/ssff

Suicide Prevention Research Center
www.suicideprc.com

Suicide and Suicide Prevention
www.psycom.net/depression.central.suicide.html

The Suicidology Web: Suicide and Parasuicide
www.suicide-parasuicide.rumos.com/en

The Aeschi Working Group
www.aeschiconference.unibe.ch

World Health Organization Suicide Prevention Efforts
www.who.int/mental_health/Topic_Suicide/suicide1.html

Youth Suicide Prevention Programs: A Resource Guide:
aepo-xdv-www.epo.cdc.gov/wonder/prevguid/p0000024/p0000024.asp

## OTHER WEB SITES OF RELATED
## INTEREST TO SUICIDE PREVENTION

Anxiety Disorders Association of America
www.adaa.org

Depression and Related Affective Disorders Association (DRADA)
www.drada.org

CRP's Internet Mental Health Resources
www.uop.edu/cop/psychology/crp/links.html

Mental Health Net
www.mentalhelp.net

National Alliance for the Mentally Ill (NAMI)
www.nami.org

National Depressive and Manic-Depressive Association
www.ndmda.org

National Foundation for Depressive Illness
www.depression.org

National Institute of Mental Health
www.nimh.nih.gov

National Mental Illness Screening Project
www.nmisp.org

Obsessive-Compulsive Foundation, Inc.
www.ocfoundation.org

Psych Central
www.psychcentral.com

# Index